Essentials of Cash Management

Fourth Edition

Editor:

Henry A. Davis
Globecon Group, Inc.

Co-Editor:

Paul J. Ruggeri, CCM
Siena College

Associate Editors:

Carol A. Levis, CCM - Chair

Paul J. Markovic, CCM

Robert J. Moerchen, CCM

J. William Murray, CCM

Treasury Management Association

All inquiries should be addressed to:

Communications Department
Treasury Management Association
7315 Wisconsin Avenue, Suite 1250W
Bethesda, Maryland 20814

ISBN 0-9614799-3-0

Table of Contents

Exhibits

Foreword

The Treasury Management Association (TMA) offered the first Certified Cash Manager (CCM) examination in 1986. As part of the development of this initial examination, the Association produced *Essentials of Cash Management, First Edition*, as the body of knowledge of cash management and as a study guide for the CCM examination.

Two subsequent editions were developed, with *Essentials of Cash Management, Third Edition*, published in 1989. Due to changes in the scope of cash management resulting from factors such as technological, regulatory and global issues, *Essentials of Cash Management, Fourth Edition,* has been developed as the current body of knowledge that constitutes the field of cash management.

In 1990, the TMA Certification Committee established the CCM Body of Knowledge Task Force to maintain, research and develop *Essentials of Cash Management, Fourth Edition*, in support of the Association's Certified Cash Manager program. This task force included: Carol A. Levis, CCM, chair; J. William Murray, CCM, vice-chair; and members Paul J. Markovic, CCM; and Robert J. Moerchen, CCM. TMA staff assistance and leadership were provided to the task force by Jacqueline Callahan, TMA Director of Professional Development.

The task force selected Henry A. Davis, Director of Research of The Globecon Group, Ltd., and Paul J. Ruggeri, CCM, Dean of Business of Siena College, as co-editors of the fourth edition. The task force worked closely with the co-editors to establish the outline, incorporate feedback received on the third edition and develop the text.

The task force and the co-editors worked diligently to provide clear and factual material because the text is used primarily as a study guide for the CCM examination. As a result, the level of detail provided for specific areas was determined in consideration of an individual with two years of experience in cash management. This edition was based on the assumption that the reader would have an understanding of, and be able to apply general mathematical principles, including algebra and business math. In addition, the text assumes an understanding of basic accounting such as cash versus accrual accounting and various financial statements including: income statements, balance sheets, and statements of cash flow.

As chapters were written, a number of volunteer reviewers, each with specific professional expertise, were used to supplement the efforts of the co-editors and the task force. All reviewers' comments were evaluated and considered as part of the detailed task force review process. Appropriate credit in this area is noted in the Preface.

The development of this edition was a lengthy and detailed process. TMA is grateful to all those named previously, whose dedication has added value to the publication of this edition. We are pleased to publish *Essentials of Cash Management, Fourth Edition*, as a comprehensive body of knowledge and the treasury profession's own contribution to the literature in the field of treasury management.

Carol A. Levis, CCM
Chair - CCM Body of Knowledge
Editorial Committee

Preface to fourth edition

The scope of treasury management has expanded dramatically during the last 10 years. New technology has bred new applications in information and payments systems. The treasury manager has become concerned with issues that go beyond the traditional definition of cash management. In response to these changes, the National Corporate Cash Management Association has become the Treasury Management Association (TMA). TMA serves as the focal point for the professional development of the treasury professional.

TMA has developed a certification program, which includes the Certified Cash Manager (CCM) examination. The *Essentials of Cash Management, Fourth Edition*, is designed as the body of knowledge for the CCM examination. It is also a useful text for those who are new to the field, or for experienced managers seeking a desk reference. Vendors of cash management services and university students may also find this book to be a valuable guide to cash management.

The *Essentials of Cash Management, Fourth Edition*, consists of 15 chapters, which are written in an integrated fashion but are meant to stand alone as an examination of each topic. Each chapter begins with an outline and a statement of learning objectives. The body of each chapter is in an outline, study-guide format. The chapter concludes with a series of study questions designed to help the reader determine whether the learning objectives have been met. The questions are not written in the multiple-choice format of the CCM examination.

The reader is assumed to have an undergraduate degree or equivalent work experience. He or she should have an understanding of basic accounting, including the preparation of financial statements and the concept of cash flow analysis. A working knowledge of financial mathematics, especially present and future value, and basic finance concepts, such as cost of capital, is also presumed.

In addition to the material in the *Essentials of Cash Management, Fourth Edition*, supplementary material can be found in a number of texts available in public or business libraries. These include:

Treasury Management Guide: D.J. Masson, editor; Treasury Management Association, Bethesda, MD, 1991.

Corporate Cash Management Handbook: Richard Bort; Warren, Gorham & Lamont, Boston MA, 1989.

The Handbook of Cash Flow and Treasury Management: Vince DiPaolo, editor; Probus Publishing, Chicago, IL, 1988.

Short-Term Financial Management (2nd ed.): Ned C. Hill and William L. Sartoris; McMillan Publishing Co., New York, NY, 1992.

Paul J. Ruggeri, CCM
Co-Editor

Acknowledgements ■

A project like this cannot be completed without the help and support of many people. I would like to second the appreciation expressed to the reviewers for their thoughtfulness and professionalism. I would also like to express my gratitude to the following:

Hal Davis, for your important contribution to this work.

The CCM Body of Knowledge Committee, Carol, Bill, Bob and Paul, for your incredible expertise, grace under pressure and your friendship.

Jacqueline Callahan, whose dedication and perseverance made this possible.

Siena, for the freedom to work.

Finally my wife Peggy and my daughter Rachel for their love and patience.

Paul J. Ruggeri, CCM
Co-Editor

CCM Body of Knowledge

Editorial Committee:

Associate Editors

The following members of the CCM Body of Knowledge Task Force have spent considerable time and effort on the development of this edition. As a result of their commitment, and as justified by their contributions, these individuals have been named Associate Editors of this text. The Co-Editors and the Treasury Management Association would like to thank these individuals for their dedication and insights and would like to thank their employers for their support of this project.

Carol A. Levis, CCM - Chair
Treasurer
Coopers & Lybrand

J.William Murray, CCM, Vice-Chair
Senior Vice President
First National Bank of Maryland

Paul J. Markovic, CCM
Vice President/Manager, Corporate Cash Manager
National City Bank

Robert J. Moerchen, CCM
Assistant Treasurer
Outboard Marine Corp.

Additional Acknowledgements

SPECIAL RESOURCE:

The following individuals provided information in the research stage of the process. The Co-Editors and the Treasury Management Association would like to thank these individuals for their assistance and for the information provided.

Douglas Anderson
Executive Vice President
CoreStates Financial Corp.

George H. Bunn, CCM
Vice President
CoreStates Financial Corp.

Michael J. Curran
Vice President
Chemical Bank

Patricia E. Dowden
Senior Vice President
CoreStates Financial Corp.

Susan Feinberg, CCM
Senior Product Manager
Bank of Boston

Mark S. Furst, CCM
Vice President
First National Bank of Maryland

Marian D. Galvin
Vice President
Continental Bank

Joseph Grimaldi
Vice President
Bank of Boston

Warren Haber
Senior Product Manager
Bank of Boston

William J. Howland
Vice President
First National Bank of Maryland

Stephen N. Kapner, CCM
Assistant Treasurer
Time Warner Inc.

Frank V. Lago
Cash Management Executive
First National Bank of Maryland

Theodore M. Mertz, CCM
Director of Product Management-Cash
Management
Bank of Boston

William F. Metzger
Vice President
CoreStates Financial Corp.

William B. Nelson, CCM
Senior Director, Network Services
National Automated Clearing House Association

Lori Nicoll
Manager of Bank Relations
Marsh & McLennan Incorporated

David M. Nygard
Senior Product Analyst
Continental Bank

William J. Osterman
Senior Vice President
CoreStates Financial Corp.

Petrina A. Rauzi, CCM
Cash Manager
Helene Curtis, Inc.

Jean H. Robinson
Vice President
Continental Bank

James P. Rossman, CCM
Director, Treasury Operations
Helene Curtis, Inc.

Michael Wilhelm, CCM
Manager of Treasury Operations
Bell & Howell Company

Nancy S. Wright, CCM
Senior Product Manager
Bank of Boston

REVIEWERS

The following individuals reviewed sections of the text for errors or misconceptions. The Co-Editors and the Treasury Management Association would like to thank these individuals for their commitment to the process and for the valuable comments provided.

Philip C. Ahwesh, CCM
Vice President
Mellon Bank

David N. Anderson, CCM
Vice President
NationsBank

Bradford G. Ankerholz, CCM
Senior Treasury Analyst
Manville Corp.

Brian P. Atkinson, CCM
Vice President
Manufacturers Bank N.A.

Susan M. Baker, CCM
Supervisor - Gas Accounting
Marathon Oil Company

Robert T.Bauter, Jr., CCM
Assistant to the Treasurer
The Copley Press, Inc.

Barbara Beausoleil, CCM
Vice President
United New Mexico Bank

Dave Berkow, CCM
Assistant Treasurer
Covia Partnership

Ellen Berkowitz, CCM
Manager of Cash & Banking
ARA Services, Inc.

John Bobko, CCM
Cash Manager
Amcena Corp.

Erik M.Bodow, CCM
Vice President
First Treasury Consolta, Inc.

James F.X. Borgia, CCM
Manager of Treasury Operations
Sprague Technologies, Inc.

Michael E. Bousman, CCM
Investment Officer
Washington Public Power Supply System

Elizabeth M. Bowerman, CCM
Staff Manager - Treasury
BellSouth Corp.

Kathryn L. Buck, CCM
Vice President
NationsBank

Guy Candido, CCM
Vice President/Manager
First National Bank of Chicago

Van L. Carmean, CCM
Assistant Treasurer
CSX Transportation

Frank A. Cesario, CCM
Vice President
Northern Trust Bank

John M. Connell, CCM
Vice President
First National Bank of Chicago

Kathryn M. Corry, CCM
Assistant Treasurer
American Television and Communications Corp.

Laura Skeel Cowan, CCM
Vice President
NationsBank

Terry W. Crawford, CCM
Vice President & Treasurer
Metmor Financial Inc.

Kent W. Crocombe, CCM
Treasurer
Aladdin Industries

W. Steven Culp, CCM
Assistant Vice President of Treasury Services
ITT Financial Corp.

Steven A. Decker, CCM
Cash Manager
Gerber Products Company

Nancy B. Levin, CCM
Director of Cash Management
The Artery Organization

Tedd Lingo, CCM
Manager, Cash Management
Goodyear Tire & Rubber Company

David W. Lubbers, CCM
Vice President
Old Kent Bank and Trust Company

William J. Luehrmann
Assistant Vice President
Caesars World,Inc.

Terry S. Maness, CCM
Chairman, Department of Finance
Baylor University

George F. Markle, CCM
Vice President
First Citizens Bank

D. J. Masson, CCM
President
Treasury Management Associates

Susan J. McComb, CCM
Assistant Vice President
First Wisconsin National Bank

Rebecca S. McCulloch, CCM
Assistant Treasurer
Brown & Root, Inc.

Jack M. Meckler, CCM
President
Phoenix-Hecht

John A. Menes, CCM
Manager Treasury Operations
USX Corp.

Stephen F. Messerly, CCM
Assistant Treasurer
Ohio State University

Phyllis C. Meyerson, CCM
Senior Consultant
J.D. Carreker and Associates, Inc.

Elizabeth C. Miller, CCM
Assistant Investment Manager
San Diego County

Richard J. Moorman, CCM
Manager, Corporate Finance
Mead Corp.

Thomas J. Nist, CCM
Vice President
Pittsburgh National Bank

J. Robert Nolley, CCM
Vice President
Signet Bank

David L. O'Brien, CCM
Director of Banking
Royal Insurance

John G. Oros, CCM
Assistant Treasurer
Welbilt Corp.

Thomas K. Patton, CCM
Senior Vice President
Wachovia Bank

Daniel J. Pavlick, CCM
Vice President
Pittsburgh National Bank

Charles R. Pierce, CCM
Vice President
Global Cash Management
Mellon Bank

Philip Pompili, CCM
Controller
T&T Companies

Marsha Prentiss, CCM
Assistant Treasurer
Hitachi Data Systems

Charles F. Racki
Treasury Manager
United Telephone Company-Midwest

Delores E. Ratliff, CCM
Senior Cash Management Consultant
Dayton Hudson Corp.

Timothy M. Roberts, CCM
Assistant Treasurer
Salt River Project

Glenn T. Roe, CCM
Vice President
Hamilton Bank

T. K. Rogers, Jr., CCM
Cash Management Director
Eastman Kodak Company

Robert A. Rudzki, CCM
Assistant Treasurer
Bethlehem Steel Corp.

George B. Rush, CCM
Vice President
Phoenix-Hecht

Bob A. Sherrill, CCM
Associate Director-Treasury Operations
Southwestern Bell Corp.

Linda P. Shields, CCM
Senior Accountant
United Gas Pipeline Company

David P. Smay
Treasurer
Chevron USA Products, Inc.

Steven W. Smith, CCM
District Manager
ADP Financial Network Services

Jamileh Soufan, CCM
Assistant Treasurer
American General Corp.

Larry R. Speer, CCM
Assistant Treasurer
Wilson Foods Corp.

Walter Szczepaniak, CCM
Director, Corporate Finance
Samaritan Health Services

Karla Sztukowski, CCM
Assistant Vice President
CoreStates Financial Corp.

Patricia J. Untermeyer, CCM
Cash Management Analyst
USAA

J. Randall Vance, CCM
Financial Analyst
Farmland Industries

Norma J. Wallace, CCM
Vice President
First Interstate Bank of Texas

Margaret L. Weber, CCM
Vice President
First National Bank Corp.

Joseph A. Wemhoff, CCM
Vice President
First Interstate Bank, Ltd.

Marilyn S. Wheaton, CCM
Vice President
Bank of Oklahoma, N.A.

Heidi Widom, CCM
Second Vice President
The Chase Manhattan Bank

James S. Wolf, CCM
First Vice President
Mellon Bank

Ken K. Wong, CCM
Corporate Cash Manager
Farmers Insurance Company

The Co-Editors and the Associate Editors would like to thank Jacqueline Callahan, TMA Director of Professional Development for her enduring assistance and support of this project. We would also like to thank the Certification Staff and the Communications Staff for their assistance and support.

Essentials of Cash Management

Introduction and Overview

Chapter 1

Overview

This introductory chapter describes a number of forces and trends in banking and corporate finance that caused cash management to develop as a discipline and continue to have an influence on the environment in which the cash manager works. The reader should focus primarily on overall trends in this chapter. This chapter introduces a number of terms and concepts that will be developed throughout the text.

Learning Objectives

Upon completion of this chapter and the related study questions, the reader should be able to do the following:

1. Identify the objectives of cash management.
2. Describe the major functions of cash management.
3. Understand the cash flow time line and the various types of float it includes.
4. Discuss the major historical developments in cash management.
5. Understand the changes in the financial market environment and their impact on cash management.

OUTLINE

I. Cash Management Functions

The general objective of cash management is the efficient utilization of cash in a manner consistent with the strategic objectives of the firm.

The major objectives of cash management include:

- **Liquidity -** Maintaining the ability of the firm to pay obligations when they become due.

- **Cash Conservation -** Establishing systems and procedures that help the firm minimize its investment in non-earning cash resources.

- **Financing -** Assisting in obtaining both short- and long-term funds in a timely manner and at an acceptable cost.

- **Risk Management -** Monitoring and controlling the firm's exposure to interest rate, foreign exchange and other risks.

- **Coordination -** Ensuring that cash management decisions are coordinated with the policy decisions and strategic objectives of other departments in the firm that affect cash.

Cash management is accomplished primarily through the following day-to-day operations:

- **Collection -** Collecting funds from customers.

- **Concentration -** Concentrating funds where they can be most efficiently deployed.

- **Disbursement -** Disbursing funds to vendors, employees, and investors.

- **Information -** Developing and maintaining appropriate information systems.

- **Forecasting -** Forecasting to predict future funds flows.

- **Investment -** Investing surplus funds.

- **Borrowing -** Borrowing to meet short-term requirements.

- **Bank Relationships -** Managing bank relationships.

II. Float and the Cash Flow Time Line

Associated with each cash transaction is a time line along which various activities and related cash and information flows can be represented (see Exhibit 1-1). The buyer's outflow time line is the seller's inflow time line. Decisions that impact any part of the time line can change the amount and/or the timing of the cash flows.

There are four major cash flows to be managed by the firm.

- **Cash Inflows -** Consisting of cash collected from customers or financial sources.

- **Internal Transfers -** Transferring funds among operating units of the firm and within the firm's banking system.

- **Cash and Near-Cash Storage -** Maintaining an inventory of liquid reserves held as cash or marketable securities.

- **Cash Outflows** - Disbursing to vendors, employees, lenders, shareholders, and other payees of the company.

Float can be caused by any type of delay along the cash flow time line.

A. **Invoicing Float** is the delay between the purchase of goods and services and the receipt of the invoice by the customer.

B. **Check Float** is caused by the delay between the receipt of the invoice by the customer and the clearing of the check.

- **Collection Float** - The delay between the time a payor mails a check and the time the payee receives available funds.

- **Disbursement Float** - The delay between the time the check is mailed and the time it is charged to the payor's account.

A company benefits from shortening all types of float associated with cash inflows, and lengthening all types of float associated with cash outflows. In principle, this is true, except that companies generally do not extend disbursement float to the point of jeopardizing their vendor relationships. Other priorities such as cost containment and the quality of information provided to management have increased in relative value to float optimization in recent years.

Exhibit 1-1

Cash Flow Time Line

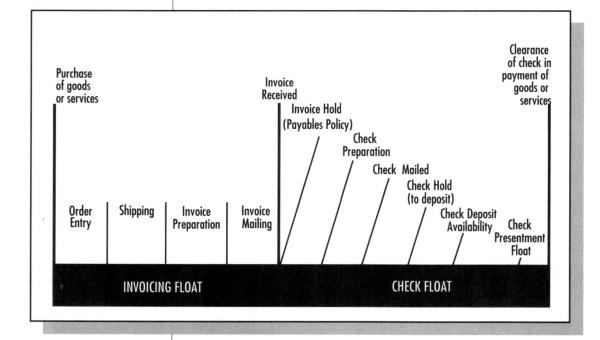

III. Role of the Cash Manager

A. Reporting Relationships

In most companies, the cash manager reports directly or indirectly to the treasurer of the company, who in turn reports to the chief financial officer. In a small company, the cash manager's job may be only a part-time responsibility of the treasurer or assistant treasurer, but in a large company, a staff of several people may be devoted to cash management and banking relations.

B. Cooperation with Other Functions

Though day-to-day monitoring of the company's cash position and maintaining banking relationships are almost always within the scope of the treasury function, other departments may have primary responsibility for some other functions such as credit management and disbursements that also have a strong impact on the time line of cash management. For example, the cash manager may share responsibility with the credit function for setting up and maintaining lockboxes operated by banks to intercept and speed the collection of checks from customers. However, the credit function sometimes reports to the controller, not the treasurer. Managing all the different types of float along the time line of cash management requires teamwork and cooperation, and the cash manager must often play an informal, influencing role with people in other departments.

C. Working Capital Management

Concern with float along the entire cash flow time line is called total working capital management. Working capital on a corporate balance sheet is the amount of current assets minus current liabilities. To manage the entire cash flow time line, a company must be concerned with its level of inventory, accounts receivable, and accounts payable, as well as its cash balances. These elements of working capital are discussed in Chapter 2, The Corporate Financial Function. Depending on company priorities and job descriptions, total working capital management may be a strategic objective to which the cash manager aspires. Many financial managers have broadened their staff members' roles so as to interact more with other functions in the corporation.

IV. Development of Cash Management in the U.S.

Cash management in the U.S. is an outgrowth of the particular features of the U.S. banking system, mail system and payment conventions. Among the features that distinguish the U.S. from other countries are a large number of banks, the lack of nationwide banking, mail delays, and a custom of paying most bills by check.

Prior to 1950, interest rates were low and the corporate treasurer did not have a large variety of external investment opportunities. There was more money in the banking system than there was loan demand. Banks funded their loans with interest-free demand deposit accounts (DDAs) and invested the excess in safe, low-yielding Government securities. Bankers competed with each other far less than they do today. They were highly selective in their corporate lending, motivating treasurers to keep large excess balances to protect credit facilities.

Key Developments in Cash Management

A.   The 1940s

The First Lockbox - RCA arranged a collection system in 1947. It was designed to accelerate payments from dealers who were borrowing from RCA to finance their inventory of RCA products.

B.   The 1960s

Negotiable Bank Certificates of Deposit (CDs) - By 1960, banks needed to buy funds and compete for deposits to support their growing loan portfolios. In 1961 the Fed authorized banks to issue negotiable certificates of deposit. The introduction of CDs provided a new source of funds for banks and an investment instrument for corporations.

Diversifying Short-Term Investments - Interest rates continued to rise in the 1960s. Treasurers diversified from low-yielding, liquid Government securities into new instruments such as municipal obligations, bankers' acceptances, commercial paper, and repurchase agreements. These instruments and how they are used are described in greater detail in Chapter 11, Investments.

Managing Bank Balances - The corporate treasurer worked cash harder, reduced bank balances and demanded more bank services for the balances on deposit. Banks, in response to this effort, expanded their corporate services and developed more formal marketing programs.

Lockbox Models - Bank-operated lockboxes became increasingly popular as corporate cash managers became more aware of collection float. In the late 1960s, a model was developed for studying mail times between one city and another. The model optimized the location of bank lockboxes in relation to the concentration of bill payors' mailing points.

C.   The 1970s

Remote Disbursement - Banks in geographically isolated locations offered significant float gains to a company that disbursed its checks from them. The remoteness of these banks meant difficulty in physically presenting checks drawn against them in a timely manner. The Federal Reserve was granting credit to the depositing bank before the check could be collected from the bank on which it was drawn. The increasing use of remote disbursement throughout the 1970s, coupled with the Fed's concern over the financial health of the banks used for this purpose, led to a program aimed at discouraging that practice and to measures aimed at reducing float.

Controlled Disbursement - Controlled disbursement was designed to take advantage of the Fed's presentment schedule. In a number of banks, the final presentment of checks from the Fed was sufficiently early in the day to enable a company to determine its check clearings, fund the account, and make investment and borrowing decisions knowing that there would be no additional clearings against the account that day.

Funds Concentration - Companies that processed credit card authorizations established services that aided in the creation of depository transfer checks. The amounts deposited in local banks would be reported by the depositing units. The information would be consolidated and relayed to the concentration bank where a depository transfer check, and later an electronic depository transfer, would be created to transfer funds from the local banks.

Bank Balance Reporting - Banks began to offer services to gather and store bank balance and transaction information which companies could access. Information from multiple banks could be consolidated into a single report.

Transaction Details and Real-Time Reporting - Customers began to get detailed transaction information on bank services. Banks offered information such as inbound money transfer amounts with accompanying reference information during the working day. Methods were developed for customers to initiate money transfers and other transactions using terminals in their offices.

Electronic Payments - Electronic payment alternatives began to be developed using the ACH. The primary applications were direct deposit of payroll and collection of life insurance premiums.

D. The 1980s

Depository Institutions Deregulation and Monetary Control Act of 1980 (DIDMCA) - Also known as the Monetary Control Act, this was was the most comprehensive banking legislation since the 1930s. This made a number of changes which were destined to have an impact on bank services and prices for years to come. A detailed discussion of its provisions is found in Chapter 3, The Banking System.

Noon Presentment and Payor Bank Services - In 1983 the Fed accelerated its presentment schedule by making second presentments later in the day as part of the float-reduction program mandated by the Monetary Control Act. This appeared at first to be a threat to controlled disbursement but the Fed developed a series of payor bank services to notify the banks electronically of the amount of the presentments.

Electronic Corporate-to-Corporate Payments - Banks began to promote corporate trade payments through the Automated Clearing House (ACH). Companies saw the efficiency of electronic payments on the one hand but were reluctant to give up disbursement float on the other.

Electronic Data Interchange (EDI) - Companies started the use of EDI. EDI is electronic, computer-to-computer communication for routine business transactions. With EDI, electronic transmission replaces paper documents throughout the business transaction cycle. Messages are coded in standard formats and sent between the buyer's computer and the seller's computer, generally through publicly available data transmission networks. This topic is discussed in greater detail in Chapter 9, Information Management.

Use of Personal Computers - The introduction of the personal computer (PC) led banks and software firms to develop the treasury workstation. Software was developed to retrieve information from banks automatically and compile it into Consolidated reports. The PC quickly replaced the paper spread sheet.

E.   Cash Management Ethics

In the early 1980s, the E.F. Hutton Company was involved in a widely discussed case concerning fair bank compensation. By channeling check deposits from Hutton branches through unsophisticated banks that treated ledger balances as though they were available balances, Hutton was effectively able to borrow interest free from the banks.

The E.F.Hutton affair put the spotlight on some questionable cash management practices. Cash management activities that are questionable risk the firm's reputation as well as that of the cash manager. Vendor, employee, and shareholder relations can be negatively affected. Procedures whose main intent is to take advantage of the banking system at the expense of the banks, or a firm's customers, invite a governmental response. Some companies developed policies designed to prevent certain practices. The Treasury Management Association (TMA) also developed Standards of Ethical Conduct.

V.   Financial Market Trends

The services, products, and technology used by the cash manager have changed through the years. The environment in which cash management is practiced has also changed. A number of fundamental trends have led to an increasingly complex financial marketplace.

A.   The Accord and the Government Securities Market

In 1951, the Federal Reserve Board of Governors reached an historic accord with the U.S. Treasury Department. It gave the Fed the right to pursue an independent monetary policy. The Fed subsequently adopted a policy of purchasing only treasury bills, letting the market determine the yield curve. The Treasury lost its captive investor and had to rely on a competitive market to raise funds. This marked the birth of a huge market of safe, liquid securities with short-, medium- and long-term maturities for companies with excess cash.

B.   Eurocurrency Markets

The Eurocurrency market developed initially in the 1960s, based on the accumulation of Eurodollars, U.S. dollars on deposit outside the U.S. The Eurodollar market broadened to become the Eurocurrency market and then expanded to become a worldwide offshore currency market.

C.   Worldwide Integration

Worldwide integration of financial markets resulted from the expansion of U.S. banks overseas and the development of international money centers. Computer and communications technology played a crucial role in forging these links and in facilitating the enormous funds flows and increasing the importance of foreign exchange management. These developments are discussed further in Chapter 13, Foreign Exchange and Interest Rate Risk Management.

D. Commercial Paper

Large corporations started to borrow short-term with commercial paper because it was less expensive than borrowing from commercial banks.

E. Financial Product Innovation

In the early 1980s, a number of capital market innovations were introduced. These new products included interest rate and currency swaps, futures, options and asset-backed securities. These are discussed further in Chapter 11, Investments, and Chapter 13, Foreign Exchange and Interest Rate Risk Management.

F. Securitization

Securitization is the pooling and packaging of similar debt obligations into securities that can be sold to investors. It started with mortgage-backed securities and spread to other assets such as automobile loans and credit card receivables. Financial institutions and corporations gained liquidity through the ability to sell short-term assets to investors.

G. Bank Creditworthiness

In the mid-1970s, several instances occurred that raised concerns about a bank's creditworthiness. The Federal Reserve showed concern over the impact a major bank failure would have on the payment system. Bankers, because of their exposure to other banks, were also worried. Treasurers who had previously shown little interest started to scrutinize the financial condition of their banks.

A key factor in judging bank creditworthiness is the bank's capital. In recent years capital adequacy ratios have been developed on a global basis. These are discussed in Chapter 4, The Payments System.

H. Payments System Risk

Payments system risk is an issue closely related to bank creditworthiness due to an increase in money transfer volume on the Fedwire and through the Clearing House Interbank Payments System (CHIPS) and the ACH. The Federal Reserve has taken numberous steps to reduce this risk. This is also explored in Chapter 4, The Payments System.

Questions

The chapter questions are to test the information in the text and are not examples of CCM examination questions nor are they in the examination format.

Answers can be found at the back of the book on p. 309.

1. What are the major objectives of cash management?

2. What are the major functions of cash management?

3. What are the four cash flows that a firm must manage?

4. What are the two types of float presented on the cash flow timeline?

5. What are the two components of check float?

6. What two disbursement products were introduced in the 1970s?

7. What banking legislation reshaped cash management in the 1980s?

8. What is securitization?

The Corporate Financial Function

Chapter 2

Overview

Chapter 1 briefly introduced the basic functions of cash management in the context of recent trends in the financial world. This chapter describes another important aspect of the environment in which cash management operates, the corporate financial function. It explains overall corporate objectives, the role of the finance function in attaining those objectives, and the basic financial and accounting concepts necessary to understand how the attainment of those objectives is measured.

Learning Objectives

Upon completion of this chapter and the related study questions, the reader should be able to do the following:

1. Discuss overall corporate objectives and the role of the finance function in attaining them.

2. Understand basic accounting and financial concepts such as the income statement, the balance sheet, the statement of cash flows, cash versus accrual accounting, the time value of money, the cost of capital, corporate financial structure, capital budgeting, and liquidity.

3. Describe the typical role of the chief financial officer, treasurer, assistant treasurer, controller, auditor, and credit manager.

4. Discuss how the cash manager fits into the treasury organization.

5. Describe the cash manager's day-to-day responsibilities.

OUTLINE

I.   **Corporate Financial Objectives**

   A.   Overall Corporate Objective

   B.   Corporate Financial Decisions

   C.   Corporate Financial Function

II.   **Accounting Concepts**

   A.   Accounting Principles

   B.   Certified Public Accountants (CPAs)

   C.   Financial Statements

   D.   Double Entry Bookkeeping

   E.   Cash versus Accrual Accounting

   F.   Accounting for Cash

III.   **Financial Concepts**

   A.   Time Value of Money

   B.   Cash Discount and Present Value

   C.   Weighted Average Cost of Capital (WACC)

   D.   Capital Structure and Strategy

   E.   Capital Budgeting

   F.   Financial Ratios

   G.   Liquidity

IV.   **The Corporate Financial Organization**

   A.   Responsibilities of the Key Players

   B.   Finance Function Organizational Structure

   C.   Responsibilities of the Cash Manager

I.   Corporate Financial Objectives

A.   Overall Corporate Objective

The primary objective of a corporation is to maximize shareholder value, that is, the value of the owners' shares in the corporation. A corporation's financial objectives are closely related to this overall objective.

B.   Corporate Financial Decisions

The most important financial decisions a corporation must make are as follows:

1. **Investment Decisions** - The firm must decide where to allocate its capital, i.e., the kinds of projects in which it wants to invest. Investment projects may range from capital equipment to corporate subsidiaries. They should be evaluated in terms of return and risk; in other words, the forecasted extra profits those projects will create, and the risk that those forecasts will not be met.

   Also, very few companies can raise unlimited capital for their projects, or have the management resources for an unlimited number of projects even if the capital is available. Therefore, one of the company's most important investment decisions is how many projects can be undertaken and how big the corporation can realistically be.

   Another type of investment decision is to sell a division or subsidiary or discontinue a product line because the company's capital resources can be more effectively deployed elsewhere.

   These are all long-term investment decisions as distinct from short-term investment decisions, which are discussed in Chapter 11, Investments.

2. **Financing Decisions** - The firm must decide how to finance its projects, either from shareholders' capital, from borrowed funds, or from a mixture of the two. As discussed in the section on leverage later in this chapter, borrowing can increase corporate earnings if project returns exceed the cost of borrowing. However, borrowing also increases risk because projections may not be met and subsequent default on a loan obligation could push a company into bankruptcy.

   Financing and investment decisions are intertwined. Whether or not a corporation invests in a given project and the total level of investment are partly determined by whether or not it can raise the capital. Companies with differing risk profiles appeal to investors with differing risk appetites.

3. **Dividend Decisions** - The company must decide how much of its earnings to distribute as cash dividends to stockholders and how much to retain and reinvest. That decision is sometimes guided by shareholders' expectations, which vary widely by factors such as the company's industry and its stage of growth. For example, the stock of an established utility may have limited capital appreciation but pay high dividends relative to other companies. In contrast, the stock of a young,

growing, high-technology company may not pay dividends at all because earnings, to the extent there are any, are being invested in the company and shareholders are investing for growth in share price rather than dividends. Also, debt agreements may restrict dividends if certain conditions are not met.

C.   Corporate Financial Function

The finance function plays a pivotal role in the achievement of a company's overall objective to maximize shareholder value. The principal roles of the finance function include the following:

1.   **Accounting** - The accounting function is in effect the scorekeeping function. Companies need to follow generally accepted principles of accounting to record assets, liabilities, revenues, expenses, and earnings.

2.   **Capital Budgeting** - The finance function is responsible for:

   - quantitatively evaluating various projects in which the corporation could invest,

   - forecasting the rate of return in relation to the cost of capital, and

   - working with top management to weigh quantitative factors against other more qualitative factors. Those factors might include whether a project fits into the firm's core strategy, and whether it is in the area where the company has maximum competitive advantage.

3.   **Funding** - The finance function is responsible for raising capital to fund the projects a company undertakes to produce earnings and enhance shareholder value.

II.   Accounting Concepts

This section describes the basic accounting and financial concepts that underlie the system of financial reporting and record-keeping used in the U.S. today.

A.   Accounting Principles

The accounting function records a company's assets, liabilities, revenues and expenses according to a detailed set of rules called Generally Accepted Accounting Principles (GAAP). These principles are developed, agreed upon, and published in the form of Financial Accounting Standards (FAS) by the Financial Accounting Standards Board (FASB), an independent, self-regulating organization, formed in 1973. Adherence to those rules is important because investors, lenders, and trade creditors rely on that financial information for their decisions as to whether to invest, lend or to provide products or services on credit terms.

B. Certified Public Accountants (CPAs)

CPAs review the methods companies use to prepare their financial statements, audit selected records to verify the accuracy of the financial statements and provide opinions as to whether the statements are in accordance with GAAP.

C. Financial Statements

The following types of accounting or financial statements are generally used to record revenues, expenses, assets and liabilities, and are prepared according to GAAP.

1. **Income Statement** - The income statement, or profit and loss statement, is a record of revenues and expenses, as illustrated in Exhibit 2-1. It describes the net change in the value of the owners' equity resulting from the operations of the firm during the accounting cycle.

   • Revenues are the total proceeds from an organization's sale of merchandise or services.

Exhibit 2-1

Income Statement

INCOME STATEMENT
Year Ended December 31, 199Y

Revenues	$15,000,000
Cost of Goods Sold	9,200,000
Gross Profit	5,800,000
Operating Expenses	4,200,000
Operating Profit	1,600,000
Interest Expense	300,000
Net Profit Before Taxes	1,300,000
Provision for Income Taxes	450,000
Net Income	$850,000
Earnings Available for Common Shareholders	850,000
Dividends	250,000
Addition to Retained Earnings	600,000
Earnings Per Share (100,000 shares outstanding)	$8.50

- The cost of goods sold represents the cost of providing goods and services for sale. It includes labor and material directly used in manufacturing a product or providing a service, as well as depreciation of the production equipment.

- Operating profit, also known as operating income, is the profit after deducting the cost of goods sold and operating expenses.

- Selling, general and administrative expenses, also known as operating expenses, are indirect expenses necessary for the conduct of the business but not tied directly to the production of goods and services.

- Net income is revenues minus cost of goods sold, operating expenses, income taxes and other expenses incurred during the accounting cycle.

2.   **Balance Sheet** - A balance sheet is illustrated in Exhibit 2-2. The balance sheet or statement of financial condition, reports the following:

- balances in a company's asset accounts, items owned by the corporation

- liability accounts, amounts owed by the corporation

- equity, the value of the owners' position in the organization.

Assets are listed at historical cost on the balance sheet. Assets that may be depreciated or amortized are shown net of depreciation. Assets are usually listed on the balance sheet in the order of decreasing liquidity. The first category at the top is current assets, which include cash, marketable securities, accounts receivable and inventories. These current assets will normally be converted to cash within one year or within the accounting cycle.

Current assets in this example include prepaid expenses. An example is insurance policies prepaid for the year. Some banks and companies may report prepaid expenses as long-term assets because they cannot readily be turned into cash.

Intangible assets are assets that lack physical substance. Examples are goodwill and patents.

- Goodwill is the excess of the purchase price of a business over the value of its net assets as reflected on its balance sheet.

- A patent is an exclusive right to a product or process.

- Both goodwill and patents are amortized over their legal or useful lives.

Property, plant and equipment, is the company's investment in fixed assets such as factories, office buildings and computers. Fixed assets, known also as long-term assets or capital assets, cannot be turned into cash as readily as current assets.

Liabilities represent obligations of the firm. They are usually listed on the balance sheet in order of increasing maturity. The first category is current liabilities, which include obligations such as accounts payable, short-term loans, wages payable, and the current portion of long-term debt (all due within one year or accounting cycle). Accounts payable are amounts due to trade creditors for items such as raw materials and office supplies. Short-

Exhibit 2-2

Balance Sheet

BALANCE SHEET
December 31, 199Y

ASSETS

Current Assets

Cash	$1,500,000
Short-Term Investments	1,300,000
Accounts Receivable	1,700,000
Inventory	2,600,000
Prepaid Expenses	900,000
Total Current Assets	8,000,000

Fixed Assets

Property, Plant and Equipment (net of depreciation)	7,500,000
Total Assets	$15,500,000

LIABILITIES AND OWNERS' EQUITY

Current Liabilities

Accounts Payable	$ 1,600,000
Short-Term Notes Payable	1,800,000
Total Current Liabilities	3,400,000

Long-Term Liabilities

Long Term Debt	3,900,000
Total Liabilities	7,300,000

Shareholders' Equity

Common Stock at Par Value	200,000
Paid-In Capital	3,600,000
Retained Earnings	4,400,000
Total Liabilities and Owners' Equity	$15,500,000

term notes payable are typically short-term bank loans or commercial paper.

Long-term liabilities are obligations such as term loans, mortgages and bonds due beyond one year.

Shareholders' equity represents the book value committed by and belonging to the owners, either in the form of investment or retained earnings.

Retained earnings is the increase in owners' equity that arises from the retention of profits in the business.

The following equations always hold true:

Assets = Liabilities plus Shareholders' Equity

Assets minus Liabilities = Shareholders' Equity

3. **Statement of Cash Flows** - Under the accrual system, the accounting period when a revenue or expense item is recognized is often different from the accounting period when the cash transaction takes place. Although the income statement based on accrual accounting is a useful indication of the company's performance, lenders are concerned with the company's cash flow because cash, not earnings, repays debt.

The Statement of Cash Flows provides an indication of the sources of a company's cash flow and how it is being used. It is divided into three sections—Operating, Investing, and Financing Activities.

Exhibit 2-3 shows how a Statement of Cash Flows can be constructed from information in the income statement and balance sheet.

Notice that more information is needed than the change in net earnings to derive the cash flow from operations. The level of depreciation is also needed to derive cash flow. The change in retained earnings on the balance sheet is equal to net income minus dividends paid. The net change in the property account reflected on the balance sheet is equal to the additions to property minus depreciation.

Other needed information comes from year-to-year changes in the balance sheet. Decreases in assets and increases in liabilities are sources of cash. Increases in assets and decreases in liabilities are uses of cash.

In examining the statement of cash flows, it can be seen that cash flow from operations was the largest source of funds, but that funds were also generated from an increase in accounts payable, a decrease in short-term investments, an increase in short-term notes payable and an increase in long-term debt. Funds were in turn used to increase the level of cash, to support increased accounts receivable, to increase inventory, to add to property, plant and equipment, and to pay dividends.

D. Double Entry Bookkeeping

For every accounting transaction, there is both a debit or series of debits, and a credit or series of credits. An addition to an asset account or a subtraction from a liability or owners' equity account is a debit. An addition to a liability account, or a subtraction from an asset account is a credit.

E. Cash versus Accrual Accounting

Some firms, particularly small ones, record their revenues, expenses and earnings strictly on the basis of when they were received or paid. This is known as cash accounting. Most large firms are required to use a system known as accrual

Exhibit 2-3

Statement of Cash Flows

STATEMENT OF CASH FLOWS

ASSETS	Prior Year 199X	Current Year 199X	Change
Cash	$ 1,000,000	$ 1,500,000	$ 500,000
Short-Term Investments	1,500,000	1,300,000	(200,000)
Accounts Receivable	1,300,000	1,700,000	400,000
Inventory	2,100,000	2,600,000	500,000
Prepaid Expenses	900,000	900,000	
Total Current Assets	6,800,000	8,000,000	
Property, Plant and Equipment	6,800,000	7,500,000	700,000
Total Assets	$13,600,000	$15,500,000	$1,900,000

LIABILITIES AND OWNERS EQUITY

	Prior Year 199X	Current Year 199X	Change
Accounts Payable	$ 1,200,000	$ 1,600,000	$ 400,000
Short-Term Notes Payable	1,300,000	1,800,000	500,000
Total Current Liabilities	2,500,000	3,400,000	
Long-Term Debt	3,500,000	3,900,000	400,000
Total Liabilities	6,000,000	7,300,000	
Common Stock at Par Value	200,000	200,000	
Paid-In Capital	3,600,000	3,600,000	
Retained Earnings	3,800,000	4,400,000	600,000
Total Liabilities and Owners' Equity	$13,600,000	$15,500,000	$1,900,000

STATEMENT OF CASH FLOWS
For the Year Ended December 31, 199X

Cash Flows From Operating Activities

Net Income $850,000

Adjustment to Reconcile Net Income to Net Cash Provided from Operating Activities

Depreciation 200,000

(More)

Exhibit 2-3 (Continued)

Statement of Cash Flows

STATEMENT OF CASH FLOWS
For the Year Ended December 31, 199X

Increase (Decrease) in Current Assets or Liabilities	
Accounts Receivable	$ (400,000)
Inventories	(500,000)
Accounts Payable	400,000
Net Cash Provided From (Used By) Operating Activities	550,000
Cash Flows From Investing Activities	
Capital Expenditures	(900,000)
Net Cash Used By Investing Activities	(900,000)
Cash Flows From Financing Activities	
Decrease in Short-Term Investments	200,000
Net Borrowing Under Bank Line of Credit Agreement	500,000
Proceeds from Issuance of Long-Term Debt	400,000
Dividends Paid	(250,000)
Net Increase (Decrease) in Cash	500,000
Cash—Beginning of Year	1,000,000
Cash—End of Year	$ 1,500,000

accounting. Accrual accounting is the approach that uses the matching concept to report the revenues and expenses in the same accounting period.

The fundamental difference between cash and accrual accounting is the timing of the recognition of income or expenses, and the actual cash flows. With the accrual accounting system, revenues may be reported but not yet collected, and expenses may have been incurred but not yet paid. It is particularly important for the cash manager, who is mainly concerned with cash flows, to understand the distinction between accounting information and cash flows.

The primary features of accrual accounting are as follows:

1. **Income Recognition** - Revenue is recognized on the income statement when the sales are made. When sales are made on credit, accounts receivable are created. This documents that the revenue from sales has been recognized, but that funds have not yet been received. When funds are collected from the customer, the accounts receivable balance is decreased, and the cash balance is increased without any effect on income.

2. **Cost Recognition** - Costs incurred in a time period prior to the sale are added to the inventory value. They are not treated as expenses when there is a cash expenditure. The expense is recognized as part of the cost of goods sold in the accounting period of the sale so as to match revenues and expenses.

3. **Capitalized Assets** - Capitalized assets are expected to have a life greater than one accounting cycle and are not considered an expense during the period in which they were acquired. The assets are carried on the balance sheet at their acquisition cost and depreciated.

4. **Depreciation and Amortization** - Accounting expense connected with a capitalized asset is recognized by depreciation in the case of fixed assets and amortization in the case of intangible, long-term assets. With both depreciation and amortization, the cost of the asset is allocated over its legal or useful life. Neither depreciation nor amortization measures a decline in the value of an asset. Both are non-cash expenses; therefore, the income statement for an accounting period understates the cash flow provided by operations, by the amount of the depreciation expense.

5. **Deferred Taxes** - Due to differences between recognition of revenue and expenses by the tax code and by accrual accounting, the cash disbursement for income taxes may be different from the taxes reported on the income statement. This difference is recognized as a deferred tax and is listed as a liability on the balance sheet.

6. **Capital and Dividends** - A number of cash flows such as capital asset additions or retirements and dividends are neither income nor expenses. The addition of capital to the firm, such as the issuance of debt or the sale of common stock, results in a cash inflow, but is not income. The cash flow for the repayment of principal in a debt obligation is not an expense. The payment of cash dividends to the owners of the firm is a distribution of profits and not an expense.

7. **Management Discretion** - A company must exercise judgement on the allocation of expenses and revenues and there is potential for companies to overstate revenues or understate expenses under the accrual system. Part of the external auditor's role is to render an opinion that revenue and expense recognition is according to GAAP.

F. Accounting for Cash

The cash balance that is reported on the balance sheet reflects cash as recorded on the company's accounting books. It is often different from the cash balance on the bank's books, primarily because of disbursement float (checks that have been written but not yet presented for payment).

Sometimes, a company's books will reflect a negative cash balance, or a red book balance. There are two ways to avoid reporting these negative balances in the company's financial statements. Instead of reporting cash as a separate item, the combined total of cash and marketable securities can be reported on the balance sheet. This, of course, assumes that the amount of marketable securities is greater than the negative cash balance. Alternatively, the company can report the bank balance in the cash account, and report checks that have been written but not yet presented for payment as a current liability under a title such as drafts payable, or checks not cleared.

III. Financial Concepts

A. Time Value of Money

The basic concepts of the time value of money are as follows: A dollar today is worth more than a dollar tomorrow because a dollar today can be invested to earn a return. It follows logically that a dollar tomorrow is worth less than a dollar today because the opportunity to earn interest is foregone. This price or rate of return that the best alternative course of action provides is called opportunity cost.

The future value of $100 invested at 10% is $110 one year from now ($100 X 1.10), and $121 two years from now ($100 X 1.10 X 1.10).

$$FV_n = P_o (1+i)^n$$

Where:

P_o = Initial Principal Invested

FV_n = Future value in "n" periods

i = Discount Rate

n = Number of Periods

The present value of $110 at a discount rate of 10% is $100. A corporate treasurer with an opportunity cost or opportunity rate of 10%, i.e., the opportunity to invest or borrow at 10%, should be indifferent to the $100 he or she received today, and the $110 received a year from now.

$$PV = \frac{FV}{(1+i)^n}$$

If the company's opportunity cost or discount rate is 10%, a project that requires an investment of $100 now and returns a total of $110 a year from now has a net present value of 0. The net present value is the present value of all the cash inflows (earnings) from a project minus the present value of the cash outflows (initial and possibly subsequent investments). When the net present value is 0, the present value of the outflows is equal to the present value of the inflows. If the company considers 10% to be its hurdle rate, the minimum return for its projects, then it could use 10% as the discount rate in a discounted cash flow analysis. Any project with a net present value of more than zero would exceed the 10% hurdle rate.

Companies often use their cost of capital as a discount rate for evaluating their projects. Companies in riskier businesses tend to have higher costs of capital and to use higher discount rates in evaluating their projects. When a given project is evaluated with higher discount rates, the net present value is lower because each future cash flow is discounted at a higher rate.

B. Cash Discount and Present Value

Present value analysis can also be applied to short-term financial decisions such as when to pay an invoice. This is illustrated in Exhibit 2-4. The most accurate cost of capital to use in this case is the weighted average cost of capital, which is described in Section C. However, depending on the nature and length of the project, other rates may be appropriate.

Exhibit 2-4

Cash Discount and Present Value

CASH DISCOUNT AND PRESENT VALUE

A company can pay an invoice of $10,000 on the tenth day to receive a 1.5% discount or pay the invoice in full on the 30th day. Credit terms are therefore 1.5/10 net 30. The opportunity cost of funds is 8.0%.

If the payment is made on the tenth day, the cash outflow is the invoice amount minus the discount:

$$\$10,000 \times (1 - .015) = \$9,850$$

The present value (PV) is calculated by the following formula:

$$PV = \frac{\text{Cash Flow to be Received } t \text{ days from now}}{[\,1 + r\,(t/365)\,]}$$

where r = the relevant interest rate over t days. Note that if an annual rate is given, to convert to a t-day rate multiply by $t/365$.

The present value of paying $10,000 on the 30th day is as follows:

$$PV = \frac{\$10,000}{[\,1 + (.08)\,(30/365))\,]} = \$9,934.68$$

The present value of paying on the tenth day is:

$$PV = \frac{\$9,850}{[\,1 + (.08)\,(10/365))\,]} = \$9,828.46$$

Therefore, in present value terms, there is a savings of $106.22 to pay the invoice on the tenth day and take the discount than to pay the net amount on the 30th day.

C. Weighted Average Cost of Capital (WACC)

Companies tend to finance with a combination of equity and debt. Equity is more expensive than debt because the shareholders' position is generally considered riskier than that of the debt holders. Interest costs are a legal obligation, whereas the payment of dividends is discretionary and may be omitted in times of poor earnings. Also, interest on debt is tax-deductible, whereas dividends on common stock are not. Therefore, debt tends to be cheaper than equity on an after-tax basis.

Many companies consider their weighted average cost of capital (WACC) to be an appropriate discount rate for evaluating their projects. A weighted average cost of capital is calculated as follows:

$$\text{WACC} = \left(\text{After Tax Cost of Debt} \times \frac{\text{Debt}}{\text{Debt} + \text{Equity}}\right) + \left(\text{Cost of Equity} \times \frac{\text{Equity}}{\text{Debt} + \text{Equity}}\right)$$

Assume that a company's long-term capital structure is 40% long-term debt and 60% equity. The company's cost of long-term debt is 12%. The corporate tax rate is 34%; therefore, the after-tax cost of debt is 12% X .66 = 7.92%. The company's cost of equity is 16%.

The WACC is calculated as follows:

$$\text{WACC} = (.0792 \times .40) + (.16 \times .60)$$

$$= .0317 + .0960$$

$$= .1277 = 12.77\%$$

D. Capital Structure and Strategy

Companies have an incentive to finance with debt for two reasons. First, as we have seen, the cost of debt is typically lower than the cost of equity. Second, from the point of view of existing shareholders, the less new stock is sold, the less equity interest in the growth of the company they are giving up, i.e., the less they are being diluted.

The use of debt to finance a company is called **financial leverage.** Assuming that there are sufficient investment projects with a return higher than the cost of debt, a company can continually increase its earnings by taking on more debt, in effect leveraging the investment of the shareholders, but leverage works both ways. Interest on debt obligations is a fixed cost, and the more debt a company assumes, the greater the risk that it will default on its debt obligations.

Each company must evaluate its own tolerance for leverage and risk and decide on a target mix between debt and equity. Investors demand higher returns for higher risks. Companies in different industries with different risk profiles attract investors with different risk appetites and return expectations.

E. Capital Budgeting

Capital budgeting is the process of evaluating alternative investment projects by methods such as net present value, and weighing other non-quantitative factors such as the company's core strategy and where the firm believes its competitive strengths lie. A company may compare the net present values of various projects using the WACC as the discount rate.

A company operating in several industries may use a higher assumed WACC and discount rate for its riskier businesses and a lower WACC for its less risky businesses. It may also evaluate projects by calculating an **internal rate of return** (IRR). The IRR is the discount rate at which the net present value is equal to zero.

F. Financial Ratios

Financial ratios are used to determine the company's creditworthiness, growth prospects and can be used for comparison to other firms in the same industry. No single ratio tells the whole story, but groups of ratios when considered together can be revealing.

1. **Advantages** - Advantages of using traditional financial ratios for analysis include the following:

    - Ratios are easily computed from the information found in publicly available financial reports.

    - Ratios are familiar to most producers and users of financial information.

    - Historical trends and variability can be observed over time.

    - Financial ratio databases allow comparison between firms.

2. **Disadvantages** - The key disadvantages of traditional ratio measures include the following:

    - Traditional ratio measures usually reflect accounting rather than economic values.

    - Ratios express static relationships and do not take the variability of cash flows into account except to the extent that the ratios themselves may vary.

    - Financial ratios provide indications but not answers. The evaluation of a firm's liquidity is a matter of judgment.

    - Ratios are affected by differing methods of depreciation and by window dressing, a practice of adjusting certain accounts just prior to the end of the accounting period to make financial statements look better.

Exhibit 2-5 contains examples of commonly used ratios.

G. Liquidity

Liquidity is the ability to convert an asset into cash or cash equivalents without significant loss. A company may be said to be liquid if it is easily able to meet its near-term financial obligations on time. Managing corporate liquidity on a day-to-day basis is an important function of cash management.

Exhibit 2-5

Examples of Financial Ratios

EXAMPLES OF FINANCIAL RATIOS

The following abbreviated financial statements can be used to calculate a number of commonly used financial ratios as shown below:

INCOME STATEMENT
Year Ended December 31, 199Y

Revenues	$	15,000,000
Cost of Goods Sold*		9,200,000
Operating Profit/Operating Income		5,800,000
Selling, General and Administrative Expenses		4,200,000
Interest		300,000
Net Profit Before Taxes		1,300,000
Provision for Income Taxes		450,000
Net Income	$	850,000
Earnings Available for Common Shareholders		850,000
Dividends		250,000
Additions to Retained Earnings	$	600,000
Earnings Per Share (100,000 shares outstanding)	$	8.50

*Includes Depreciation of $200,000

BALANCE SHEET
December 31, 199Y

ASSETS
<u>Current Assets</u>

Cash	$	1,500,000
Short-Term Investments		1,300,000
Accounts Receivable		1,700,000
Inventory		2,600,000
Prepaid Expenses		900,000
Total Current Assets		8,000,000

<u>Fixed Assets</u>

Property, Plant and Equipment (net of depreciation)		7,500,000
Total Assets	$	15,500,000

Exhibit 2-5 (Continued)

Examples of Financial Ratios

LIABILITY AND OWNERS' EQUITY

<u>Current Liabilities</u>

Accounts Payable	$	1,600,000
Short-Term Notes Payable		1,800,000
Total Current Liabilities		3,400,000

<u>Long-Term Liabilities</u>

Long-Term Debt	3,900,000
Total Liabilities	7,300,000

<u>Shareholders' Equity</u>

Common Stock at Par Value	200,000
Paid-In Capital	3,600,000
Retained Earnings	4,400,000
Total Liabilities and Owners' Equity	$ 15,500,000

RATIO CALCULATIONS

WORKING CAPITAL POSITION RATIOS

Working capital position ratios measure the extent to which the firm's current liabilities are covered by current assets.

Current Ratio = Current Assets/Current Liabilities

$$\frac{\$8,000,000}{3,400,000} = 2.35$$

Quick Ratio = (Current Assets minus Inventory)/Current Liabilities

$$\frac{\$8,000,000 - 2,600,000}{3,400,000} = 1.59$$

Net Working Capital/Total Assets = (Current Assets minus Current Liabilities)/Total Assets

$$\frac{\$8,000,000 - 3,400,000}{15,500,000} = 29.7\%$$

WORKING CAPITAL ACTIVITY RATIOS

Working capital activity ratios measure how rapidly the corresponding asset is turned into cash.

Sales/Inventory

$$\frac{\$15,000,000}{2,600,000} = 5.77$$

Cost of Goods Sold/Accounts Receivable

$$\frac{\$9,200,000}{1,700,000} = 5.41$$

Exhibit 2-5

Examples of Financial Ratios

RATIO CALCULATIONS

LEVERAGE RATIOS
Leverage ratios are often included as liquidity measures because they indicate borrowing capacity.

Debt/Total Assets = [Current Liabilities + Long-Term Debt]/ Total Assets

$$\frac{\$\,3,400,000 + 3,900,000}{15,500,000} = 47.1\%$$

Debt/Equity = Total Debt/Shareholders' Equity

$$\frac{\$\,3,400,000 + 3,900,000}{200,000 + 3,600,000 + 4,400,000} = 89.0\%$$

Long-Term Debt/Total Capitalization

$$\frac{\$\,3,900,000}{3,900,000 + 200,000 + 3,600,000 + 4,400,000} = 32.2\%$$

Note: Total Capitalization = Long-term Debt + Shareholders' Equity

PERFORMANCE RATIOS
Performance ratios such as return on investment or return on assets measure the company's earnings capability.

Return on Investment

Net Income/Shareholders' Equity = $\$\dfrac{850,000}{8,200,000} = 10.37\%$

Return on Assets

Net Income/Total Assets = $\$\dfrac{850,000}{15,500,000} = 5.48\%$

1. **Sources of Liquidity** - A company can safeguard its liquidity in the following ways:

    - By having continuing cash flow from operations,

    - By having sufficient cash and easily liquidated short-term investments to take care of temporary cash shortages, and

    - By having ample unused short-term borrowing facilities.

2. **Why Liquidity is Needed** - According to traditional economics, there are three primary reasons a firm needs liquidity. These are:

    - *Transactions Requirement* - A firm's cash inflows and outflows are not perfectly synchronized. The transaction liquidity balance is a reserve containing cash and near-cash resources held to provide for future funds requirements.

    - *Precautionary Requirement* - A firm's cash inflows and outflows are not known with perfect certainty. Furthermore, unanticipated cash needs may arise after budgets are established. The precautionary liquidity balance is a reserve in which cash and near-cash resources are held to provide for unexpected requirements for funds.

    - *Speculative Requirement* - If the firm expects interest rates to rise in the near future, it may invest in maturities with the shortest term, say less than seven days, and wait to invest in longer maturities, say three to six months, assuming that rates rise. On the other hand, if rates are high and the firm expects them to decline in the near future, it may want to invest in longer maturities. Having extra liquid resources helps a firm take advantage of such investment opportunities.

3. **Determining the Right Level of Liquidity**

    - *Insufficient Liquidity* - There are a number of costs associated with not having sufficient liquidity. These are:

    Transaction costs are the brokerage and administrative costs incurred when securities are sold or a line of credit is exercised to replenish a firm's cash balance. These costs are incurred more frequently when a firm maintains a smaller cash balance.

    Cash shortage costs are the costs of not having cash available when it is required. While these costs range from minor to very significant, they are more likely to be incurred when the firm maintains a smaller liquid reserve. Examples include:

    The costs of delaying payments, such as damage to the firm's credit standing, lost cash discounts, and interest penalties.

    The opportunity cost of foregoing advantageous purchases or investment opportunities.

    Additional interest cost from unanticipated borrowing.

    At the extreme, a firm with inadequate liquidity may become insolvent, and be forced to seek court protection by filing for bankruptcy. The resulting liquidation or reorganization creates bankruptcy costs such as legal fees, time requirements by management, low employee morale, a negative public image, and foregone investment opportunities.

- *Excess Liquidity* - Conversely, too much liquidity also has disadvantages. The opportunity cost of holding cash and near-cash assets results from the inability to invest these resources in opportunities that are more profitable.

The dollar volume of cash inflows and outflows is a major determinant of the level of liquidity needed, but there are other important factors as well. Even slight timing differences between cash inflows and outflows can cause a large drain on cash resources. Individual remittances may be relatively large in proportion to the size of the firm, and, therefore, only a few days delay in a customer payment can cause substantial problems. The firm's sales may fluctuate from month-to-month while expenses are incurred at a steady rate. All of these factors require a firm to maintain substantial safety reserves.

4. **Measuring Liquidity** - Measuring liquidity is important to the company's internal management for determining the adequacy of the firm's liquidity policies, setting policy guidelines, and reporting to outside creditors such as banks. Bankers and trade creditors need to measure liquidity as part of their evaluation of the company's creditworthiness. Methods for measuring liquidity include:

- **Current Ratio** $= \dfrac{\text{Current Assets}}{\text{Current Liabilities}}$

The current ratio measures the degree to which current obligations are covered by current assets. Example is from Exhibit 2-5.

$$\$8,000/3,400 = 2.35$$

- **Quick Ratio** $= \dfrac{\text{Current Assets minus Inventory}}{\text{Current Liabilities}}$

The quick ratio is a more conservative liquidity ratio. Inventory is not included in current assets in the quick ratio because it is not so easily turned into cash. Example is from Exhibit 2-5.

$$\$(8,000-2,600)/3,400 = 1.59$$

- **Cash flow to total debt** is defined as net income plus depreciation divided by total long-term and short-term debt. Studies of failed firms have found this ratio to be historically accurate in predicting financial failure. A relatively low ratio is indicative of an inability to repay debt. Example from data in Exhibit 2-5.

$$\$\dfrac{(850 + 200)}{1,800 + 3,900} = \dfrac{1,050}{5,700} = .184$$

- The **Cash Conversion Cycle** approaches liquidity from a different angle. By adding the average age of the inventory and the accounts receivable and subtracting the average age of the accounts payable, this measure indicates how efficiently a company is using its current assets and liabilities. The formula is:

$$\text{Cash Conversion Cycle} = \frac{\text{Inventory}}{\text{Cost of Goods Sold}} \times 365 + \frac{\text{Accounts Receivable}}{\text{Sales}} \times 365$$

$$- \frac{\text{Accounts Payable}}{\text{Purchases}} \times 365$$

Purchases = Ending Inventory + Cost of Goods Sold - Beginning Inventory:

$$\text{Purchases} = 2{,}600 + 9{,}200 - 2{,}100 = 9{,}700$$

$$\left(\frac{2{,}600}{9{,}200} \times 365\right) + \left(\frac{1{,}700}{15{,}000} \times 365\right) - \left(\frac{1{,}600}{9{,}700} \times 365\right) = 103 \text{ days} + 41 \text{ days} - 60 \text{ days} = 84 \text{ da}$$

This indicates the company cycles through its cash every 84 days.

- **Cash Turnover** is the number of cash conversion cycles per year.

$$\text{Cash Turnover} = \frac{365}{\text{Cash Conversion Cycle}}$$

$$\frac{365}{84} = 4.35$$

The cash conversion cycle and cash turnover are measures of efficiency that can be compared to those of similar companies in similar industries.

- **Minimum Liquidity Requirement** or Minimum Operating Cash is equal to the total annual cash outlays for the year divided by the cash turnover.

$$\text{Minimum Liquidity Requirement} = \frac{\text{Total Annual Cash Outlays}}{\text{Cash Turnover}}$$

If the company in this example has $85 million in total outlays for the year then it will need:

$$\frac{\$85{,}000{,}000}{4.35} = \$19{,}540{,}230$$

as its minimum liquid balance. Any policy that can speed up the cash cycle will reduce this need and free up the funds for investment in more profitable activities.

IV. The Corporate Financial Organization

A.   Responsibilities of the Key Players

1.   **Chief Financial Officer (CFO)** - The CFO is normally a member of the top management team of the firm reporting to the chief executive officer. In a large company, the CFO oversees the treasury and accounting functions, and plays an important strategic planning role as the pivotal person in the

capital budgeting and investment decision making process. Selecting and rejecting investment projects is part of the way a company carries out its strategic plan. Final decisions on building a plant, buying or selling a subsidiary or closing down a product line may be made by the chief executive officer or the board of directors, but the CFO plays a central role in spelling out and quantifying decision alternatives, and measuring the financial results of those decisions once they are made.

2. **Treasurer** - The treasurer is usually responsible for arranging external financing, managing relationships with banks and other financial institutions, and overseeing day-to-day liquidity management. Other functions that may report to the treasurer include credit management, dividend disbursement, insurance and pension management. In a large company, some of these responsibilities may be delegated to an assistant treasurer.

3. **Controller** - The controller is normally responsible for internal accounting, preparation of the company's financial statements, internal auditing, coordination with the company's external auditors, preparing budgets and taxes, and capital budgeting.

4. **Internal Auditor** - The internal auditor is responsible for determining that controls and operating procedures are in place to protect the company from losses caused by inefficiency, inaccuracy, or fraud. The internal auditor often reports to the controller but may also report to the CFO.

5. **Credit Manager** - The credit manager, who may report either to the controller or to the treasurer, is responsible for setting corporate credit policies, approving the extension of credit terms to customers, establishing information systems to monitor accounts receivable, and monitoring accounts receivable on a day-to-day basis.

6. **Cash Manager** - The cash manager is part of the treasury function and is concerned primarily with the management of day-to-day cash flows and banking relationships. Responsibilities of the cash manager are discussed in Section C.

B. Finance Function Organizational Structure

1. In a large company, the treasurer and the controller often report to the CFO.

2. Some firms have a flatter organizational structure in which the following functions report to the CFO:

   • Treasury

   • Control

   • MIS

   • Audit

   • Strategic planning

   • Financial analysis

3. Exhibit 2-6 illustrates how the cash manager typically fits into the treasury function of a large corporation.

Exhibit 2-6

*Organization of The
Treasury Function*

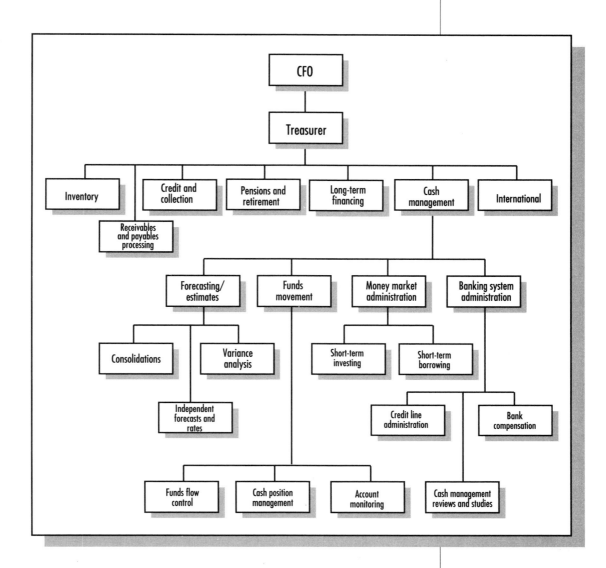

C. Responsibilities of the Cash Manager

Although the cash manager's position may vary from firm to firm, there are several functions that typically fall under the cash manager's responsibilities:

1. **Funds Movement**

   • Monitoring the firm's daily cash position

   • Controlling balances at major banks

   • Moving funds from concentration accounts and other cash pools to where they are needed

2. **Banking System Administration**

   • Managing bank relations and compensation

   • Conducting analytical reviews and feasibility studies

3. **Money Market Administration**
   - Short-term borrowing
   - Short-term investing

4. **Forecasting**
   - Projecting cash needs and excesses
   - Monitoring the accuracy of such projections

Questions

The chapter questions are to test the information in the text and are not examples of CCM examination questions nor are they in the examination format.

Answers can be found at the back of the book on p. 310.

1. What are the three major financial decision areas for a firm?

2. What is the primary objective of corporate financial management?

3. What is GAAP?

4. What are the three sources of cash flow represented in the statement of cash flows?

5. What is a red book balance and how may its reporting be avoided?

6. What is the present value of $1,500 two years from now if the opportunity cost is 5%?

7. A firm has a $500 invoice with terms of 2/10 net 30. How much will it save by taking the discount if the opportunity cost of funds is 10%?

   Questions 8-9 pertain to the following balance sheet and income statement:

   Balance Sheet
   Dec. 31, 199X

   Assets
   Current Assets
   Cash $ 100,000
   Short-term Investments   50,000
   Accounts Receivable   300,000
   Inventory   500,000
   Prepaid Expenses   20,000
   Total Current Assets   970,000

Fixed Assets

Property Plant and Equipment	<u>1,000,000</u>
Total Assets	<u>1,970,000</u>

Liabilities and Owners' Equity
Current Liabilities

Accounts Payable	290,000
Short-Term Notes Payable	<u>300,000</u>
Total Current Liabilities	$ 590,000

Long-Term Liabilities

Long-Term Debt	<u>800,000</u>
Total Liabilities	$ 1,390,000

Stockholders' Equity

Common Stock at Par Value	100,000
Paid-In Capital	400,000
Retained Earnings	<u>80,000</u>
Total Liability and Owners' Equity	$ <u>1,970,000</u>

Income Statement
Year Ended Dec. 31, 199X

Revenues	$ 1,000,000
Cost of Goods Sold	700,000
Operating Profit	3,000,000
Selling, General and Administrative Expenses	100,000
Interest	50,000
Net Profit before Taxes	150,000
Provision for Income Taxes	60,000
Net Income	90,000
Earnings Available for Common Shareholders	90,000
Dividends	36,000
Addition to Retained Earnings	54,000
Earning Per Share (10,000 shares outstanding)	$ 5.40

8 -1. What is the current ratio?

8-2. What is the debt to equity ratio?

9. What is the return on investment?

10. What are the reasons a firm needs to be liquid?

11. What are the major areas of responsibility for the cash manager?

The Banking System

Chapter 3

Overview

This chapter describes the role of the various types of financial institutions in the U.S. economy, the agencies that supervise them, and the legislation and regulations that govern the services they provide to the treasury function. The primary focus is on the role of the commercial bank, but the chapter also illustrates how various other types of financial institutions are competing with commercial banks, and how the distinction among the ranges of services provided by various types of financial institutions has begun to blur.

Learning Objectives

Upon completion of this chapter and the related study questions, the reader should be able to do the following:

1.   Explain the principal functions of financial institutions such as commercial banks, investment banking firms, savings banks and finance companies.

2.   Explain the functions and structure of the Federal Reserve System, the Federal Deposit Insurance Corporation and the Office of the Comptroller of the Currency.

3.   Discuss how the banking system evolved through significant legislative developments.

4.   Explain the more important Federal Reserve regulations as they pertain to cash management.

5.   Discuss the more important competitive, regulatory and safety issues in the banking system today.

6.   Understand the impact of the relevant parts of the Uniform Commercial Code on the practice of cash management.

OUTLINE

I. **Financial Institutions and Their Role**

   A.   Commercial Banks

   B.   Investment Banking and Brokerage Firms

   C.   Savings Institutions

   D.   Credit Unions

   E.   Mutual Funds

   F.   Non-Bank Financial Institutions

II. **Regulatory Agencies and Their Role**

   A.   Federal Reserve System (Fed)

   B.   Office of the Comptroller of the Currency (OCC)

   C.   Federal Deposit Insurance Corporation (FDIC)

   D.   Resolution Trust Corporation (RTC)

   E.   Securities and Exchange Commission (SEC)

   F.   Department of Justice

   G.   State Banking Boards and Commissions

III. **Federal Legislation**

   A.   Federal Reserve Act (1913)

   B.   Edge Act (1918)

   C.   McFadden Act (1927)

   D.   Glass Steagall Act (Banking Act of 1933)

   E.   Electronic Funds Transfer Act (EFTA) (1978)

   F.   Depository Institutions Deregulation and Monetary Control Act (DIDMCA) (1980)

   G.   Garn-St. Germain Depository Institutions Act (1982)

   H.   Expedited Funds Availability Act (EFAA) (1988)

   I.   Financial Institutions Reform, Recovery and Enforcement Act (FIRREA) (1989)

OUTLINE (Continued)

IV. **Federal Reserve Regulations**

    A.   Regulation D

    B.   Regulation E

    C.   Regulation J

    D.   Regulation Q

    E.   Regulation CC

V. **The Uniform Commercial Code**

    A.   Article 3—Commercial Paper

    B.   Article 4—Bank Deposits and Collections

    C.   Article 4A—Payment Instruments

    D.   Article 5—Letters of Credit

I. Financial Institutions and Their Role

This section discusses the role played and the types of services provided by commercial banks and other types of financial institutions.

A. Commercial Banks

The term bank originally applied to a money changer's table in ancient times. Money changers gradually began to accept wealthy customers' deposits and lend them to farmers and merchants. The commercial bank as it exists today is a complex institution. It may range in size from a small community bank with a few million dollars in assets to a large money center bank with more than $100 billion in assets. Commercial banks can offer a wide variety of services though even the largest do not offer all of them. This section describes the principal roles commercial banks play in the domestic and international financial markets and the services that fall under each role.

1. **Intermediation Role** - Banks act as custodian for the savings of households and the transaction balances of businesses, lend funds to businesses to fulfill seasonal working capital and long-term expansion needs, and act as intermediaries between borrowers and investors. Services include:

   • *Deposit Accounts* - An important function of a commercial bank is to serve as a depository for a firm's or individual's cash. There are two basic types of depository accounts, demand and time, and there are also interest-paying accounts that combine the features of demand and time deposits.

     * *Demand Deposit Accounts (DDAs)* are also known as checking accounts. Funds can be transferred from the account and paid to a third party with a check, wire transfer or ACH transfer. By law, interest cannot be paid on demand deposits held by businesses except those that are sole proprietorships, partnerships or not-for-profit organizations. Balances held in demand deposit accounts may include:

       Transaction Balances are deposits held by firms for collection and disbursement activity.

       Compensating Balances are deposits held by firms in the form of collected balances used to pay for bank services.

       Correspondent Balances are balances from another bank held to facilitate check clearing, securities, letter of credit and other transactions.

     * *Time Deposits* are deposits that must be held at a bank for a specified period. They consist primarily of savings accounts and certificates of deposit (CDs).

       Savings Accounts or Passbook Savings Accounts pay interest on maintained balances. They are held mainly by individuals and not-for-profit institutions but companies may hold them too.

       Certificates of Deposit (CDs) are negotiable or non-negotiable obligations of a bank that may have fixed or variable interest rates. Jumbo

CDs are deposits of $100,000 or more; they are sold to individuals and companies. Maturities range from 7 days to several years.

Negotiable CDs are generally sold in $1,000,000 blocks to companies, money market funds, and other large investors. By being negotiable, they can be sold to another investor prior to maturity. Maturities range from seven days to several years.

Individual Retail CDs are non-negotiable CDs sold to retail investors in amounts as low as $500.

* *Other Interest-Paying Accounts* have some of the features of both demand and time deposits.

Money Market Deposit Accounts, created by the 1982 Garn-St. Germain Act, pay an unregulated rate of interest determined by the bank, and allow limited check-writing. They are available to all types of businesses.

Negotiable Order of Withdrawal (NOW) accounts, offer unrestricted check writing and pay unregulated rates of interest. They are limited to individuals, sole proprietorships, partnerships, not-for-profit organizations, and governmental bodies.

• **Credit Services** - Banks provide loans to companies of all sizes, to not-for-profit organizations and to individuals.

* *Short-term loans* are usually for working capital purposes, for example, to support temporary or seasonal increases in inventory or accounts receivable. Short-term loans are expected to be repaid from the current assets they finance. Short-term borrowing is often under a line of credit which allows a company to borrow up to a specified amount, repay, and borrow again at any time. Lines of credit and revolving credits are covered in Chapter 12, Borrowing.

* *Long-term loans* for up to 10 years are made primarily for capital improvements such as plant and equipment. The source of repayment is generally expected to be earnings from the project being financed.

* *Leasing* - Banks provide leases as alternatives to the use of long-term loans for financing capital equipment. Leasing is discussed in Chapter 12, Borrowing.

* *Mortgages* - Commercial banks provide mortgage financing for commercial and residential real estate.

* *Investment Banking Services* - In the last 10 years, large companies have funded themselves to an increasing degree in the commercial paper market rather than with short-term bank loans because the cost is considerably less. Commercial banks have responded to the competition by moving into investment banking services to the extent allowed by Federal legislation, and have campaigned for legislation to increase their investment banking powers. The more important investment banking services provided by commercial banks today include:

* *Commercial Paper (CP)* - CP consists of unsecured, short-term promissory notes issued by companies. Banks act as agents to place the commercial paper of their customers with investors. Commercial banks have recently won regulatory approval to perform this investment banking privilege, helped by an interpretation that they were acting in an agent rather than in an underwriting capacity.

* *Loan Sales* - Banks provide lending facilities structured so that short-term loans can be sold to other banks and investors.

* *Private Placements* - Banks work with their customers to place long-term loans with institutional investors such as insurance companies.

* *Corporate Bonds* - Some of the largest banks have recently been permitted to underwrite corporate bonds in limited amounts through special-purpose subsidiaries.

2. **Payments and Collections Role** - Banks assist companies by making and receiving payments, by acting as clearing agents for checks, and by acting as initiating and receiving points for wire transfers and automated clearing house (ACH) transfers. This role is discussed in detail in Chapter 4, The Payments System.

3. **Guarantor Role** - Banks act as guarantors in standing behind their customers to pay obligations in the event the customer is unable to do so. The role of guarantor is fulfilled by the following services:

   • *Letters of Credit (LCs)* are documents issued by a bank, guaranteeing the payment of a customer's draft up to a stated amount for a specified period if certain conditions are met. A letter of credit substitutes a bank's name and credit for that of the buyer. LCs are further described in Chapter 15, International Cash Management.

   • *Standby Letters of Credit (Standby LCs)* are guarantees issued on behalf of a bank's customer in favor of a beneficiary promising that the bank will pay the latter upon presentation of a letter stating that the bank's customer has not met the terms of the contract.

   • *Credit Enhancement Standby Letters of Credit* are guarantees by the bank that the investor will be paid if the issuer (the borrower) under a commercial paper or other underwritten facility defaults.

4. **Agency or Fiduciary Role** - In an agency role, a bank or trust institution manages assets in which title remains with the owner. A fiduciary is an individual or institution to whom certain property is given to hold in trust according to a trust agreement. Banks act to manage or protect their customers' property in several ways. These include:

   • *Trust Services* - Banks invest, manage and distribute monies as instructed in wills, trusts, and estates.

- *Investment Management* - Banks manage portfolios of investments for their customers.

- *Corporate Pension Plans* - Banks act as agents for corporations in establishing and managing employee pension programs.

- *Corporate Trustee* - As a trustee for a corporate bond or preferred stock issue, a bank monitors compliance with the indenture agreements. These are formal agreements between an issuer of bonds and a bondholder.

- *Transfer Agent* - A transfer agent is an individual or firm that keeps a record of the shareholders of a corporation by name, address and number of shares. Banks serve as transfer agents by keeping records of the sale and purchase of stocks and bonds.

- *Registrar* - Banks serve as registrars by maintaining lists of current stockholders and bondholders for the purpose of remitting dividend and interest payments.

- *Paying Agent* - Banks receive funds from an issuer of stocks or bonds and in turn pay principal and interest to bondholders and dividends to stockholders.

5. **Consulting Role** - Banks provide consulting services for corporate customers in areas such as mergers and acquisitions, corporate financial structure and cash management. Bank consulting services generally relate closely to other types of transactions and products that a customer might use on a continuing basis.

6. **Risk Management Role** - Banks offer services such as interest rate and currency swaps, options and futures and interest rate caps (maximums) floors (minimums) and collars (maximums and minimums) to help their customers protect against interest rate and currency volatility. These risk management tools are explained in Chapter 13, Foreign Exchange and Interest Rate Risk Management.

7. **Broker and Dealer Role** - Banks act as brokers and dealers for certain permissible investment securities and foreign currencies, and trade for their own account as an extension of that role.

B. Investment Banking and Brokerage Firms

Investment banking and brokerage firms provide a wide range of services. Not every firm is a full service provider. Some specialize more in investment banking, others more in brokerage. Some brokers deal more with institutional customers, others more with retail customers.

1. **Stock and Bond Underwriting** - Underwriting is the principal function of investment banking. When an investment banking firm underwrites a stock or bond offering, it assures the issuer of a definite sum of money for the issue at a definite time. In purchasing the entire issue from the issuer, the underwriter assumes the risk of price and marketability. The investment banker's intermediation function is often described as having two

components, origination and distribution. Underwriting is the origination function, and selling the securities to investors is the distribution function.

2. **Commercial Paper (CP)** - Investment bankers have traditionally acted as underwriters and dealers for commercial paper. Commercial banks have recently started to compete with investment bankers in selling commercial paper.

3. **Institutional and Retail Brokerage** - Stock brokerage, selling shares to institutional and retail customers, is the distribution side of the investment banker's intermediation function.

4. **Investment Research** - Investment banking firms have research analysts who generally specialize by industry and provide advice to large institutional and personal clients.

5. **Investment Advisory and Portfolio Management** - Similar to commercial banks, investment banking firms provide investment advice and manage investment portfolios for large institutional and personal clients.

6. **Risk Management** - Investment banking firms compete with commercial banks in offering interest-rate and currency risk management products such as interest rate and currency swaps, options and futures.

C. Savings Institutions

Savings institutions have traditionally been depositories that accept consumer deposits and lend money primarily in the form of home mortgage loans. Until 1980, they were allowed by law to offer 1/4 of 1 percent more on savings accounts than commercial banks. The *Depository Institutions Deregulation and Monetary Control Act of 1980 (DIDMCA)* provided for a phase out of interest rate ceilings for savings institutions and commercial banks and allowed savings institutions to make commercial and consumer loans. There are two types of savings institutions:

1. **Savings and Loan Associations (S&Ls)** are state chartered and owned by either shareholders or depositors. Their deposits are federally insured by the **Savings Association Insurance Fund (SAIF)**, which is administered by the **Federal Deposit Insurance Corporation (FDIC)**, a regulatory agency described in detail in Sections II and III.

2. **Savings Banks or Mutual Savings Banks** have historically been state chartered and owned by depositors but the Garn St. Germain Depository Institutions Act of 1982 allowed them to switch to a federal charter and to convert to stock ownership. Their deposits are insured by the **Bank Insurance Fund (BIF)**.

D. Credit Unions

Credit unions are not-for-profit financial corporations created by Federal or state charter. Membership in a credit union is restricted to people with a common bond such as an employer, association or community organization. Credit unions can provide retail financial services similar to those offered by other types of financial institutions. Members/owners often enjoy higher savings and lower lending rates. Deposits in most credit unions are insured by the National Credit Union Administration (NCUA) Share Insurance Fund.

E. Mutual Funds

Mutual fund providers are investment companies that sell shares to investors, offering those investors diversification and professional portfolio management. Shares may be redeemed through the investment company which provides liquidity. Prices fluctuate with the performance of the fund. Money market mutual funds invest in short-term securities such as Treasury bills, bank certificates of deposit and commercial paper. They have limited check-writing privileges. The majority are managed by brokerage or investment companies and compete with similar accounts offered by commercial banks.

F. Non-Bank Financial Institutions

1. **Industrial Credit and Capital Companies** - Subsidiaries of large industrial corporations raise funds in the commercial paper market and lend to companies and individuals. Some, known as **captive finance companies**, lend only to finance the purchase of their companies' products. Others compete across the full range of commercial lending services.

2. **Factors** - Factors provide short-term financing to companies by purchasing their accounts receivable at a discount and assuming the responsibility and the risk for collecting them.

3. **Insurance Companies** - Insurance companies are primarily long-term lenders to companies. They extend loans for terms up to fifteen years while banks usually do not go beyond ten years. Insurance companies have started to compete with banks for medium-term loans as well. Insurance companies also compete with banks in providing guaranteed income contracts (GICs) and in providing universal life insurance policies with long-term savings features.

4. **Consumer Credit Companies** - Consumer loan and sales finance companies extend credit to individuals at relatively high rates. Many of these companies also lend to businesses. The larger, well-known consumer finance companies raise funds in the commercial paper market.

II. Regulatory Agencies and their Role

The U.S. has a dual banking system. It is regulated at the federal level and by state banking commissions. At the federal level, bank supervision is shared primarily by three agencies, the Board of Governors of the Federal Reserve System, the Federal Deposit Insurance Corporation (FDIC), and the Office of the Comptroller of the Currency (OCC). The Securities and Exchange Commission (SEC) and the Department of Justice have regulatory roles as well.

A. Federal Reserve System (Fed)

The Federal Reserve System (Fed) is an independent agency of the U.S. government. The following is a description of the roles and structure of the Federal Reserve System:

1. **Roles** - The Fed has four principal roles. It acts as a supervisor of member banks and bank holding companies, as the manager of U.S. monetary policy, as a wholesaler of banking services, and as the fiscal agent of the U.S. Treasury.

   - *Supervision* - The Board of Governors of the Federal Reserve System is charged with examination of state-chartered member banks and bank holding companies. It also regulates Edge Act banks, the U.S. banking activities of foreign owned banks and the foreign activities of U.S. member banks.

   - *Monetary Policy* - The Board controls the money supply through bank reserve requirements, the discount rate for bank borrowing at the Fed, and open market operations.

     * *Reserve Requirements* - All depository institutions must maintain a specified percentage of their deposits in cash or on deposit with the Fed. These deposits earn no interest. The required level of reserves is established by averaging reservable liabilities over a 14-day period. Reserve requirements are not changed often, but when they are, the effect is either an expansion or contraction of lendable funds and a resulting multiplier effect throughout the economy.

     * *Discount Rate* - The Fed sets the discount rate for loans to depository institutions. The discount rate is viewed as an indicator of interest rate movements.

     * *Open Market Activities* - One of the most influential roles of the Fed is exercised through the Open Market Committee. It is charged with promoting economic growth, full employment, stable prices and a balance in international trade and payments.

       Its primary activities involve the sale and purchase of government securities. The sale of securities from the Fed's portfolio reduces the money supply by taking cash out of the economy. Conversely, buying securities in the open market increases the money supply because the Fed makes purchases by crediting the seller's account.

   - *Banking Service* - For a commercial bank, the Fed is both a regulator and a provider of services. It oversees the payments system, operates a nationwide check clearing system, operates the Fedwire, a money transfer system, and is the main operator of the Automated Clearing House (ACH). The Fed's role in the domestic payments system centers on the following:

     * *Check Clearing* - The Fed receives check deposits from depository institutions and then clears checks back to the drawee banks.

* *Wire Transfers* - It operates Fedwire, the major large-dollar domestic wire transfer system.

* *Automated Clearing House (ACH) System* - The Fed is the main operator of this system, which settles electronic payments.

- *Fiscal Agency* - The Reserve Banks and their branches function as the banker for the Federal Government. They maintain the Treasury Department's checking accounts, clear Treasury checks drawn against them, accept payments for Federal taxes on behalf of the Internal Revenue Service (IRS), and act as fiscal agent for the Treasury Department to issue, redeem and transfer ownership of government securities.

2. **Organization** - The Federal Reserve System has three components, the Board of Governors, the Federal Open Market Committee (FOMC), and the 12 Federal Reserve Banks and their branches.

- *Board of Governors* - Each of the seven members is appointed to a 14-year term by the President of the U.S. and confirmed by the Senate. Primary functions include formulation of credit and monetary policy, and supervision of the Reserve Banks, state-chartered member banks and bank holding companies. The President appoints one governor as chairman and another as vice chairman; each serves a four-year term and may be reappointed.

    The Board is advised by three committees. These are:

    * *Federal Advisory Council* consists of one member from each of the Fed districts. Each member is elected to a one-year term. The Council meets with the Board at least four times a year to review business and financial conditions and to make recommendations.

    * *Consumer Advisory Council* consists of representatives from the consumer sector and institutions granting credit to consumers.

    * *Thrift Institutions Advisory Council* consists of members from savings and loan associations, mutual savings banks, and credit unions

- *Federal Open Market Committee (FOMC)* - The FOMC implements monetary policy, principally by the conduct of open market operations. There are 12 committee members, including seven members of the Board of Governors, the president of the Federal Reserve Bank of New York and presidents of four other Federal Reserve Banks.

- *Federal Reserve District Banks* - There are 12 Federal Reserve districts with one Reserve Bank serving each district. The 12 reserve banks have 25 branches and 11 additional regional check processing centers (RCPCs). Commercial banks in the region hold the stock of the Reserve Banks and are represented on their boards, but do not maintain control the way stockholders normally do. The Board of Governors appoints part of each Reserve Bank's board as well as its chairman. A map of the Federal Reserve System is shown in Exhibit 3-1.

B. Office of the Comptroller of the Currency (OCC)

The Office of the Comptroller of the Currency (OCC) grants charters to, and regulates, supervises and examines national banks. It monitors bank performance, issues supervisory agreements, and determines loan credit quality ratings.

C. Federal Deposit Insurance Corporation (FDIC)

1. **Deposit Insurance -** The primary role of the FDIC is to protect depositors from losses caused by bank insolvency.

   - It insures deposits up to $100,000 per personal or corporate depositor per institution in all banks that have FDIC insurance, all federally chartered and most state banks. The rate is set by the FDIC as a percentage of deposits.

     - The FDIC manages two deposit insurance funds— the Bank Insurance Fund (BIF) and the Savings Association Insurance Fund (SAIF).

2. **Supervision -** The FDIC supervises, examines, and regulates insured banks that are not Federal Reserve members.

3. **Role in Bank Failures -** One of the FDIC's most important roles is in determining the course of action in the event of bank failure. The FDIC usually makes the decision that a bank is insolvent, and the FDIC is usually appointed receiver. The agency is charged with finding a merger partner or liquidating the bank's remaining assets and paying insured depositors

D. Resolution Trust Corporation (RTC)

In 1989, the Resolution Trust Corporation (RTC) was established as a provision of the Financial Institutions Reform, Recovery and Enforcement Act (FIRREA). The RTC has two major functions:

1. It manages and resolves troubled savings institutions that have been turned over to the RTC.

2. It manages and liquidates assets controlled by insolvent S&Ls.

E. Securities and Exchange Commission (SEC)

1. Must approve any public offerings of debt or equity securities by banks or bank holding companies as well as all other corporations.

2. Sets financial disclosure standards for corporations that sell securities to the public.

3. Requires filing of quarterly and annual financial statements by companies with publicly owned securities.

4. Under some legislative proposals to give banks increased investment banking powers, underwriting and related activities by bank subsidiaries would come under SEC supervision.

Exhibit 3-1

Federal Reserve Check Processing Regions

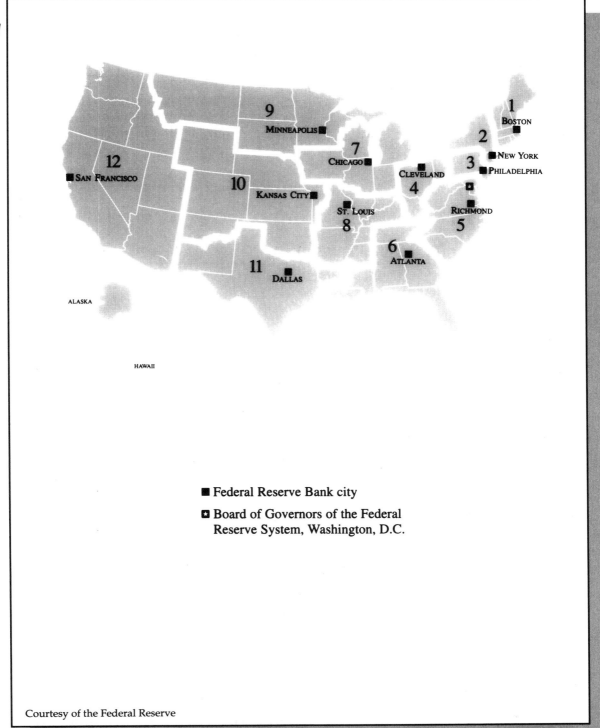

■ Federal Reserve Bank city

✪ Board of Governors of the Federal Reserve System, Washington, D.C.

Courtesy of the Federal Reserve

F.   Department of Justice

Reviews and approves proposed bank mergers and holding company acquisitions to determine their effect on competition as part of overall antitrust supervisory responsibility.

G.   State Banking Boards and Commissions

1.   Issue charters for new banks.

2.   Supervise and regularly examine all state-chartered banks.

3.   Reserve the right to approve all applications of banks operating within state borders to form holding companies, to acquire affiliates or subsidiaries, or to establish branch offices.

4.   Reserve the right to impose liquidity requirements and minimum equity capital requirements on state-chartered banks.

III. Federal Legislation

The following selected chronology of bank legislation shows how the U.S. banking system evolved into its current form.

A.   Federal Reserve Act (1913)

1.   The Federal Reserve Act provided the foundation for the current banking system.

2.   The Fed was granted supervisory power over member banks. Chartered national banks were required to become members and to comply with reserve requirements.

3.   The Act also empowered the Fed to create a check collection and settlement system through member banks.

B.   Edge Act (1918)

1.   The Edge Act permitted U.S. banks to invest in corporations that engage in international banking and finance.

2.   Subsidiaries could be established to conduct international banking business such as import and export financing, foreign exchange, letters of credit and documentary collections in other cities in the U.S. as well as overseas. This legislation has helped banks establish a presence and be closer to their customers in other cities, even though the units could not take in domestic deposits and were limited to providing services related to international trade.

C.   McFadden Act (1927)

1.   The McFadden Act established the state boundary as the primary limit for bank expansion by prohibiting banks from accepting deposits across state lines.

2. It prohibited branching across state lines unless approved by state governments, thereby relegating to the states the power to decide the extent of bank branching within and outside state borders.

3. The **Douglas Amendment** in 1956 allowed banks to merge across state lines if each state permitted it, but did not allow bank holding companies to acquire banks across state lines. Recent legislation enacted by individual states has allowed bank holding companies to acquire banks and bank holding companies in states both within and outside their regions.

D. Glass Steagall Act (Banking Act of 1933)

1. Prohibited commercial banks from securities underwriting except for government issues.

2. Prohibited securities firms from engaging in bank-like activities such as deposit gathering.

3. Required the Fed to establish interest-rate ceilings on all types of accounts and prohibited the payment of interest on demand deposits.

4. Created the Federal Deposit Insurance Corporation (FDIC) to guarantee the public's deposits up to a stipulated maximum amount.

E. Electronic Funds Transfer Act (EFTA) (1978)

Defined the rights and responsibilities of individuals using EFT services except for wire transfers. It limits customer liability for unauthorized banking transactions involving Automated Teller Machines (ATMs) and Point of Sale (POS) terminals provided the customer notifies the bank or other institution that issued the card.

F. Depository Institutions Deregulation and Monetary Control Act (DIDMCA) (1980)

1. Required all deposit-taking institutions to maintain reserves at the Fed.

2. Made Fed services such as the discount window and check clearing available to all deposit-taking institutions.

3. Mandated the Fed to reduce and/or price float in the system.

4. Priced previously free Fed services according to the standards of a tax-paying vendor.

5. Provided for phasing out of Regulation Q interest rate ceilings over a five-year period through 1986.

6. Permitted banks to offer Negotiable Order of Withdrawal (NOW) accounts, check writing accounts with an unregulated interest rate for individuals and not-for-profit organizations.

G. Garn-St. Germain Depository Institutions Act (1982)

1. Extended banks' legal lending limit to 15% of capital and surplus unsecured and 25% for secured loans.

2. Allowed FDIC to arrange mergers of banks across state lines when suitable intrastate partners could not be found.

3.   Allowed banks to offer accounts fully competitive with money market mutual funds. Allowed banks in need of capital to issue net worth certificates to the FDIC in return for promissory notes that could be held as assets.

H.   Expedited Funds Availability Act (EFAA) (1988)

Defined check availability time periods, payable-through draft and check return procedures. Provisions of this act are incorporated in Federal Reserve Regulation CC.

I.   Financial Institutions Reform, Recovery and Enforcement Act (FIRREA) (1989)

1.   Consolidated Federal Savings and Loan Insurance Corporation (FSLIC) resources under FDIC and established two insurance funds, the Savings Association Insurance Fund (SAIF) and the Bank Insurance Fund (BIF).

2.   Dismantled the Federal Home Loan Bank Board (FHLBB) and established the Office of Thrift Supervision (OTS) to assume the FHLBBs supervisory responsibilities.

3.   Established the Resolution Trust Corporation to make timely disposal of assets of failed S&Ls.

4.   Gave the FDIC increased flexibility to raise deposit insurance premiums charged to banks and savings and loan associations.

IV. Federal Reserve Regulations

A.   Regulation D

Imposes uniform reserve requirements on all depository institutions with different levels of reserves for different types of deposits.

B.   Regulation E

1.   Establishes the rights, liabilities and responsibilities of parties to consumer-related electronic funds transfers (EFT) and protects consumers using EFT systems.

2.   Provides for documentation of electronic transfers.

C.   Regulation J

Establishes procedures, duties and responsibilities for check collection and settlement through the Federal Reserve System.

D.   Regulation Q

Prohibits depository institutions from paying interest on corporate demand deposit accounts.

E.   Regulation CC

1.   Establishes policies on holding funds, as provided in the Expedited Funds Availability Act (EFAA), and requires banks to disclose their availability policies to their customers.

2.   Establishes rules designed to speed the collection and return of checks and imposes a responsibility on banks to return unpaid checks expeditiously.

3.   Establishes endorsement standards for banks and companies to follow in depositing and clearing checks.

V.   The Uniform Commercial Code

The Uniform Commercial Code (UCC) is a uniform set of laws governing commercial transactions enacted separately by each state. The UCC defines the rights and duties of the parties in a commercial transaction and provides a statutory definition of commonly used business practices.

The three articles most relevant to the cash manager are:

A.   Article 3—Commercial Paper

1.   **Negotiable Instruments -** Article 3 defines a negotiable instrument and the forms it may take, including a draft, a check, a certificate of deposit and a note. These items will be defined in Chapter 4, The Payments System.

2.   **Accord and Satisfaction -** A current change to Article 3 of high relevance to cash managers is in the section titled "Accord and Satisfaction by Use of Instrument." Originally, this section was drafted to permit a check to constitute a payment made in full, i.e., accord and satisfaction, when a message to that effect was written on the face of the check and the check was deposited. This allowed for the possibility of inadvertent accord and satisfaction when the customer wrote "paid in full" on a check for a disputed claim, and the check was deposited, for example, through a lockbox. The revised section permits avoidance of inadvertent accord and satisfaction if the payee discovers the inadvertence and returns the check to the payor within a reasonable time period, not to exceed 90 days.

3.   **Unauthorized Signatures -** Changes have occurred in the interpretation of who is responsible if a check is paid and contains an unauthorized signature. A bank's failure to examine a forged drawer's signature is not failure to exercise ordinary care to the extent such failure does not violate the bank's procedures and that these procedures do not unreasonably vary from general banking procedures. At the same time, a bank can only charge a customer's account for checks which are properly payable, and an unauthorized signature does not pass this test. However, if a company does not exercise ordinary care related to check issuance and does not notify the bank of multiple forgeries by the same wrongdoer in a timely manner, it may be held liable.

B. Article 4—Bank Deposits and Collections

1. **Bank Parties** - Article 4 defines the various bank parties to the deposit and collection process and their respective rights and duties.

2. **Relationship Between Payor Bank and Customer** - Article 4 defines the following:

   • When a bank may charge a customer's account.

   • Bank's liability to customer for wrongful dishonor.

   • Customer's right to stop payment.

   • Bank's option not to pay an item more than six months old (stale date).

   • Customer's duty to report unauthorized signature or alteration.

3. **Recent Changes** - Under the changes to UCC 4, a company has the duty to examine bank statements within a reasonable time, not to exceed 30 days, and to report to the bank any unauthorized signatures or alterations. This, coupled with the Ordinary Care provision of UCC 3, makes it imperative that companies reconcile their accounts on a timely basis.

C. Article 4A—Payment Instruments

Article 4A provides a legal framework that outlines the risks, rights and obligations of parties in connection with an electronic payment.

1. **Transactions Covered** - The new article governs wire transfers through Fedwire, CHIPS, and SWIFT, and book transfers and wholesale credit transfers through the ACH and SWIFT transfers. (Because SWIFT is an international payment mechanism, it is not clear to what extent Article 4A may apply. However, Article 4A may apply to those transaction segments which occur in the U.S. prior to the transmission overseas or after receipt in the U.S. via SWIFT facilities.)

2. **Security Procedures** - Article 4A uses the concepts of commercially reasonable security procedures and verified payment orders to determine when the purported sender of an unauthorized payment instruction will be obligated to make the payment. The bank must make security procedures for verifying payment orders available to the customer, and the bank and the customer must agree that those procedures are commercially reasonable. Some common security measures include the use of Personal Identification Numbers (PINs), callbacks, encryption and message authentication.

3. **Consequential Damages** - Banks are not responsible for consequential damages, which are losses resulting from the action or error made by the bank beyond the simple loss of funds. A bank incorrectly executing a payment order remains liable for interest losses or incidental expenses. The bank is liable for consequential damages only if it agrees to assume this liability in a written agreement with the customer.

D. Article 5—Letters of Credit

Article 5 covers commercial letters of credit requiring documentary drafts or documentary demands for payment. It does not cover standby letters of credit. It defines a letter of credit, a documentary draft or documentary demand for payment, the roles of the issuer of the letter of credit, the customer for whom the credit is issued, the beneficiary of the credit, the advising bank, and the confirming bank. The article defines the issuer's obligation to the customer, including the duty to examine documents to see that they comply with the terms of the credit. It also states that the issuer must honor a demand for payment which complies with the terms of the credit, and the issuer is entitled to immediate reimbursement by the customer.

E. Payments System Risk

Payments system risk is an issue closely related to bank creditworthiness due to an increase in money transfer volume on the Fedwire and through the Clearing House Interbank Payments System (CHIPS) and the ACH. The Federal Reserve has taken numerous steps to reduce this risk. This is also explored in Chapter 4, The Payments System.

Questions

The chapter questions are to test the information in the text and are not examples of CCM examination questions nor are they in the examination format.

Answers can be found at the back of the book on p. 313.

1. What are the major roles of commercial banks?

2. What is the principal function of an investment banking firm?

3. Who charters savings and loan institutions?

4. In what ways are credit unions different from banks?

5. What is a captive finance company?

6. What is the dual banking system in the U.S.?

7. What are the four major roles of the Federal Reserve?

8. Who grants charters to national banks?

9. What two insurance funds are operated by the Federal Deposit Insurance Corporation (FDIC)?

10. What legislation permits U.S. banks to invest in corporations engaged in international banking and finance?

11. What legislation prohibits banks from accepting deposits across state lines?

Questions (Continued)

12. What legislation separates commercial from investment banking?

13. What legislation mandated the Federal Reserve to reduce and/or price float?

14. What legislation created the Resolution Trust Corporation?

15. What Federal Reserve regulation prohibits the payment of interest on corporate demand deposits?

16. What Federal Reserve regulation requires the disclosure of check availability policies by banks?

17. What article of the Uniform Commercial Code permits avoidance of inadvertent accord and satisfaction?

18. Under UCC Article 4, what is the maximum time a firm has to examine bank statements and report unauthorized signatures?

19. Under UCC Article 4A, is a bank responsible for consequential damages?

The Payments System

Chapter 4

Overview

This chapter deals with the basic structure of the U.S. domestic payments system which consists of paper-based and electronic payments. It is important to understand the mechanics of each of the major payment systems, the regulatory and institutional constraints, and, most important, the key corporate applications.

Learning Objectives

Upon completion of this chapter and the related study questions, the reader should be able to do the following:

1. Understand the mechanics and applications of the principal paper instruments such as checks, payable through drafts, preauthorized drafts, and depository transfer checks.

2. Understand the mechanics and applications of the principal electronic payment instruments such as Fedwire, CHIPS, and ACH.

3. Discuss payments system risk and measures that the Federal Reserve and the banking industry are taking to reduce it.

OUTLINE

I.   **Overview of Payment Methods**

II. **Paper-Based Payment Instruments**
     A.   Overview of Domestic Check System
     B.   Magnetic Ink Character Recognition (MICR) Line
     C.   How Checks are Cleared
     D.   Ledger and Collected Balances
     E.   Availability Schedules
     F.   Federal Reserve Float
     G.   Return Items
     H.   Other Check-Like Payment Instruments

III. **The Automated Clearing House (ACH) System**
     A.   Objectives
     B.   Structure
     C.   ACH Payment Formats
     D.   Corporate Applications
     E.   Processing
     F.   Participants
     G.   How an ACH Transaction Works
     H.   Settlement
     I.   Prenotification
     J.   Advantages of Using ACH
     K.   Disadvantages of Using ACH
     L.   Recent ACH System Developments

OUTLINE (Continued)

IV. **Large-Dollar Payment Systems**

    A.   Fedwire

    B.   Mechanics of a Fedwire Transfer

    C.   Clearing House Interbank Payments System (CHIPS)

    D.   Society of Worldwide Interbank Financial Telecommunications (SWIFT)

    E.   Payments System Risk

I. Overview of Payment Methods

While the great majority of payment transactions are by check, far more dollar value is transferred through the electronic payment networks. The dollar volume of electronic transfers is growing substantially, especially through the ACH.

Although electronic payments receive more publicity, it is apparent that the check will be an extremely important payment mechanism for years to come. For this reason, it is necessary for cash managers to understand the mechanics of the paper-based clearing system, the methods of granting availability and the implications of the timing of the system's activities. These issues are discussed in the first part of this chapter. The remainder of the chapter describes electronic payments, including transfers for same-day value (through Fedwire or CHIPS) and for delayed value (through the ACH system).

II. Paper-Based Payment Instruments

A. Overview of Domestic Check System

A check is a demand instrument used to transfer funds from the payor to the payee.

1. **Payor** - The payor is the party that writes or draws the check to remit funds.

2. **Payee** - The payee is the party to whom the check is made payable

3. **Drawee Bank** - The drawee bank is the bank on which the check is drawn, the payor's bank.

4. **Signature** - A check requires the signature of the payor. Sometimes there are joint payors and sometimes more than one signature is required. For some companies, mechanically generated signature facsimiles are often used. Some firms use computer-typed names in the signature block; that method produces a check in one pass through the computer and avoids multiple handling.

5. **Provisional Credit** - The payee receives ledger credit when the check is deposited. The credit is provisional, subject to final clearing of the check.

6. **Check Clearing** - To effect final settlement, the check must be presented to, and accepted by the institution on which it is drawn, the drawee bank. This process is called check clearing.

   Exhibit 4-1 illustrates how a check is used to transfer funds from Company A (the payor) to Company B (the payee). The central event in the check clearing process is presentment, the delivery of a check to the payor's (drawee's) bank. At the time of presentment, value is subtracted from the bank's account with the Fed, correspondent bank or other clearing institution. Generally, the amount is also subtracted from the payor's account the same business day.

Exhibit 4-1

**Steps in Check
Clearing System**

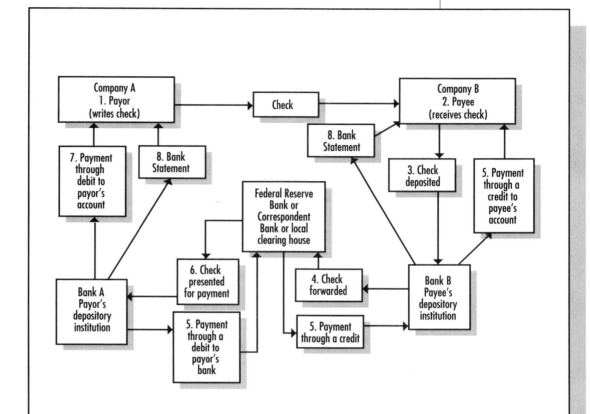

STEPS IN THE CHECK-CLEARING SYSTEM

Step :1   Company A prepares and mails a check to Company B.

Step 2:   Company B receives and processes the check.

Step 3:   Company B deposits the check in its account at Bank B.

Step 4:   Bank B processes the check and transports it to a clearing system.

Step 5:   The clearing system gives value to Bank B in the amount of the check and subtracts value from Bank A for
           the same amount. The clearing agent (if any) can be the Federal Reserve System, a correspondent bank or a
           local clearing house.

Step 6:   The check is physically presented by the clearing agent to Bank A where the amount is deducted from
           Company A's account. This step may occur simultaneously with step 5.

Step 7:   This step does not come at a predetermined time in the cycle, but on the day of posting, Company A must
           have funds available in Bank A to cover the amount of the check.

Step 8:   Both banks provide reports to their respective companies in the form of periodic bank statements.

7. **Role of Drawee Bank** - In the check clearing process, the drawee bank is responsible for inspecting the check for proper signature, alterations, appropriate dating and stop payments or alerts in effect.

   • The account is reviewed for active account status, adequate funds, whether or not there are holds in place (instructions not to debit the account or not to draw the account below a certain balance) or any other problems with the disbursement account.

   • The paying bank has until its close of business on the day following presentment to conduct this review and to authorize final payment. If the check does not pass the review process, it must be returned to the bank of first deposit to reverse the provisional credit provided earlier to the payee.

   • If the check exceeds $2,500 the drawee bank must notify the depository bank electronically, by the close of business two days after presentment, that the check will be returned. The notification must include all pertinent data from the check. Rules on check return are included in Federal Reserve Regulations J and Regulation CC, and are described in Chapter 3, The Banking System.

B. Magnetic Ink Character Recognition (MICR) Line

The information necessary to process checks by machine is contained in the **Magnetic Ink Character Recognition (MICR)** line printed with special characters on the lower portion of the check. These characters can be read by scanning equipment. The MICR information is used by the depository institution to identify the drawee bank and to route the check back to the bank and the account on which it was drawn. The information contained in the MICR line of a business check is illustrated in Exhibit 4-2. The MICR line for a personal check has a different sequence. Following the exhibit is an explanation of each segment of the MICR line corresponding to item numbers in the diagram.

The bank's reader-sorter equipment endorses and microfilms the checks, sorts them according to the clearing channels that will be used and sends the clearing data to the bank's computers to allow deposit updating and float assignment.

C. How Checks Are Cleared

Check clearing is the process of presenting a check to the drawee bank to effect final payment. Checks are sent from one bank to another in cash letters. Often banks make direct sends to other banks or Federal Reserve Banks in other districts. A variety of clearing channels are used.

1. **Cash Letter** - A cash letter is a bundle of checks accompanied by a list of individual items and dollar amounts, together with deposit tickets and other control documents. Checks are usually presented by a bank to the Fed or another bank via a cash letter.

2. **Direct Sends** - Banks often bypass the Fed with direct sends, which are arrangements to send cash letters directly to correspondent banks or to a non-local Federal Reserve bank, to meet various deposit deadlines and

Exhibit 4-2

Sample Business Check

Name of Payor

Check No: 12345

February 10, 19XX

Pay to the Order of: _____ NAME OF PAYEE _____

Dollars amount: _____ One thousand & thirty four _____ $1,034.00

Name of
Drawee Bank

Payor's Signature

_____

000012345	02	12	0001	2	0310987654	0000103400
Field 6	1	2	3	4	5	7

Transit Routing Number. The first four entries described below are collectively known as the transit routing number.

1. **Federal Reserve Bank Code** - Two digits (01 to 12) identify the drawee bank's Federal Reserve district. Numbers greater than 12 identify a non-bank depository institution such as a thrift.

2. **Federal Reserve Office** - The first digit identifies the Fed branch responsible for handling the drawee bank. The second digit is the availability classification.

3. **Bank Identification Number** - Four digits make up the bank's ABA identification number. That number designates the bank and location to which the item must be delivered. A number of banks have more than one identification number, which facilitates the handling of certain types of checks.

4. **Check Digit** - This digit, when combined with the other numbers, enables the computer to verify the accuracy of the routing number for the benefit of the automated routing process.

5. **Payor's Account Number** - This number is assigned to the payor by the drawee bank.

6. **Sequence Number** - Also called the auxiliary on-us field on a business check.

   - This number is frequently the check number.

   - It assists the drawee bank in providing a variety of account reconcilement services, for example sorting the cleared checks before returning them to the payor.

   - It may also be used for identification codes of divisions or subsidiaries.

   - It is a key to providing stop payment services.

7. **Encoded Amount of Check** - This number should agree with the amount placed on the check by the payor. The amount is typically encoded on the check by the bank in which the check is first deposited.

thereby achieve faster clearing times than they would by clearing them through the local Fed. The sending bank maintains a deposit account with the correspondent bank. The correspondent bank credits the account of the sending bank with proceeds of the checks.

3. **Clearing Channels** - Selection of the appropriate channel to use is a function of deposit bank processing time, geographic location and the availability schedules of clearing agents. Availability, when funds deposited will become available for use, is granted to the clearing bank if the check reaches the endpoint (or location established by the clearing agent) prior to a pre-arranged deposit deadline. Availability schedules define the number of days delay for each endpoint; they are discussed in more detail in Section E of this chapter. Channels that the bank of first deposit can use for clearing checks back to the payee bank include the following:

   - *On-Us Check Clearing* - The payee deposits the check in the same bank on which it is drawn. Clearing the check is accomplished by charging the payor's account, crediting the payee's account and returning the check to the payor.

   - *Local Clearing House* - These are either formal or informal associations formed by banks in a geographic area to permit the exchange of items drawn on the other participants. Representatives from each bank meet daily to present checks to each other. The net value is transferred by debiting and crediting correspondent accounts or through the reserve accounts each bank maintains with the local Fed.

   - *Federal Reserve Bank* - A key role of the Fed is to act as a check clearing agent. A bank deposits checks into its own account at the Fed. The Fed gives credit for the checks according to its availability schedule. It then sorts the checks and transports them to the drawee bank. When a check is presented to the drawee bank, the Fed subtracts the amount of the check from the drawee bank's Fed account. A bank may deposit checks at its local Fed or direct send them to other Federal Reserve banks.

   - *Correspondent Bank* - The sending bank or bank of first deposit maintains a deposit account with the correspondent bank. The correspondent bank credits the account of the sending bank with proceeds of the checks.

4. **Drawee Endpoints** - The classification of drawee endpoints is as follows:

   - *City Items* - Checks drawn on banks located in Federal Reserve cities.

   - *RCPC Items* - Checks drawn on banks serviced by a Fed regional check processing center (RCPC).

   - *Country Items* - Checks drawn on banks located outside the area served by a Fed city or RCPC.

   - *High Dollar Group Sort (HDGS) Items* - Checks drawn on RCPC or country banks. HDGS is the Fed's program to expedite the processing of high-dollar checks through the system.

* The HDGS program involves making a second presentment to banks with more than $10 million of checks presented from outside their Fed district.

* The program has allowed banks to make presentments of checks drawn on HDGS banks at a later time.

5. **Deposit Deadlines**. Each type of item has a specific deposit deadline that must be met if the clearing bank is to receive the designated availability.

D. Ledger and Collected Balances

Banks differentiate between ledger and collected balances in deposit accounts.

1. **Ledger Balances** - Ledger balances are bank balances that reflect all accounting entries that affect a bank account, regardless of any deposit float. Ledger balances are important for accounting purposes but not usually for compensation. If the ledger balance is negative, there is a ledger overdraft. There is often a service charge and/or an interest penalty for such an overdraft

2. **Collected Balances** - Collected balances are the differences between ledger balances and deposit float.

   • *Deposit float* is the sum of each check deposited multiplied by its availability in days.

   • The collected balance reflects when credit is actually given for the deposit. For example, a $1,000 check deposited on Tuesday is granted one-day availability. This means that the bank gives the customer availability (the deposit becomes good funds) after a delay of one business day. While the ledger balance increased by $1,000 on Tuesday, the collected balance would not increase until Wednesday.

   • Checks are generally granted immediate (same day), one or two business days' availability. The assignment of availability is usually in whole numbers of business days. Checks presented for payment against the account are deducted from both the collected and ledger accounts on the same day. The ledger balance is usually larger than the collected balance. The collected balance may dip below zero without creating a ledger overdraft, but banks may consider a collected overdraft equivalent to a loan and charge interest and/or service fees.

3. **Deposit Float** - There are several ways a bank can compute deposit float:

   • *Proof of Deposit (POD) or Item-by-Item* - Banks assign availability to each check as it passes through the automated check processing system. Availability is assigned based on the time of deposit and endpoint. This is the most accurate method and most major cash management banks have this capability.

   • *Bank Average* - Banks that lack POD capabilities often compute an average availability that applies to all checks. This average is applied to each customer. This method may or may not benefit a customer depending on whether its mix of check deposits has more or less float than average.

- *Company Sample* - Some banks take a sample of check deposits for a specific firm and track the average availability for a period of time. The float based on the sample is then applied to that firm's deposits.

- *Negotiated Availability* - In some cases the bank and the firm may negotiate an average availability that applies to all checks.

E. Availability Schedules

An availability schedule specifies when a bank or the Fed grants credit for deposited checks in the form of an increase in the depositor's available or collected balance. The assignment of availability is usually in whole business days, and checks are generally assigned zero, one or two days' availability. The Fed has availability schedules for banks, and banks have availability schedules for their customers. Many banks have multiple availability schedules. The schedule a bank offers to a particular customer is a marketing decision.

An example of a corporate availability schedule is shown in Exhibit 4-3.

Exhibit 4-3

Example of Availability Schedule

TR No.	Deposit Endpoint	Availability	Deposit Deadline	Days Covered
0210-0000	NYC Banks	0	10:00 a.m.	Monday - Friday
0531-0000	Charlotte RCPC	1	5:00 p.m.	Monday - Thursday
1210-0000	L.A. City	0	1:00 a.m.	Monday - Friday
0865-0000	St. Louis Country	1	6:00 a.m.	Monday - Thursday

1. **Ledger Cut-Off Times** - A bank's ledger cut-off time is the time after which deposits are credited as of the following business day.

2. **Constructing the Schedule** - To construct the availability schedule, the clearing bank examines clearing times for important endpoints, determines endpoints for direct sends, determines costs, and works back from deposit deadlines for those endpoints to establish its own deposit deadlines for customers.

3. **Factors Determining Availability** - The following factors influence the availability a bank assigns to a particular check:

   - *Drawee Location* - Checks drawn on distant banks or banks in remote locations generally have longer availability times than those drawn on nearby banks.

   - *Time of Deposit* - Checks must reach the processing center by a certain time of day in order to qualify for the designated availability. Some financial institutions also have deadlines by which checks must be proofed and encoded.

   - *Degree of Sorting* - If a customer sorts its own checks by transit routing number, the bank may grant better availability. Also, the bank may charge a lower processing fee and/or grant a later deposit cutoff for sorted checks.

   - *Encoding* - If a customer MICR-encodes the check dollar amount on the checks it deposits, the bank may grant faster availability, a later cutoff time, and/or reduced service charges.

   - *Reject Items* - Checks that are rejected by a bank's deposit processing equipment are likely to miss critical deposit deadlines and are likely to receive longer availability.

4. **Availability Adjustments** - Banks make adjustments to a customer's availability in several ways:

   - *As-of Adjustments* - An as-of adjustment is the adjustment of the value date of a transaction for the purpose of calculating collected balances to a different date than the date the transaction occurred. For example, if a bank originally granted one-day availability but actually cleared the check in two days, it would add one more day of float in calculating collected balances.

   - *Fractional Availability* - A bank may experience an average availability of one day under normal circumstances, but its availability deadlines may be missed on 5% of the days of the year. Therefore, it assigns availability of 1.05 days to its customers.

   - *Guaranteed Availability* - Some banks offer a guaranteed availability schedule, which is not subject to deposit adjustments. The customer is given the availability on the schedule regardless of whether the bank is delayed in clearing the checks.

F. Federal Reserve Float

In the process of clearing checks, banks will sometimes receive availability from the Fed before the Fed can generate the offsetting debit. Fed float is the difference between the availability granted a clearing bank and the time required to present the item to the drawee bank. Fed float represents interest-free loans to banks and, indirectly, to companies. The elimination of this Fed float subsidy was mandated by the 1980 Depository Institutions Deregulation and Monetary Control Act. Fed float is priced to banks through as-of adjustments, clearing balance requirements or interest at the Fed funds rate. Because the Fed charges the bank for float, the bank may similarly charge the company.

Bank methods of charging for Fed float vary. Some banks subsidize their customers by ignoring these charges, while others charge back through as-of collected balance adjustments, explicit interest charges or by granting fractional availability.

G. Return Items

Return items are checks rejected by the payee bank. They may be redeposited or charged back to the depositor's account. Some banks charge for redeposits as well as return items. For checks over $2,500, Federal Reserve Regulation CC requires the returning institution to notify the drawee bank electronically that the check is being returned.

H. Other Check-Like Payment Instruments

A number of other payment instruments have check-like attributes and clear through the same channels.

1. **Payable Through Draft (PTD)** - A payable through draft is a payment instrument resembling a check that is drawn against the payor and not the bank. The payor has a period of time in which to honor or refuse payment. Insurance companies often use PTDs for claim reimbursement, partially because the PTD gives them an opportunity to verify the signature and endorsements before honoring it. The return process has very strict guidelines defined by both Fed Regulation CC and local clearing house rules. Regulation CC requires the same time for the return process as for checks.

2. **Government Warrant** - Similar to a PTD, it is issued by a government agency for a specified purchase or service.

3. **Pre-Authorized Draft** - The payor authorizes the payee to draw a check against the payor's account. The payee, rather than the payor, initiates the transaction. Mortgage, insurance and other recurring payments are often made in this way.

4. **Money Order** - The payor first purchases the money order from a third party (such as the Post Office or a bank). The draft then becomes the obligation of the third party.

5. **Traveler's Checks** - Such instruments are prepaid drafts, similar to money orders. An additional signature is required at the time of use.

6. **Depository Transfer Checks (DTCs)** - These are checks used in moving funds from one account to another account held by the same firm, usually in cash concentration systems. No signature is required, but for security there is often a payee restriction. Normally the payee can only be an account at the concentration bank.

7. **Sight Draft** - While a check is payable when presented, a sight draft must generally be accompanied by other documents showing that the terms of transaction have been met. Sight drafts are primarily used in foreign trade transactions.

8. **Time Draft** - This payment mechanism is like a sight draft but is not payable until a specified future date. Time drafts are used in foreign trade transactions that by contract call for delayed payments.

III. The Automated Clearing House (ACH) System

A. Objectives

The financial industry developed the ACH system to automate its payments system, designing it to parallel the paper check system. An ACH transfer can contain more information than a check. The information is processed electronically instead of manually, increasing reliability, efficiency and cost-effectiveness.

B. Structure

There are currently 42 local ACH associations. Of these, 29 are owned by regional member institutions, banks and other depository institutions. Twelve are single-bank ACH associations; one is VISANET, owned by VISA.

Most regional ACHs are operated by the Fed under contract with the ACH. However, the New York ACH is privately operated, and, in 1985, Calwestern ACH (serving California, Nevada and Arizona) switched some of its operations to a private-sector service provider, currently VISANET.

The **National Automated Clearing House Association (NACHA)** is a membership organization that provides marketing and education assistance and establishes the rules, standards and procedures that enable financial institutions to exchange ACH payments on a national basis.

C. ACH Payment Formats

There are ACH formats for both consumer and corporate payments. All ACH payment formats move funds in essentially the same manner. The most appropriate format for a particular payment need is determined by the relationship between the parties, the amount of funds and information exchanged, and the types of ACH payment services offered by the participating banks.

There are both ACH credit transactions and ACH debit transactions. ACH credit transactions move funds from the originator's account to the receiver's account. ACH debit transactions move funds to the originator's account from the receiver's account.

The NACHA operating rules require all financial institutions participating in the ACH to accept all types of ACH entries and post the dollar amounts to the proper accounts, though many institutions do not have the capability to process addenda records. Addenda records are records with remittance detail that follow the standard payment information in ACH payment messages.

The format of an ACH payment message is identified by a three-letter standard entry class in the header of the message.

The most commonly used formats are as follows:

1. **Prearranged Payment and Deposit (PPD)** - The PPD format is the payment application by which consumers may authorize debits or credits to their accounts by a company or financial institution. These are normally recurring payments in fixed amounts for standing obligations.

    - *Credits* - Examples of credits to the consumer are payroll, expense reimbursement, dividends, social security, retirement benefits and tax refunds. The Federal Government currently accounts for about 40 percent of ACH volume with its direct deposit of Social Security payments.

    - *Debits* - Examples of debits to the consumer are rent and mortgage payments, subscriptions, dues and memberships, insurance premiums, installment debt payments and utility payments.

2. **Cash Concentration and Disbursement (CCD)** - CCD is an electronic payment format used for concentration and disbursement of funds within or between companies. A single 94-character record contains the standard entry class indicating the type of transaction, transit routing numbers for the originating and receiving financial institutions, and the payor's and payee's account numbers. CCD is the only corporate ACH format that does not have space for an additional addenda record, but it contains space for a reference number.

3. **Cash Concentration and Disbursement Plus Addendum (CCD+)** - CCD+ is used for the U.S. Treasury Vendor Express program and for corporate-to-corporate payments. It is useful when only a limited amount of information must be transmitted. This format is the identical to CCD but with an addenda record. The addenda record is a free-form data space for up to 80 characters of descriptive data.

4. **Corporate Trade Payment (CTP)** - This format is used for corporate-to-corporate payments. The CTP format consists of a standard ACH payment transaction and a message addendum for remittance information. The message addendum can carry remittance information in fixed-field format with up to 4,990 records, 80 characters each.

5. **Corporate Trade Exchange (CTX)** - The CTX format, like the CTP format, is designed for corporate-to-corporate trade payments. It consists of a standard ACH payment transaction and a variable-length message addendum designed to convey remittance information in the ANSI X12 data standard. The addendum can accommodate 4,990 records, 80 characters each. CTX is useful for payments related to multiple invoices and substantial invoice detail.

D.   Corporate Applications

The most important corporate applications are in cash concentration and disbursement funding. Many corporations use ACH debits to consolidate funds deposited in field banks. This is particularly well suited to corporate lockbox and retail branch deposits. By virtue of its next-day availability an ACH debit may be used by creditworthy companies to fund disbursement accounts. This provides effective day-in-advance notification of the amount of funds required at the concentration bank, and it eliminates the timing problems associated with the late and/or large second presentments. In general, ACH payments can be used in place of more costly wire transfers when the amounts are known at least one day in advance.

E.   Processing

The ACH system is a batch process, store-and-forward system. Transactions received by the bank during the day are stored and processed later in a batch mode. This provides significant economies of scale. It also provides faster processing than paper checks, which must be physically handled. To improve the system further, banks are being encouraged by the Fed to transmit and receive ACH transaction files electronically. They will be required to do so by July 1, 1993. These transmissions use encrypted lines for security. This and other security related concepts are discussed later in the chapter.

F.   Participants

Exhibit 4-4 shows the relationship between parties to an ACH transaction. The sequence of payment instructions illustrated can apply to either a debit or credit.

G.   How an ACH Transaction Works

Instead of using paper to carry the necessary transaction information (as a check does), an ACH transaction carries the information electronically, usually by direct transmission. The data are essentially the data on a check's MICR line and additional information on the sending and receiving accounts. Transactions may be either debits or credits.

Exhibit 4-5 shows the steps in a typical ACH credit transaction in which Company A pays its payroll by direct deposit. An ACH debit transaction is

Exhibit 4-4

ACH Transaction Participants

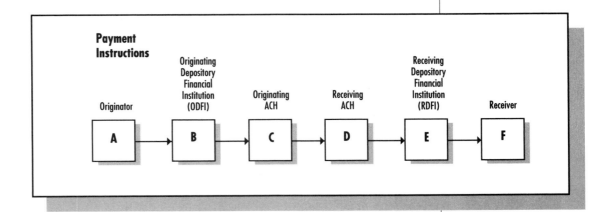

Exhibit 4-5

**An ACH Credit
Transaction (Direct
Deposit of Payroll)**

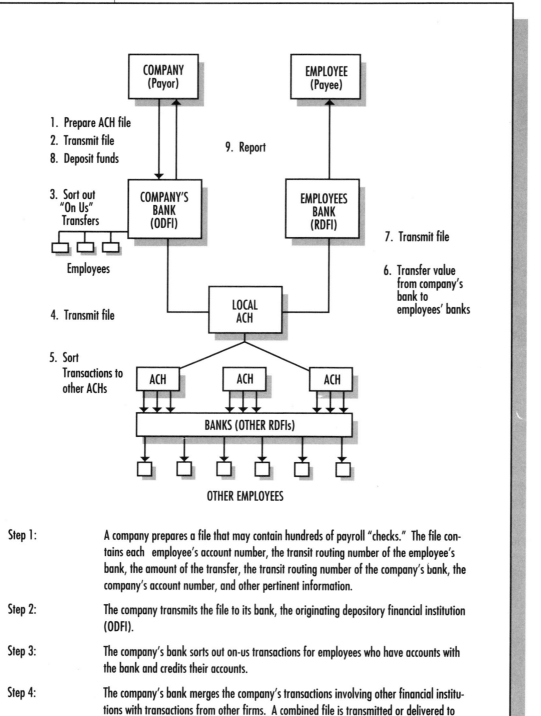

1. Prepare ACH file
2. Transmit file
8. Deposit funds

9. Report

3. Sort out "On Us" Transfers

7. Transmit file

6. Transfer value from company's bank to employees' banks

4. Transmit file

5. Sort Transactions to other ACHs

Step 1: A company prepares a file that may contain hundreds of payroll "checks." The file contains each employee's account number, the transit routing number of the employee's bank, the amount of the transfer, the transit routing number of the company's bank, the company's account number, and other pertinent information.

Step 2: The company transmits the file to its bank, the originating depository financial institution (ODFI).

Step 3: The company's bank sorts out on-us transactions for employees who have accounts with the bank and credits their accounts.

Step 4: The company's bank merges the company's transactions involving other financial institutions with transactions from other firms. A combined file is transmitted or delivered to the ACH servicing the originating institution.

Exhibit 4-5 (Continued)

An ACH Credit Transaction (Direct Deposit of Payroll)

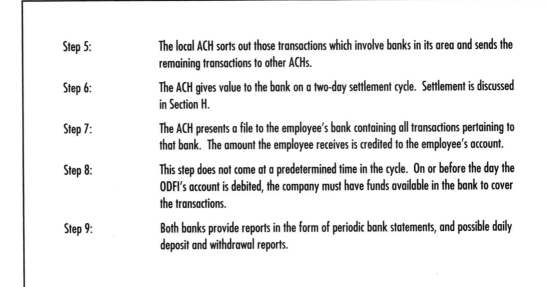

Step 5:	The local ACH sorts out those transactions which involve banks in its area and sends the remaining transactions to other ACHs.
Step 6:	The ACH gives value to the bank on a two-day settlement cycle. Settlement is discussed in Section H.
Step 7:	The ACH presents a file to the employee's bank containing all transactions pertaining to that bank. The amount the employee receives is credited to the employee's account.
Step 8:	This step does not come at a predetermined time in the cycle. On or before the day the ODFI's account is debited, the company must have funds available in the bank to cover the transactions.
Step 9:	Both banks provide reports in the form of periodic bank statements, and possible daily deposit and withdrawal reports.

identical to the credit transaction outlined in the exhibit, except that the file contains a code indicating that the account at the receiving depository financial institution (RDFI) is to be debited instead of credited.

H. Settlement

ACH transactions carry settlement dates that determine the availability of funds. Transactions are settled one or two business days after the payment information is initiated into the payment system. Both the receiver and the originator are settled simultaneously, thereby eliminating float.

1. Most consumer debit and credit transactions are entered into the system two days prior to settlement.

2. Corporate debits are usually entered one day prior to settlement, although some companies use the two-day cycle for concentrating smaller amounts. Large-dollar concentration debits usually are initiated as late as possible to allow the maximum dollar amount to be deposited.

3. Cutoff times and possible charges for input vary by originating bank.

4. Memo posting is posting an ACH credit or debit on a memo basis early in the day when the actual credit or debit will not be posted until later in the day. This allows the beneficiary such as an employee in a direct deposit of payroll program use of the funds during the day.

5. Some financial institutions and ACHs will accept files over the weekend for Monday settlement.

I.   Prenotification

Prenotifications (Prenotes), are zero-dollar entries sent through the ACH system at least ten days prior to live entries. Prenotes provide a verification function at the receiving bank before entries for settlement are processed. For example, when a company adds a new employee to its direct deposit payroll program, it uses prenotification to ensure that the bank transit routing number and the employee's personal bank account number(s) are correct.

Account holders receiving ACH transactions must give prior consent by signing an agreement that authorizes the ACH transaction process. Prenotes are required for all PPD entries and CTP and CTX debits. They may be made but are not required on CCD entries and on CTP and CTX credits.

J.   Advantages of Using ACH

The ACH system provides numerous advantages to companies. These include:

1. **Reduced Banking Costs** - An ACH transfer is usually less expensive than a check and much less expensive than a wire transfer.

2. **Reduced Reconciliation and Cash Application Costs** - Because payments are automated, reconciliation time is reduced. Cash application is more automated than in manual systems that deal with paper checks.

3. **Faster Inflows** - The use of ACH debits can accelerate cash inflow by reducing invoicing, customer processing, mail delays, internal processing, and availability delays.

4. **Control of Payment Timing** - The use of ACH debits and credits can increase control of payment initiation and funds availability and help cash forecasting.

5. **Reliability** - ACH transactions reach their destination in a timely and predictable manner.

6. **Enhanced Service** - Customers and employees benefit from enhanced service, for example, automatic bill paying and direct deposit of payroll.

7. **Flexibility** - Input can be in a wide variety of media, such as magnetic tape, electronic, and PC transmission.

K.   Disadvantages of Using ACH

The following are considered disadvantages of the ACH system:

1. **Reduction in Disbursement Float** - The payor may lose float benefits accruing from mail, customer processing and clearing delays.

2. **Loss of Control in Initiating Payments** - When the payee directly debits the payor's account, the payor may lose the use of accounts payable as a discretionary source of short-term funds.

3. **System Start-up Costs** - Development costs for such items as computer software and hardware can be incurred.

4. **Renegotiation** - Before switching to electronic payments, payors and payees often renegotiate payment terms.

L. Recent ACH System Developments

1. **Improved Controls** - To ensure that an ACH file is not processed multiple times, banks have implemented new controls. Those controls include warnings when two files have the same header information or total dollar amount and communication between the bank and the ACH both before and after a file is transmitted.

2. **Increased Membership** - An increasing number of banks and other financial institutions are now members of the ACH system.

3. **PC ACH Software** - Software for originating ACH entries via a PC has become widely available and is more cost effective.

4. **Return Items** - The automation of return items from the Federal Reserve banks has accelerated the return process.

5. **Direct Transmission**. Banks are encouraging electronic transmission of data rather than physical tape delivery.

6. **Electronic Payment Authorization** - New software has been developed to prevent unauthorized debit and credit activity or amounts in excess of preapproved limits.

7. **All Electronic ACH** - Banks will be required by the Fed to transmit and receive ACH files electronically by July 1, 1993.

IV. Large-Dollar Payment Systems

A. Fedwire

The Fedwire is the Federal Reserve's funds transfer system. It is a real-time method of transferring immediate funds and supporting information between two financial institutions using their respective Federal Reserve accounts. The system is reliable and secure but relatively expensive for companies, compared to checks and ACH transactions.

1. **Communications and Settlement** - Fedwire is both a communication and a settlement system operated by the Fed through its 12 district banks. Funds are moved almost instantaneously once the request has been received by the originating bank except for delays that might result from either a customer or bank temporarily reaching a daylight overdraft limit. The transaction is final once it has been sent by the originating bank and receipt is confirmed by the Fed.

2. **Hours of Operation and Deadlines** - Interdistrict Fedwire service is open from 9:00 A.M. to 6:30 P.M. local time. A bank's deadline for originating a transfer to a third party is 6:00 P.M. The deadline for a bank-to-bank transfer is 6:30 P.M. Banks establish earlier cutoff times for customers and other internal departments to allow for processing.

3. **Types of Fedwire Funds Transfers** - A customer can instruct a bank to do repetitive, semi-repetitive, non-repetitive, and drawdown transfers:

   - *Repetitive* - Repetitive transfers are used when a company makes a transfer frequently between the same debit and credit parties. The bank has a record of the debit and credit parties and receives electronic and telephonic instructions to make the transfer. A line number is used to identify each transfer. Only the date and dollar amount may be changed.

   - *Semi-Repetitive* - With semi-repetitive transfers, the debit and credit parties remain the same but the description may be changed along with the date and dollar amount. They allow some of the control of repetitive transfers and some of the flexibility of non-repetitive transfers.

   - *Non-Repetitive* - With non-repetitive transfers, the debit and credit parties are different each time. Additional security steps such as callbacks may be required.

   - *Drawdown* - A company initiates instructions to debit its own or another party's account. The party being debited must authorize these transfers. Drawdowns are most frequently used as part of a company's concentration system.

4. **Pricing** - The total price to a user of a wire transfer varies significantly. Both the sending institution and the receiving institution may impose a charge.

5. **Payment Finality** - In the event of the sending bank's failure to settle, the Federal Reserve guarantees the transferred funds to the receiving bank.

B. **Mechanics of a Fedwire Transfer**

1. **Example**. Firm A wants to send $5,000,000 to Firm B via a Fedwire transfer.

   Firm A notifies its bank (Bank A) in one of the following ways:

   * *Written Request* - A letter signed by an authorized signatory of the company is delivered to the bank.

   * *Telephone Request* - This type of payment instruction can be verified in several ways. The caller can give the bank prearranged codes. The bank can call the customer to verify the transfer instructions. Sometimes a telephone request must be confirmed later by written request. Most calls are recorded for security purposes and to resolve any disputes.

   * *Terminal Initiation* - A bank may provide a firm with the capability of requesting transfers via personal computer.

   - Bank A deducts $5,000,000 from Firm A's ledger and collected balance.

   - Bank A notifies the Fed of the transfer to Bank B in favor of Firm B. An on-line financial institution is connected directly to the Fedwire computer system; most major cash management banks are on-line. An off-line financial institution does not have such a direct link and must phone in wire transfer requests, use a PC link with a Fed to receive and send wire transfers or process wire transfers through a correspondent bank.

- The Fed subtracts $5,000,000 from Bank A's reserve balance and adds $5,000,000 to Bank B's reserve balance.

- The Fed notifies Bank B of the transfer. If Bank B is in a different Fed district from Bank A, the information is routed through the Fed's communication network to the appropriate receiving Fed.

- Bank B credits Firm B's ledger and collected balance with $5,000,000, and notifies Firm B through a phone call, balance report and/or written communication.

2. **Timing** - The entire process generally takes minutes. However, since it is labor- and systems-intensive, the cost for a company is significantly more than for a check or an ACH transfer.

C. Clearing House Interbank Payments System (CHIPS)

CHIPS is an independent message-switching system that permits international financial transactions to be settled among New York banks.

1. **Background** - CHIPS is operated by the New York Clearing House Association. It was established in 1970 to substitute electronic payments for paper checks arising from international dollar transactions such as Eurocurrency or foreign exchange between foreign and American banks. It is also used for payments under letters of credit and documentary collections and for small third-party transfers. Other institutions outside New York City use their New York Edge Act subsidiaries as agents or have access to CHIPS through correspondents.

2. **Operation** - Transfers between member banks are received and authenticated during the day. Transfers are batched, and at the end of the day net amounts due to, or from each of the settling participants are settled using the Clearing Banks or the Fed. Non-settling participants settle with the larger banks via correspondent banks. Transfers are executed on a same-day basis and may be unwound (i.e., reversed) only if a member bank cannot honor its net debit position.

D. Society for Worldwide Interbank Financial Telecommunications (SWIFT)

SWIFT is the major international interbank telecommunications network that transmits international payment instructions as well as other financial messages. It is not a funds transfer network. Messages are transferred requesting debits and credits to correspondent accounts (in addition to other types of messages). Settlement occurs through Fedwire, CHIPS, correspondent accounts, or other means.

E. Payments System Risk

Federal Reserve concern with payments system risk started in the mid 1970s as payment volume grew and several large banks failed.

1. **Types of Risk** - Today's payments system creates three kinds of risk for banks:

   - **Sender risk** is undertaken by a bank on behalf of the paying customer. If the bank makes a payment and thereby allows its customer to incur an overdraft, it runs the risk of not recovering funds from its customer.

   - **Receiver risk** is undertaken by a bank when it lets its receiving customer use funds before settlement. A bank participating in CHIPS may notify its customer of funds credited, and the customer may use those funds long before settlement at the end of the day.

   - **Systemic risk** is the risk that the failure of one major bank participant could cause other banks to fail. The cancellation of the failed participant's payments and receipts on the day of failure, could cause a chain of payment failures and liquidity shortages, and seriously endanger the liquidity of other bank participants.

2. **Daylight Overdrafts** - A daylight overdraft is an intra-day exposure occurring when an account is in an overdraft position during the business day. Controlling daylight overdrafts has been one of the primary elements in recent Federal Reserve measures to control risk on the large-dollar payment networks.

   - Bank members may have daylight overdrafts in their Federal Reserve Bank accounts, and companies may have daylight overdrafts in their accounts at commercial banks.

   - Examples of transactions that inherently create daylight overdrafts include the following:

     * A bank may repay Fed funds borrowed for the previous night in the morning, and not receive the proceeds of new borrowings until the afternoon.

     * A bank customer that issues commercial paper may repay funds to investors in the morning and not receive funds from renewals and new investors until the afternoon.

   - In order to control this risk, in March 1986, the Fed mandated that all banks using the large-dollar payment systems must have in place a sender net debit cap, which limits the intra-day overdraft that the bank can incur over all the large-dollar systems, and must establish bilateral net credit limits which defined the maximum amount of net payments that the bank was receiving from another bank over private networks such as CHIPS. The reason for the net credit limits is that payments on CHIPS are not settled until the end of the day, and a higher amount of payments received and credited to beneficiaries means a higher exposure to the sending bank's failure to settle at the end of the day.

   - The caps are based on a Fed schedule relating to a bank's self-evaluation of its overall creditworthiness as an institution, its credit policies, and operational controls. The self-evaluation must be approved by the bank's board of directors.

- Daylight overdraft limits have not had a major gridlock effect on corporate money transfers, though there are occasional delays when companies or banks reach their limits.

- Progress has been made on the issue of CHIPS finality. The receiving bank that credits a commercial customer and allows that customer to use the funds has always borne the risk that the sending bank will not settle. Recently, a settlement fund consisting of collateral posted by all members has been established to insure against the failure of a participant, and has, in effect, raised the level of confidence in the finality of CHIPS payments.

- The Fed, working with representatives of the banking industry, has decided that pricing will be the primary approach for controlling the level of daylight overdrafts. In effect, this is a market, rather than a regulatory solution.

Questions

The chapter questions are to test the information in the text and are not examples of CCM examination questions nor are they in the examination format.

Answers can be found at the back of the book on p. 315.

1.   With a check, who is the payee?

2.   What is the portion of the Magnetic Ink Character Recognition (MICR) line which includes the Federal Reserve Bank Code and office and the bank identification number?

3.   What is a cash letter?

4.   What is a direct send?

5.   What is an on-us item?

6.   What is a country item?

7.   What is the difference between a ledger balance and a collected balance?

8.   How is deposit float calculated?

9.   What factors determine availability?

10. What is Federal Reserve float?

11. Why is a payable through draft (PTD) not a check?

12. What differentiates a time draft from a sight draft?

Questions (Continued)

13. What are the most commonly used ACH formats?

14. When does settlement occur in an ACH transaction?

15. How does settlement through Fedwire differ from settlement through the ACH?

16. What is a repetitive wire transfer?

17. What is the major difference between CHIPS and S W I F T ?

18. Why is the Federal Reserve concerned about daylight overdrafts and what action has it taken to address this concern?

Accounts Receivable and Credit Management

Chapter 5

Overview

This chapter describes how companies offer credit to their customers and how they manage accounts receivable.

Learning Objectives

Upon completion of this chapter and the related study questions, the reader should be able to do the following:

1. Describe the objective of the corporate credit function.
2. Describe how the credit function fits into the corporate finance organization.
3. Discuss how corporations develop credit policies.
4. Define commonly used credit terms.
5. Explain how companies make customer credit decisions.
6. Explain how the costs and benefits of credit policies are calculated.
7. Describe how accounts receivable are measured and monitored.
8. Discuss how accounts receivable may be financed.
9. Discuss legislation that affects credit and collections.

OUTLINE

I. **Objectives of Credit Management**

II. **The Credit Management Function**
   A. Responsibility for Credit Management
   B. Importance for the Cash Manager

III. **Credit Policies**
   A. Reasons to Offer Credit
   B. Credit Policy Constraints
   C. Financial Implications

IV. **Forms of Credit Extension**
   A. Open Account
   B. Installment Credit
   C. Revolving Credit
   D. Letter of Credit

V. **Credit Terms and Considerations**
   A. Common Credit Terms
   B. Credit Term Considerations
   C. Cost of Trade Credit

VI. **Credit Standards**
   A. Potential Errors in Credit Decision-Making
   B. Information Sources
   C. Qualitative Analysis
   D. Quantitative Analysis
   E. Billing and Collection Policies

Outline (Continued)

VII. Costs and Benefits of Credit Policies
    A. Seller's Benefits and Costs
    B. Analysis of Credit Policy Alternative

VIII. Financing Accounts Receivable
    A. Unsecured Bank Borrowing
    B. Secured Bank Borrowing
    C. Captive Finance Company
    D. Third-Party Financing Institution
    E. Credit Card
    F. Factoring
    G. Private Label Financing

IX. Monitoring and Control
    A. Purpose
    B. Days Sales Outstanding (DSO)
    C. Aging Schedule
    D. Receivables Balance Pattern

X. Legislation Affecting Credit and Collections
    A. Pricing and Interest Charge Restrictions
    B. Consumer and Commercial Credit Legislation
    C. Uniform Commercial Code (UCC)
    D. Bankruptcy and Reorganization

I. Objectives of Credit Management

The objectives of credit management include the following:

- Set credit policies and communicate them to other areas such as sales and marketing.

- Make customer credit decisions.

- Ensure prompt and accurate customer billing.

- Maintain up-to-date records of accounts receivable.

- Follow up on overdue accounts and initiate collection procedures when necessary.

II. The Credit Management Function

A. Responsibility for Credit Management

1. Credit policy is generally administered by the credit manager.

2. The marketing function may work with credit management, as credit policy can have an influence on winning or losing sales, as well as maintaining customer relationships.

3. Captive finance companies, discussed later in this chapter, assume responsibility for credit management in some companies.

B. Importance for the Cash Manager

Working relationships with the credit function are important for the cash manager.

1. **Organizational Relationship** - Credit policy and accounts receivable collection time have a predominant influence on the time line of cash management, but often they are not under the cash manager's control.

2. **Need for Interaction** - A strong information link and a cooperative working relationship are needed between the credit and cash management functions for the following reasons:

   - *Customer Payments* - The cash manager is responsible for establishing and maintaining the banking network. The credit management function needs to have input to, and receive feedback from this network.

   - *Forecasting* - The credit department is an important resource for the cash manager in forecasting, since credit policies affect the accuracy, nature and time frame of cash flow forecasts. For example, a company that sells only on a cash basis must forecast daily sales for the next seven days to forecast cash inflows for the next week. On the other hand, a company that sells completely on credit terms of net 30 has already realized the sales that will generate the cash inflows for the next few weeks.

III. Credit Policies

Corporate credit policies concern credit standards, credit terms, and collection policy. If credit is to be offered, a number of decisions must be made by the company:

- **Credit Standards** - Granting credit has two stages, establishing credit standards and determining whether an applicant meets those standards.

- **Credit Terms** - The terms of the sale must be clearly specified.

- **Collection Policy** - A company must establish policies and procedures to collect payment when a credit customer fails to pay according to the specified terms.

It is important that the company have written policies and procedures in place to ensure consistency and objectivity. After a company has established its basic credit policies, it must develop the procedures and information systems necessary to monitor the accounts receivable for compliance with credit terms and to detect changes in payment patterns.

A. Reasons to Offer Credit

The primary reason for a company to offer credit terms to its customers is to increase sales. Companies may choose to offer credit for other reasons such as the following:

1. **Competition** - Matching competitors' terms may be a sales necessity.

2. **Promotion** - A company may offer special credit terms as part of a promotion program for a product.

3. **Credit Availability** - Some buyers may not have access to any credit other than trade credit. In tight credit times, seller trade terms or financing may be necessary.

4. **Convenience** - The buyer may prefer the convenience of an open account trade credit arrangement. Trade credit does not require the documentation or the explicit agreement on the repayment date that some forms of bank or finance company credit do.

5. **Profit** - A company extending credit may earn interest above its cost of funds.

B. Credit Policy Constraints

A company's credit policy is influenced by the following:

1. **Industry Convention** - The credit terms customarily offered in many industries have not changed for a long time. It is difficult for a seller to make a change unilaterally unless the buyer is offered some value such as a discount in return.

2. **Legal Constraints** - The Robinson-Patman Act prohibits various forms of price discrimination, as discussed in Section X of this chapter. Also, state law may dictate terms for certain goods and services.

3.   **Contractual Obligations** - A covenant in a loan agreement may have a current ratio limitation. If accounts receivable and related short-term borrowing are increased by the same amount, working capital will stay the same but the current ratio will decrease, possibly in violation of a loan covenant.

C.   Financial Implications

A company's credit policies, together with the pattern of its sales, determine the level of accounts receivable.

1.   **Use of Capital and Liquidity** - For companies that offer credit, a certain minimum level of accounts receivable is unavoidable. However, a delay in customer payments and corresponding increase in accounts receivable must be financed and can cause a liquidity problem if the company does not have additional sources of financing.

2.   **Source of Liquidity** - Accounts receivable can also be a source of liquidity to the extent they can be used as the basis for short-term borrowing or sold to other parties through factoring or securitization, both discussed later in the chapter and in Chapter 12, Borrowing. These may be attractive sources of financing because a company's customers may be better credits than the company itself. For example, some captive finance companies have better credit ratings than their parents.

IV. Forms of Credit Extension

Credit can be extended to a customer in the following ways:

A.   Open Account

This method, sometimes called open book credit, is the most common type of commercial trade credit in the U.S. The seller issues an invoice, which is formal evidence of the obligation, and records the sale as an account receivable. The customer is billed for each transaction by an invoice and/or by a monthly statement covering all invoices generated during the billing period.

B.   Installment Credit

The amount of the sale, as well as any interest, is paid in periodic installments, usually in equal monthly amounts. Frequently, the seller requires the buyer to sign a contract specifying the terms of the obligation. This form of credit is most common for high-value consumer durables such as automobiles. A contract explaining credit terms and disclosing rates to retail consumers is required under Federal Reserve Regulation Z (Truth in Lending).

C.   Revolving Credit

Under revolving credit terms, credit is granted without requiring specific approval of each transaction as long as the account is current. The account is usually considered current if the credit outstanding is below an established credit limit and minimum payments have been made on time.

The term revolving credit also refers to a type of bank loan which is described in Chapter 12, Borrowing.

D. Letter of Credit

The seller may require the buyer to open a letter of credit through a bank, wherein the bank guarantees that the seller will be paid if certain specified conditions are met by a certain date. This method is sometimes used domestically, but is more common in international trade. It is described in detail in Chapter 15, International Cash Management.

V. Credit Terms and Considerations

A. Common Credit Terms

Credit terms are the contract between the buyer and seller. They stipulate the form and timing of payments. They are usually specified on an invoice and/or on legal documents. The following are the credit terms used most commonly.

1. **Cash Before Delivery (CBD)** - CBD requires payment, often in the form of a check. A cashier's or certified check may be required before the order is shipped. CBD is used when the buyer is considered a greater credit risk than the seller is willing to accept.

2. **Cash on Delivery (COD)** - Goods are shipped, and the buyer must pay upon delivery. The seller may have to pay the shipping costs to return the goods if the payment is not made.

3. **Cash Terms** - The buyer generally has a week to ten days to make the payment. This method is frequently used in sales of highly perishable items.

4. **Ordinary Terms** - The seller specifies a net due date by which the full amount must be paid and the discount date by which the buyer must pay to take advantage of the stated discount. These dates are usually calculated from the invoice date, although other dates, such as the delivery date, are occasionally specified. Terms of 2/10 net 30 mean that the total amount is due within 30 days of the invoice date, but the buyer can take a 2% discount if payment is made within 10 days.

5. **Monthly Billing** - A monthly statement is issued for all invoices dated prior to a cutoff date, such as the 25th of the month. Payment is due by a specified date the following month. Cash discounts may also be incorporated. For example, 1/10, Prox net 30 means that a discount of 1% can be taken if payment is made by the 10th day of the following month; the total amount is due on the 30th day of the following month.

6. **Draft/Bill of Lading** - This collection method is also known as a documentary collection. The seller collects payments through a bank. Having shipped goods to the buyer, the seller sends shipping and title documents to its bank. The seller's bank sends the documents to the buyer's bank. The buyer gains possession of the documents upon paying the bank or upon signing a draft agreeing to pay. This method is more common in international than domestic trade.

7. **Seasonal Dating** - Payment is due near the end of the buyer's selling season when the buyer has cash. This is a way for a manufacturer to help finance a buyer. It is common in industries with distinct seasonality of sales such as toys, greeting cards, garden supplies, sporting goods, or textbooks. Sliding discounts may be available to encourage early payment.

8. **Consignment** - Under a consignment agreement, the seller ships the goods to the buyer with no obligation to pay until the goods have been sold or used. The title to the goods remains with the seller until that date. The buyer is usually required to segregate the consigned inventory and the proceeds from the sale of consigned items, as well as to provide periodic accounting of the inventory on hand. Sometimes the buyer is invoiced after each accounting.

B. Credit Term Considerations

1. **Penalty Fees** - In addition to offering credit terms, firms often assess a penalty fee for payments received past the due date. This fee is usually a percentage of the past due amount. The fee should be clearly stated at the time of the sale and shown on the invoice. These fees are generally shown as an annualized rate, e.g., 21% per annum, or as a daily rate.

2. **Credit Limits** - The aggregate amount of credit to be granted to a customer must also be determined. A new customer that meets the standards is often granted credit at the lowest limit. After some time period of satisfactory experience (for example, six months), the credit limit is raised to the next level. Credit limits are usually reviewed annually.

3. **Eligibility for Discount** - Companies usually use the postmark date or the date funds are received as the benchmark date for determining eligibility for discounts. Industry standards dictate the method used.

C. Cost of Trade Credit

With the exception of the cost of not taking a discount for early payment (if one is offered), there usually is no explicit charge included in the terms of sale for trade credit. For example, assume the credit terms for the purchase are 1/10 net 30. The payment will be 99% of the invoice price if it is made by the 10th day or 100% of the price if payment is made between the 11th and the 30th day.

This means that 1% of the invoice can be considered the amount of interest paid to borrow (the discounted amount of the purchase) from the supplier for 20 additional days - from the discount date to the net payment date. The choice of payment dates can be evaluated by comparing the effective interest cost of missing the discount with the cost of alternative sources of credit. The effective annual interest cost of making the net payment on the due date instead of the discounted payment on the discount date is shown in Exhibit 5-1. In this example, the buyer is essentially borrowing from the supplier at 37.24%. If the buyer can borrow at a lower rate, it would probably be better off borrowing the funds necessary to pay on the tenth day. In general, if the effective rate computed by the formula is greater than the company's alternative cost of borrowing, the discount should be taken.

Exhibit 5-1

Trade Credit Borrowing Calculation

Effective annual percentage cost for terms of d/t net n

$$i = \frac{d}{1-d} \times \frac{365}{n-t}$$

where:

i = the effective interest rate

d = the discount percentage

n = date the payment is made

t = last day for the discount to be taken.

<u>Example</u>

With payment terms of 2/10 net 30, the effective cost of paying on day 30 instead of day 10 is:

$$i = \frac{.02}{.98} \times \frac{365}{30-10} = 37.24\%$$

VI. Credit Standards

A. Potential Errors in Credit Decision-Making

There are two types of potential errors in the granting of credit.

1. **Rejection of an Acceptable Credit Risk** - If a company rejects a customer who is a good risk, the company loses potential sales.

2. **Acceptance of a Substandard Risk** - If the company accepts a customer who does not pay according to the specified terms, the company incurs collection, monitoring and/or bad debt costs.

Making credit standards more stringent will in general reduce the frequency of the second type of error but will also increase the frequency of the first type. In practice, the costs of these two types of errors are very hard to quantify.

B. Information Sources

The type, quantity and cost of information must be considered in establishing the company's method of analyzing credit requests. With a sequential approach, credit information can be gathered in stages, and at each stage, the costs of additional information may be weighed against the benefits. Information sources can be internal or external.

1. **Internal Sources** - The most important sources of internal information are the applicant's credit history and the new customer's credit application. Internal information is generally used first in the decision- making process.

2. **External Sources** - There are a wide variety of external sources that can be used to assist in determining the creditworthiness of a credit applicant.

    - *Financial Statements* - Financial statements provide important information on corporate credit applicants.

    - *Trade References* - Other firms describe their payment experiences with the applicant. These are usually reliable indicators of when payment will be made.

    - *Banks* - The customer's bank can also be a valuable source of information about the customer's financial condition and available credit, though banks are generally reluctant to discuss their experience with trade creditors.

    - *Agencies* - There are local as well as nationwide agencies that collect, evaluate and report information on credit history, including past payment history, financial information, maximum outstanding credit amounts, length of time credit has been available and any actions that have been necessary to achieve collection.

C.   Qualitative Analysis

Qualitative analysis naturally depends upon the type of information available and the cost/benefit tradeoff. The traditional qualitative approaches are based on the five Cs of credit:

1. **Character** - The perceived honesty or integrity of the individual applicant, or the officers of a corporate applicant, is used as an indication of the intent or willingness to pay. This can be evidenced by the company's payment history.

2. **Capacity** - A measure of the customer's current resources to pay the obligation when due, as measured by financial liquidity.

3. **Capital** - The customer's long-term financial resources that could be called upon if the immediate cash flow were insufficient.

4. **Collateral** - Assets available to satisfy the obligation if payment is not made.

5. **Conditions** - The general economic environment and economic conditions of the customer and the seller affect the ability of the customer to pay and the willingness of the company to grant the credit.

D.   Quantitative Analysis

There are quantitative methods for both corporate and consumer credit analysis. These are:

1. **Business Credit Analysis** - Quantitative analysis of credit information begins with an examination of the credit applicant's financial statements,

frequently through ratio analysis, to assess the customer's financial condition. The measures used most often include the quick ratio, turnover ratios and a measure of financial leverage. Ratios must be compared to industry standards published by credit rating agencies and other associations for the exchange of credit information.

2. **Consumer Credit Analysis** - Major issuers of retail credit, such as department stores, use quantitative credit scoring models, often developing a different model for each billing region. The quantitative approaches are cost effective, and can aid in complying with consumer credit legislation which is discussed later in the chapter. Formal statistical analysis is often used to identify the factors that distinguish paying customers from non-paying customers. One type of analysis, credit scoring, is a technique used to estimate the creditworthiness of applicants. Credit scoring follows three steps:

   - *Standard and High-Risk Accounts* are defined based on historical data. Characteristics are compiled to discriminate between the two types of accounts. Variables such as monthly income, monthly obligations, and time on the job might be used for a consumer credit applicant.

   - *Weighting of Characteristics* distinguishes between standard and high-risk accounts, thus creating an aggregate credit score that measures creditworthiness.

   - *Cutoff Scores* are set - An applicant with a score above the higher cutoff is granted credit while one below the lower limit is denied credit. An applicant with a score between the two limits is usually referred for further analysis before a decision is made.

E. Billing and Collection Policies

The type of credit adopted has an important influence on the characteristics of the collection system. The major objective of a collection policy is to speed the conversion of accounts receivable to cash, while minimizing bad-debt losses.

1. **Invoicing** - The first step in collecting an account is to send prompt and correct invoices with the terms of payment clearly stated. One of the major problems with cash management is invoicing float, the delay between the purchase of goods and services and the receipt of the invoice. This can add days or even weeks to the cash flow time line.

2. **Statements** - Most companies bill their wholesale customers by invoice with each shipment because that method helps both the buyer and the seller reconcile the invoice with the shipment of goods. A statement may be sent periodically as a reminder. Monthly statements listing goods or services purchased are common in retail consumer billing.

3. **Delayed Payments** - When payment is delayed beyond the due date, the company has several options. These include:

   - Send a duplicate invoice.

   - Mail a form letter or series of form letters.

- Make telephone calls, which will also determine if there is a perceived dispute or need for a duplicate invoice.

- Visit the customer in person.

- Suspend further sales until past due items are paid, i.e., putting the customer on credit hold.

- Negotiate with the customer for payment of past due amounts.

- Attempt to negotiate a corporate or personal guarantee or try to obtain a lien on specific assets.

- Consider legal action.

- Turn delinquent accounts over to a collection agency. The charge is usually a percentage of the amount collected.

- Use credit insurance as a means of shifting part of the risk of extraordinary losses to a third party. Credit insurance usually has a contractual deductible amount and coinsurance.

VII. Costs and Benefits of Credit Policies

Credit policies create costs and benefits for both the seller and the buyer.

A. Seller's Benefits and Costs

The seller can expect the following benefits and costs from setting a credit policy:

1. **Benefits**

   - *Increased Sales* - The purpose of extending credit is to increase sales, resulting in increased profits for the firm.

   - *Interest Income* - Funds received from interest on installment or other forms of credit are a benefit to the seller.

2. **Costs**

   - *Credit Evaluation* - This may include personnel costs, data processing costs and the costs of obtaining credit information.

   - *Accounts Receivable Carrying Cost* - Accounts receivable, like any other asset on the corporate balance sheet, have a cost. The company may consider that cost to be the weighted average cost of capital or the marginal cost of borrowing to support the receivables.

   - *Discounted Payments* - Customers that take a discount pay a lower price. If the volume of sales does not increase, this reduces the total net revenue. The loss of revenue is partially offset by a reduction in accounts receivable carrying costs.

   - *Bad Debts* - The timing and volume of bad-debt chargeoffs is an important component of credit policy.

- *Collection Expenses* - These include the cost of processing payments as well as the cost of pursuing accounts that are not being paid in a timely manner.

- *Selling and Production Costs* - A liberalized credit policy may contribute to an increase in sales, but sales and production expense may increase at the same time.

B. Analysis of Credit Policy Alternatives

A company can analyze the effects of increasing credit terms by comparing the expected profitability of increased sales with the associated costs. Those costs include the cost of supporting increased accounts receivable and the cost of additional bad-debt losses.

Exhibit 5-2 is an illustration of how these benefits and costs are calculated. A company with $2,200,000 in sales is assumed to generate a 10% increase in sales as a result of changing its credit terms from net 30 to net 60.

- The marginal profitability of the additional sales is assumed to be 25%.

- The actual collection period is expected to increase from 35 days to 65 days, resulting in an additional investment in receivables of $220,000.

- The cost of supporting additional receivables on the balance sheet is assumed to be the company's weighted average cost of capital (WACC), which is assumed to be 15%. WACC is explained in Chapter 2, The Corporate Financial Function.

- Additional bad-debt losses are assumed to be 3% of sales.

- The result of the company's new collection policy is an increase in profits of $15,400.

VIII. Financing Accounts Receivable

A. Unsecured Bank Borrowing

A company that offers credit may borrow unsecured funds from a bank to support additional accounts receivable if it has sufficient credit standing.

1. The major advantages are that the company realizes the marketing benefits of extending credit and has the ability to approve the customers who purchase goods and services on credit.

2. The major disadvantage is that the company absorbs the costs of running the credit operation, financing the accounts receivable, and collecting the accounts and the bad-debt losses.

B. Secured Bank Borrowing

If the company cannot finance its accounts receivable with unsecured borrowings, it may be able to pledge its receivables as collateral and borrow on a secured basis.

C. Captive Finance Company

A company may be able to create a wholly owned subsidiary to perform the credit operations and to obtain receivables financing. Since the finance company is a subsidiary of the parent company, the advantages and disadvantages listed earlier, apply. In addition, because of its greater liquidity, the captive finance company may be able to obtain financing at a lower cost than the parent company.

Exhibit 5-2

Costs and Benefits of Extending Credit Terms

Step A: Additional Sales	
= Percent increase x Present sales	
= 0.10 x $2,200,000	$220,000
Marginal Profitability of additional sales	
= Profit contribution ratio x Additional sales	
= 0.25 x $220,000 =	$55,000
Step B: Additional investment in receivables	
= New average balance - Present average balance	
= $\dfrac{\text{New annual sales}}{365}$ x New average	
collection period - $\dfrac{\text{Present average sales}}{365}$	
x Present average collection period	
= $\dfrac{\$2,420,000}{365}$ x 65 - $\dfrac{\$2,200,000}{365}$ x 35	
= $430,959 - $210,959	$220,000
Cost of additional investment in receivables	
= Additional investment in receivables x Required pretax rate of return	
= $220,000 x 0.20	$44,000
Step C: Additional bad-debt loss	
= Bad-debt loss ratio x Additional sales	
= 0.03 x $220,000	$6,600
Step D: Net change in pretax profits	
= Marginal returns - Marginal costs	
= A - (B + C)	
= $55,000 - ($44,000 + $6,600)	+$4,400

Reprinted by permission from p. 725 of **Contemporary Financial Management, 5E**, By Moyer, McGuigan, Kretlow; Copyright © 1992 by West Publishing Company. All rights reserved.

D. Third-Party Financing Institution

The company may collect the information necessary to complete a credit application and forward the completed application to a financial institution which makes the credit decision, and, at its option, grants the credit. Because of the administrative costs involved, this is most common for large-ticket items such as production machinery.

1. The advantage of this alternative is that the company avoids most of the costs of operating a credit department and frees up the funds that otherwise would be tied up in financing accounts receivable.

2. The disadvantage is that the company loses control over the type of customer accepted for credit and loses some of the marketing opportunities. The company may have to pay a fee in the form of a discount of the face value of the sale to compensate the third party.

E. Credit Card

A third party, usually a bank or other financial institution, may offer a credit card that a merchant accepts as payment. The agreement between the seller and the financial institution specifies that the seller is paid in cash at a discount of the face value of the purchase at a specified time after the credit sale ticket is deposited.

1. The advantages of using credit cards are as follows: The seller bears none of the direct costs of running a credit department. Depending upon the agreement, the seller has little or no funds tied up in financing accounts receivable. Finally, the third party and the seller have many options in sharing or absorbing bad-debt losses.

2. The disadvantages in using credit cards for customer financing are as follows: The seller loses control over the determination of acceptable credit customers and many of the promotional aspects of having its own list of credit customers. Also, a major direct cost is the discount of the face value which may be as high as 5%, depending upon the average size of the sale and the total volume.

F. Factoring

Another important third-party financing option is factoring, which is the sale or transfer of title of the accounts receivable to a factoring company. The factor provides credit evaluation and collection services. The degree to which factoring is considered acceptable and the degree to which it is actually used vary by industry and region. It has historically been widely used in the textile and garment industries.

1. **Recourse** - When factoring is done with recourse, the seller is still liable if the factoring company cannot collect an account receivable. Most factoring is without recourse.

2. **Notification** - Most factoring is on a notification basis. The buyer is notified that the account has been sold and is informed to remit the funds directly to the factor.

3. **Maturity and Discount Factoring** - Under maturity factoring, the funds are available to the seller on the average collection date from the customers. In this case, the seller is using the factor more for protection against bad debts than for receivables financing.

   With discount factoring, funds are made available to the seller prior to the average collection date from the customers.

   The amount available is usually the face value of the invoice less any cash discounts and an allowance for returns, adjustments and bad debts.

4. **Advantages of Factoring** - Factoring has the following advantages:

   • It reduces or eliminates the cost of maintaining a credit department.

   • The factor absorbs the uncertainty in the timing of the payment and any extraordinary bad-debt losses.

   • Because of the ability to spread risks, the factor may be able to accept some credit customers that the seller has to reject.

   • The factor may have better credit information and be able to make better credit decisions.

5. **Disadvantages of Factoring** - Disadvantages of factoring include the following:

   • The fees charged in a typical non-recourse agreement may be quite high.

   • The seller loses control over who is granted credit and may require its own credit operation to assess those customers rejected by the factor.

   • Some companies believe that having their receivables factored conveys a sign of financial weakness, though in some industries, factoring is a standard practice.

G.   Private Label Financing

With private label financing, a third party operates the credit function in the name of the seller. From the customer's perspective, the credit appears to be arranged through the seller.

1. **Advantages**:

   • The seller retains many of the promotional aspects of conducting its own credit function.

   • It has neither the costs of the credit operation nor the requirement to finance accounts receivable.

2. **Disadvantages**:

   • The seller does not receive the full face value of the sale.

- The seller may lose the authority to decide on acceptable credit customers.

IX. Monitoring and Control

Accounts receivable should be tracked both by individual customer and in the aggregate. An aging schedule is a useful method for tracking individual receivables, and a report of days sales outstanding is a useful measure of total accounts receivable.

A. Purpose

Monitoring of accounts receivable should be performed on both an individual and an aggregate level.

1. Individual accounts should be monitored for the following reasons:

   - Some customers may intentionally delay payment until a follow-up is initiated.

   - A change in financial condition may alter the ability of a customer to make the payments.

2. Aggregate accounts receivable should be monitored because of the following reasons:

   - Aggregate accounts receivable are the basis for future cash receipts.

   - A significant change in the level of accounts receivable may be a symptom of a change in business that could affect the company's financing needs and should be analyzed to determine underlying causes and any actions to be taken. Potential variables that could create significant changes are:

     * sales volume

     * credit standards

     * economic conditions

B. Days Sales Outstanding (DSO)

The most commonly used measurement of accounts receivable is days sales outstanding (DSO), which is calculated by dividing accounts receivable outstanding at the end of a time period by the average daily credit sales for the period.

DSO is easy to calculate and gives a single number that can be compared to the stated credit terms or to a historic trend. It may be distorted by changing trends in sales volume, payment pattern or by a strong seasonality in sales.

Exhibit 5-3 describes a basic method for calculating DSO. Average sales of $3,444.44 is computed without considering the pattern of sales for the period.

C. Aging Schedule

An aging schedule is a list of the percentages and/or amounts of outstanding accounts receivable classified as current or past due, in 30-day increments. Its

Exhibit 5-3

Days Sales Outstanding (DSO) Calculation

Assume:

Outstanding receivables of $285,000

Credit terms of net 60

Sales history:

Month 1 = $ 90,000

Month 2 = $105,000

Month 3 = $115,000

In Month 1, the four weeks of sales are $40,000, $20,000, $20,000 and $10,000.

$$\text{Average sales} = \frac{90000 + 105000 + 115000}{90} = 3444.44$$

$$\text{DSO} = (\$285,000)/\$3,444.44 = 82.7$$

Average past due is 22.7 days, which is calculated by subtracting the credit terms of net 60 from the 82.7 days, sales outstanding.

main use is to identify past-due accounts. This is important because the older a receivable becomes, the less likely it is to be collected.

With credit terms of net 30, the aging schedule in Exhibit 5-4 shows that 30% of the receivables are overdue. The aging schedule can be a more informative breakdown than DSO because it provides information on the distribution, not just a single average. However, the aging schedule suffers from the same potentially misleading signals as DSO when sales vary from month to month.

D.   Receivables Balance Pattern

A receivables balance pattern is based on aging schedules. It specifies the percentage of credit sales in a time period, usually a month, that remains outstanding at the end of each subsequent time period. The normal balance pattern is identified by examining the company's collection history. The balance experience at any point in time is then evaluated for any shifts by comparing it to the normal balance experience.

For example, assume that the pattern shown in Exhibit 5-5 is typical of the accounts receivable pattern for the company over time. At the end of March,

Exhibit 5-4

Example of an Aging Schedule

Age of Accounts	Accounts Receivable	% of Accounts Receivable
0-30 days	$1,750,000	70%
31-60 days	375,000	15%
61-90 days	250,000	10%
91 + days	125,000	5%
Total	$2,500,000	100%

95% of sales for March, 55% of sales for February and 20% of sales of January are still in accounts receivable.

The balance pattern gives a more complete distribution of the collection experience. Furthermore, it is not directly affected by variation in sales; thus, it is not subject to misleading signals because of sales changes.

The balance pattern can be used to project accounts receivable levels and collections and can be used as a basis for preparing cash flow forecasts.

X. Legislation Affecting Credit and Collections

A. Pricing and Interest Charge Restrictions

Because the credit option is a benefit to the buyer, terms can be considered a part of the price of the product or service being offered.

1. **Robinson-Patman Act** - The Robinson-Patman Act specifically prohibits price discrimination among customers where a cost basis cannot be demonstrated as the reason for price differences. Different credit terms are acceptable if they are industry practice or in cases in which cost differences can be substantiated.

2. **Usury Laws** - Usury laws, which vary significantly from state to state, restrict the interest rates that firms can charge on installment credit or penalty fees.

B. Consumer and Commercial Credit Legislation

A number of laws regulate the statement of terms, the credit analysis and approval process and the collection practices that can be employed when sell-

Exhibit 5-5

*Example of a
Receivables Balance
Pattern*

Month Sales	Sales	Accounts Receivable End of Month 3	Accounts Receivable % of Sales
January	$250	$ 50	20%
February	300	165	55%
March	400	380	95%
April	500	*	*

The estimate of cash inflows for April = 5% of April sales + 40% of March sales + 35% of February sales + 20% of January sales.

= (.05 x $500) + (.40 x $400) + (.35 x $300) + (.20 x $250) = $340

ing on a credit basis to consumers. Some of the more important Federal legislation and regulations are:

1.   **Truth in Lending Act (1969)** - Requires lenders to disclose the true annual interest rate and the total dollar cost on most types of loans.

2.   **Fair Credit Reporting Act (1971) -** Gives a borrower, an applicant for an insurance policy or a job applicant the right to learn the contents of his or her own credit file at any credit bureau.

3.   **Fair Credit Billing Act (1975) -** An amendment to the Truth in Lending Act that protects charge account customers against billing errors by permitting credit card customers to use the same legal defenses against banks or other "third party" credit card companies that they could previously use against merchants.

4.   **Equal Credit Opportunity Act (1975) -** Prohibits creditors from discriminating against credit applicants on the basis of sex, marital status, race, color, religion, national origin, age, or receipt of public assistance.

5.   **Fair Debt Collection Practices Act (1978) -** An amendment to the Consumer Practices Act designed to eliminate abusive and unfair debt collection practices such as threats of financial ruin, loss of job reputation, and late evening telephone calls.

C.   Uniform Commercial Code (UCC)

In general, revolving credit, installment credit and sales finance transactions are covered by provisions of the Uniform Commercial Code, which is the model for many state laws.

D.   Bankruptcy and Reorganization

Under the Federal Bankruptcy Reform Act of 1978, a company may file for liquidation under Chapter 7 or reorganization under Chapter 11. Individuals typically file for reorganization under Chapter 13. Reorganization allows a company to pay off debts gradually and operate under a court supervised plan for returning to financial soundness. Filing of a petition protects the debtor from a list of actions by creditors. The law established a federal bankruptcy court system with exclusive jurisdiction over bankruptcy cases.

Questions

The chapter questions are to test the information in the text and are not examples of CCM examination questions nor are they in the examination format.

Answers can be found at the back of the book on p. 317.

1. What are the major objectives of credit management?

2. What are the three elements of a credit policy?

3. What are revolving credit terms?

4. What is seasonal dating?

5. What is the effective cost of not taking a discount under terms of 3/20 net 60?

6. What are the five Cs in the qualitative analysis of credit?

7. What is credit scoring?

8. A company with $100,000 in sales is anticipating a 15% increase in those sales if credit terms are changed from net 10 to net 30. If the marginal profitability of those sales is 20%, the firm's weighted average cost of capital is 10%, the average collection period is expected to increase from 15 to 35 days, and bad debts will remain at 2% of sales, is this change in credit terms profitable?

9. What is factoring?

10. A firm has outstanding receivables of $125,000. Its credit terms are net 30. If during the past three months sales are $75,000, $100,000 and $90,000, how many days' sales are outstanding?

11. What Federal legislation prohibits price discrimination?

12. What Federal legislation requires disclosure of the true cost of a loan?

Collections

Chapter 6

Overview

An organization may collect funds at several locations and deposit them into one or more banks. To do so effectively, it develops systems to collect payments from customers. This chapter discusses the objectives of a collection system, the principal methods that companies and other organizations use to collect payments and the role of the commercial banking system in the collection process.

Learning Objectives

Upon completion of this chapter and related study questions, the reader should be able to do the following:

1. Describe the objectives of a corporate collection system.

2. Compare and contrast alternative over-the-counter, mail and electronic collection methods.

3. Describe the components of collection float.

4. Understand how a collection processing system is selected.

5. Calculate the cost of float and the dollar savings from a lockbox.

6. Explain and contrast the function and performance criteria of wholesale and retail lockboxes.

7. Understand the basic design for a lockbox study.

8. Compare the service features of bank lockbox providers.

9. Describe the function of field deposit systems.

10. Describe the function and application of ACH corporate-to-corporate payments, credit and debit cards, and preauthorized credits and debits.

Outline

I. **Objectives of a Collection System**

II. **Collection Methods**
   A. Over-the-Counter/Field Deposit Systems
   B. Mail
   C. Electronic

III. **Collection System Considerations**
   A. Payment Practices
   B. Payments System
   C. Nature of the Business
   D. Payment Instrument Characteristics
   E. Float/Administrative Cost Tradeoff
   F. Wholesale and Retail Payments

IV. **Collection Float**
   A. Collection Float Components
   B. Float Measurement

V. **Mail Payment Processing Systems**
   A. Company Processing Center
   B. Lockbox

VI. **Over-the-Counter/Field Deposit Systems**
   A. Location
   B. Branch Banking
   C. Compensation
   D. Deposit Reconciliation Services
   E. Preprocessing Check Deposits
   F. Cash Processing

VII. **Electronic Collection Systems**
   A. Wire Transfers
   B. ACH Corporate-to-Corporate Payments
   C. Preauthorized Payments

VIII. **Other Collection Systems**
   A. Net Settlement Systems
   B. Retail Collection Systems

I. Objectives of a Collection System

A collection system is a set of arrangements and management procedures used to collect and process customer payments. The broad objectives of a corporate collection system are the following:

- **Mobilize Funds** - Move funds from a customer (payor) into the collecting company's (payee's) banking system as quickly and cost effectively as possible. To do this, the company's collection system must be well integrated with its concentration system.

- **Access Information** - Provide accurate and timely information on cash flows, the level of bank balances and availability of funds in a manner that integrates easily with other parts of the company's treasury management information system.

- **Update Accounts Receivable** - Update accounts receivable records promptly and accurately. Credit management and treasury management systems must be linked closely together. Mistakes or failure to update customer files can jeopardize potential sales because of credit limitations and damage customer relationships.

- **Support Audit Trails** - Support audit trails for the company's internal and external auditors.

II. Collection Methods

Companies collect payments from their customers over-the-counter, through the mail, and through electronic networks.

A. Over-the-Counter/Field Deposit Systems

Various businesses may collect receipts over-the-counter at field locations. Methods used by retail establishments to collect at the point-of-sale include cash, checks, debit cards, and credit cards. A wholesale customer or its agent may deliver checks or cash to a vendor's office, or a vendor, or its agent may pick up checks or cash from the customer, for example, when making a delivery. An important design issue is the selection of banks for deposits made by field units. (This topic is discussed in Section VI of this chapter.)

B. Mail

Companies receive checks from individual consumers and from other businesses in the mail directly or through lockboxes.

C. Electronic

A company can receive a payment via wire transfer or ACH. Wire transfers are typically used for large payments that must be received with good value on the same day. Electronic payments through the ACH are less expensive than wire transfers, but payment instructions must be submitted to the bank one or two days prior to settlement.

Companies may receive payments in several different ways such as checks through a lockbox, wire transfers and ACH payments. Some banks have expanded the lockbox concept to include electronic lockboxes for wire transfers and ACH payments. They can normally provide customers with consolidated reports of all electronic and check payments received. Those reports may be paper or electronic.

Exhibit 6-1 illustrates various collection methods used by companies.

III. Collection System Considerations

In designing a collection system, a company must take into consideration commonly accepted payment practices, the nature of the payments system, the nature of its own business, characteristics of the payment instrument used, float and administrative costs.

A. Payment Practices

Checks are the most frequently used payment instrument for both corporate and consumer bill paying, though the use of electronic payments is increasing. Some believe that electronic payments offer strong cost saving potential for corporate payors and receivers in the future, especially if they become the predominant method of payment and are used as an integral part of an EDI business strategy. However, in today's environment checks provide the payor with disbursement float and are an established way of doing business acceptable to most trading partners.

B. Payments System

The collection system must be designed in light of the particular strengths and limitations of the payments system in the country concerned. For example, features that distinguish the U.S. payments system from many other countries' systems include the use of checks for the majority of payments, unpredictable delays in the mail system, a large number of small banks and a lack of banks with nationwide branch systems.

C. Nature of the Business

Often the collection method a company uses is determined by the nature of its business. A fast food store receives virtually all of its payments in cash. A time-critical transaction such as a securities settlement or a real estate closing, or simply a very large dollar amount may require a wire transfer with same-day value. A supplier usually sends an invoice to its customer and receives a check as payment. It is generally accompanied by information regarding invoices paid, partial payments, discounts and deductions.

D. Payment Instrument Characteristics

Each payment instrument has different levels of cost, speed, security, finality, information content, float and payor convenience. Often, the instrument used is a matter of negotiation between the payor and the payee. The most preferred method for the payee may not be best for the payor and vice versa.

Exhibit 6-1

Collection Systems

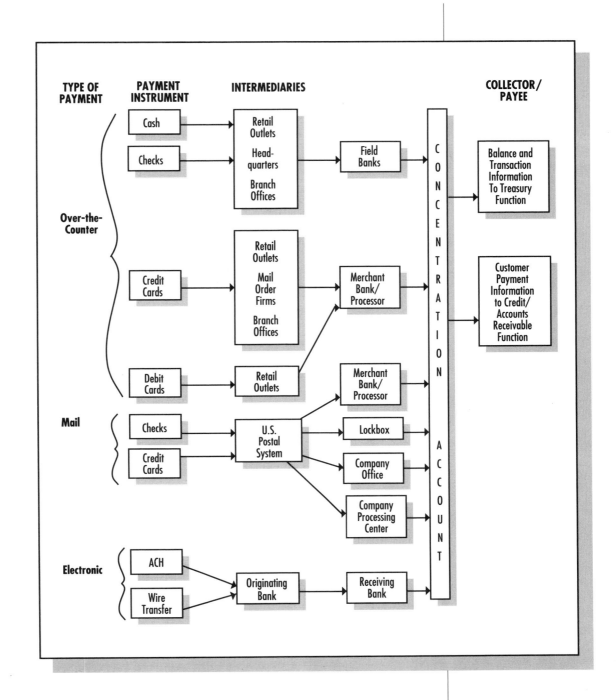

1. **Wire Transfer** - A wire transfer is secure and fast, and the payment is final, but a wire transfer is relatively expensive for the payor, and only a brief explanatory message can be sent to help the payee apply the payment.

2. **Check** - A check is used for most corporate and consumer bill payments. It is inexpensive, can be accompanied by unlimited information, and provides the payor the benefit of float until it is deposited and cleared. However, a check can be lost in the mail, stolen or returned for insufficient funds. Also, check collection float works to the detriment of the payee.

3. **ACH** - An ACH payment is relatively inexpensive compared to a wire transfer. Settlement is predictable in contrast to less predictable check collection float. However, while all banks should be able to receive ACH payments, the ability of banks to process accompanying remittance information varies.

4. **Cash** - Accepting cash is essential in most retail businesses. Cash provides the payee immediate availability but the payee also may incur additional charges for transportation to a depository bank and cash processing.

5. **Credit Cards** - Credit cards are often considered a marketing necessity by retailers. Whether credit card charges are processed manually or electronically, the merchant generally receives availability from the merchant bank/processor in one or two days. Costs for the retailer include a merchant discount (processing fee), authorization charges, supplies, and in the case of electronic processing, terminal rental or purchase. Throughout the month, chargebacks for returned charges and adjustments for addition errors are made to the merchant's account.

6. **Debit Cards** - Debit cards provide the retailer with zero-to-two-day availability. The merchant bank/processor charges a fee.

E. Float/Administrative Cost Tradeoff

An optimal collection system minimizes the sum of float costs and processing and administrative costs. If a firm chooses to use a lockbox, it must determine the number and location of lockboxes. Additionally, each customer must be assigned to a specific lockbox if more than one is used. Adding more collection points generally reduces float, but increases administrative and processing costs.

F. Wholesale and Retail Payments

1. **Wholesale** - Wholesale, or corporate-to-corporate payments, are generally for large amounts and in response to specific invoices. Often several invoices are paid with one check. Usually detailed information is required of the invoices paid, discounts taken, returns and allowances. Wholesale collection systems emphasize: (1) float reduction and (2) timely handling of information related to the invoices being paid.

2. **Retail** - In retail systems, payors are generally consumers. Payments are often small-dollar amounts, and frequently involve installments or recurring payments. Because of the large number of items to be handled, processing cost is a more critical consideration than float reduction in a retail collection system.

IV. Collection Float

Converting accounts receivable expeditiously into collected funds requires minimizing collection float. Collection float is the delay between the time when the payor mails the check and the time when the payee receives available funds.

A. Collection Float Components

Collection float has three components. These are mail float, processing float and availability float. Each represents a collection delay along the time line of cash management.

1. **Mail Float** - Mail float is the delay between the time a check is mailed and the date it is received by the payee or at the processing site. It usually ranges from one to five calendar days or more.

2. **Processing Float** - Processing float is the delay between the time the payee or the processing site receives the check and the time the check is deposited. It can range from less than one day to three calendar days or more.

3. **Availability Float** - Availability float is the delay between the time a check is deposited and the time the firm's account is credited with collected funds. It typically ranges from zero to two business days, and is determined by the depository bank's availability schedule.

The components of collection float are illustrated in Exhibit 6-2.

B. Float Measurement

Float is usually measured in **dollar-days** and is a function of the dollar amount and the number of days delay. The float on an individual check is calculated by multiplying the dollar amount by the number of days delay.

Exhibit 6-3 is an example of float measurement. Each of the three batches of checks has a different number of calendar days of float. The dollar-days of float are calculated for each batch and then for the total of the three batches. The average daily float is calculated by dividing the total dollar-days of float by the number of calendar days in the period, and the average delay—the average number of days of float—is calculated by dividing the total dollar-days of float by the total receipts.

The annual cost of float is calculated by using the company's opportunity cost of funds. A company may consider its opportunity cost to be a marginal cost such as interest on funds that have to be borrowed because receivables are still in collection. It may also use the opportunity cost of funds that could have been invested or its weighted average cost of capital, as discussed in Chapter 2, The Corporate Financial Function.

V. Mail Payment Processing Systems

For payments received in the mail, a company may use either its own processing center or a lockbox. Deciding which method to use depends primarily on the volume of

Exhibit 6-2

*Components of
Collection Float*

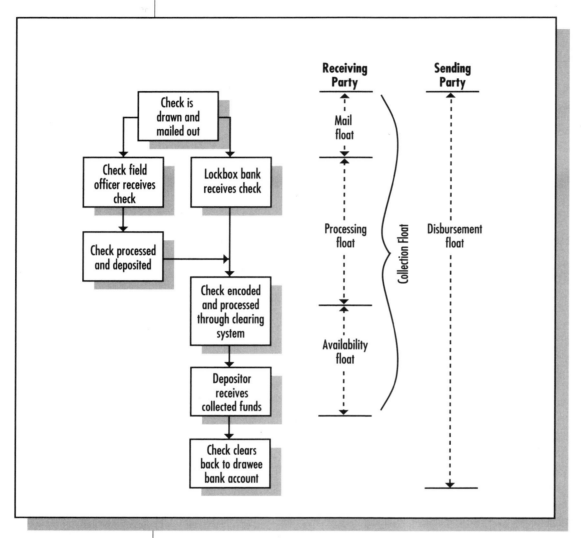

the checks processed and the dollar amount of the checks. For example, a high volume of checks for small-dollar amounts could justify an internal company processing center.

A. Company Processing Center

With a company processing center, a company does its own processing and deposit preparation. It is typically used by a company with a large volume of relatively small-dollar payments.

1. **Advantages:**

    *   The company maintains total control over the operation.

    *   It is easier to make changes in an internal system than it is in a lockbox processor.

Exhibit 6-3

Example of Float Measurement

Batch	Dollar Amount	Calendar Days of Float	Dollar Days of Float
1	$1,500,000	x 4 =	$ 6,000,000
2	4,500,000	x 2 =	9,000,000
3	3,000,000	x 6 =	18,000,000
	$9,000,000		$33,000,000

Note: In this example there are 30 calendar days in the month and the opportunity cost of funds is 9%.

$$\text{Average daily float} = \frac{\text{Total Dollar Days of Float}}{\text{Total Calendar Days in Period}}$$

$$\text{Average daily receipts} = \frac{\text{Total Dollar Amount}}{\text{Total Calendar Days in Period}}$$

$$\text{Average delay} = \frac{\text{Total Dollar Days of Float}}{\text{Total Dollar Amount}}$$

$$\text{Annual cost of float} = \text{Average Daily Float} \times \text{Opportunity Cost of Funds}$$

$$\text{Average daily float} = \frac{\$33,000,000}{30} = \$1,100,000$$

$$\text{Average daily receipts} = \frac{\$9,000,000}{30} = \$300,000$$

$$\text{Average delay} = \frac{33,000,000}{9,000,000} = 3.67 \text{ days}$$

$$\text{Annual cost of float} = \$1,100,000 \times .09 = \$99,000$$

- Processing is geared to the company's needs rather than to a general standard of a lockbox processor.

- Updating of payor information may be faster.

- With large volume and small dollars, a company may find internal processing less expensive than paying a bank for the same amount of work because the company can realize the same economies of scale as the bank.

- The company is assured of future processing capability, as opposed to relying on a lockbox processor that may eliminate the service.

2. **Disadvantages:**

- The company has to dedicate personnel and equipment to the processing center. Check volume must be large for the company to have a cost-efficient operation.

- Compared to a lockbox, there may be a greater time lag between processing the items and depositing the checks.

- Company processing centers may not receive mail through a unique zip code resulting in longer mail times.

- Company processing centers are likely to be located where the company has operations, which is not necessarily at a point that minimizes mail float.

B. Lockbox

With a lockbox, a bank or third party receives mail at a specified lockbox address, processes the remittances and deposits them in the payee's account. Lockboxes have been used since the late 1940s and remain one of the more important cash management tools.

1. **Advantages** - The advantages of a lockbox are as follows:

- *Reduction of Collection Float.*

    * *Mail Float* - Mail float is reduced in the following ways:

        A lockbox processor may use its own unique zip code to further speed mail delivery.

        Lockbox processors pick up the mail as often as hourly, seven days per week.

    * *Processing Float* - Processing float is reduced in the following ways:

        Remittances are mailed directly to the lockbox processor, eliminating the company's intermediary role in receiving and processing checks and delivering them to the bank.

        Lockbox operations are designed specifically for the efficient processing of remittances and deposits.

Some lockbox processors operate 24 hours a day, 7 days per week, with emphasis on when most mail arrives.

* *Availability Float* - Availability float is reduced in the following ways:

    Lockbox processors handle remittances so that checks meet critical availability deadlines. These are deadlines by which checks must reach the bank's proof and transit area, where they are sorted and encoded, to be assigned a certain availability. For example, 8 A.M. could be the deadline for receiving same-day availability for checks drawn on banks in the same city, or next-day availability for checks drawn on banks in certain cities.

- *Processing* - Lockboxes provide efficient processing through economies of scale, trained specialists processing the work for a particular account, and other people trained to back-up these specialists

- *Audit and Control* - A lockbox establishes an audit trail outside the company for payments received, and segregates the function of opening mail and depositing checks from other accounts receivable management functions. A lockbox may be required by company auditors even when it is not economically justified.

2. **Disadvantages** - The potential disadvantages of a lockbox include:

- *Operational Control* - The company has less control over the operation than with a company processing center.

- *Cost* - A company with very high volume may be able to run its own processing center at a cost that is lower than the cost for a lockbox.

3. **Optimizing Float and Processing Cost** - A company could continually add lockbox collection points, and theoretically each additional point reduces mail collection float. Each new point also adds administrative and processing costs, and the overall improvement for each new point diminishes as the total number increases. Lockbox studies seek to optimize the dollar benefit of reducing mail float and the cost of adding lockboxes.

4. **Wholesale and Retail Lockboxes**

- *Wholesale Lockboxes* - Wholesale lockboxes are used for corporate-to-corporate payments. The wholesale lockbox customer usually receives a small-to-moderate number of large-dollar remittances. The most important concerns are to minimize collection float and to provide accurate and timely information on payments received. Payments are usually made for specific invoices. Adjustments are often made for discounts, returns and allowances. Invoices are sometimes partially paid, and often one payment is for several invoices. There is not a standard format for the remittance information accompanying the payment, and each collecting company's information requirements may be different. Processing can be customized to meet the specific needs of the company.

Detailed deposit information, often including a breakdown of the total amount by days of availability, is usually transmitted daily to the company or to its concentration bank either by telephone or by electronic means. Detailed remittance data may be sent by courier, by mail, or electronically.

- *Retail Lockboxes* - Retail lockboxes are used by companies that receive large volumes of relatively small-dollar remittances, usually from consumers. Because of the large volume, minimizing costs is generally more important than reducing collection float.

  A retail lockbox is characterized by a remittance advice, sometimes called a return document, which is part of the invoice sent to the consumer. The consumer is asked to send the return document with the check. The return document usually has a scan line which contains information such as the payor's account number, the total amount due, the minimum amount due and the due date. The scan line is read by automated processing equipment to capture data which is used to update a company's accounts receivable. The data captured is usually transmitted electronically to the company.

  In addition to capturing information on the scan line, a retail lockbox usually has equipment that accelerates opening the mail and preparing the return documents for scanning. A retail lockbox is oriented toward processing remittances at the lowest possible cost.

5. **Lockbox Operations**

- *Wholesale Lockbox Operations* - While processing varies by processor, the typical steps in a wholesale lockbox operation are described below and illustrated in Exhibit 6-4.

  * *Mail Check* - The payor is instructed by the company to mail checks to a lockbox address.

  * *Pick Up Mail* - Mail is picked up throughout the day and night.

  * *Sort Mail* - The processor sorts mail by lockbox number.

  * *Open Mail* - The mail is opened.

  * *Examine Checks* - Checks are examined for acceptable payees, post-dated checks and missing signatures.

  * *Separate Checks and Envelopes* - Checks are separated from remittance advices and other contents.

  * *Photocopy Checks* - If required the checks are photocopied.

  * *Prepare Deposit* - Check amounts are added, balanced and deposit tickets are prepared.

  * *Endorse and Encode Checks* - Checks are encoded with a dollar amount and endorsed.

  * *Clear Checks* - Checks are sent to the proof and transit department for clearing.

Exhibit 6-4

Example of Wholesale "Lockbox" Processing

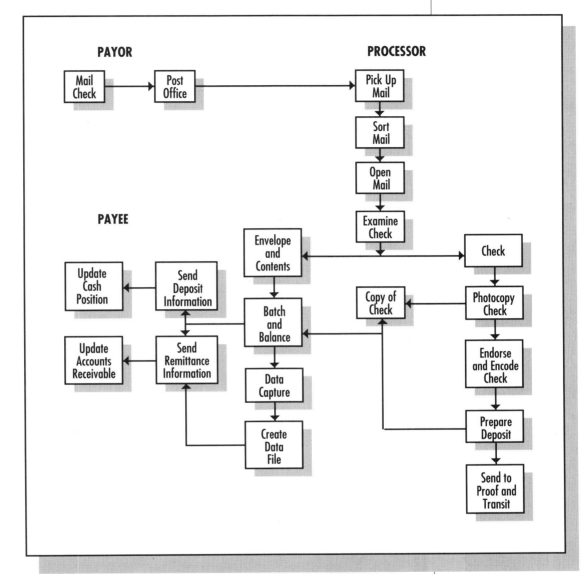

* **Send Information to Customer -** The processor provides both deposit information, such as the amount of deposit and availability, and remittance information, such as invoices paid, deductions, and discounts taken. The lockbox processor may capture data electronically or key enter from the check or remittance advice and transmit it to the company.

• **Retail Lockbox Operations -** There are differences between most wholesale and retail lockbox operations. In order to reduce costs, retail lockbox operations are more automated. Mail is typically opened by special equipment. The process of examining checks for acceptable payees, post dated checks and missing signatures is usually done at the same time the mail is being opened and remittances prepared for scanning.

The scan line on the return document is read by automated equipment to capture information that will later be used to update accounts receivable. The dollar amount of the check is often encoded in this process. Information captured from the scan line is usually electronically transmitted to the company.

6. **Lockbox Information** - A lockbox processor normally sends information to both the company's treasury and credit/accounts receivable functions.

   - *Treasury Function* - The treasury function may receive deposit information on lockbox deposits either directly from the lockbox operation or through an information reporting system.

   - *Credit/Accounts Receivable Function* - This function usually receives the envelopes, contents and photocopies of checks. The credit/accounts receivable function may receive information to update accounts receivable via hard copy, magnetic tape, or electronic transmission on a same-day or next day basis.

   - *How Information is Transmitted*

     * *Wholesale Lockboxes* - Detailed deposit information, often including a breakdown of the total amount by days of availability, is usually transmitted daily to the company through an information reporting system or other means such as hard copy, fax or voice.

       Remittance data concerning the payment of invoices may be key entered and transmitted to the customer electronically. The format and type of information varies from one company to the next. Both the Bank Administration Institute (BAI) and the American National Standards Institute (ANSI) have standards to facilitate electronic data transmission.

       A company may use information contained in the MICR line of a check to update accounts receivable automatically. The company keeps an electronic file of customers' bank transit routing and/or account numbers, cross-referenced to its internal customer account numbers, and uses an algorithm to apply payments to invoices.

     * *Retail Lockboxes* - Detailed deposit information is sent in a manner similar to wholesale lockboxes.

       Machine-readable MICR or OCR return documents may be used for capturing data and transmitting it electronically to the company. These documents are normally provided as part of the invoice by the collecting company and sent back with the check by the payor. They are commonly used in retail lockboxes for consumer payments such as utility bills and insurance premiums.

7. **Lockbox Cost Benefit Analysis** - The economic benefit of using a lockbox is usually a tradeoff between reducing collection float and paying fees to a lockbox processor over and above internal processing costs.

- *Float Savings* - A lockbox can create float savings by reducing some combination of mail, processing and availability time.

- *Fixed and Variable Costs* - Lockboxes have both fixed and variable components. The company should compare both the fixed and the variable costs per item between a lockbox and a company processing center. Banks have many ways of charging, but the following are some basic concepts:

  * *Fixed* - Fixed monthly charges may include fees for preparing deposit tickets, renting the post office box, sending remittance data to the customer, balance reporting and account maintenance. Often several of those charges are wrapped into a lockbox maintenance charge. Account maintenance charges may be higher for lockboxes than for over-the-counter deposits. In addition, there may also be a charge for transferring funds to a concentration bank.

  * *Variable* - Variable costs may include per-item deposit and processing charges and the charges for transmitting remittance data, photocopying and microfilming. These and other custom processing charges are often on a per-item basis. Some costs, for example, deposit ticket preparation, may be considered either fixed or variable, depending on the bank.

- *Calculation of Net Benefit* - The net benefit from a lockbox is equal to the reduction in float opportunity costs plus the reduction in internal processing cost minus lockbox processing costs. Float opportunity cost is a function of the dollar amount of the collected items, the total collection time of items and the current investment/borrowing rate.

Exhibit 6-5 is an example of a lockbox cost benefit analysis, including the trade-off between the savings from float reduction and the cost of a lockbox.

8. **Lockbox Studies**

- *Benefits* - Lockbox studies are useful for companies considering lockboxes for the first time and also for existing lockbox users who want to reevaluate their lockbox configurations because of changes in businesses and products, locations of customers, interest rates, mail times, and bank prices and availability schedules. Often, this leads to the fine tuning of a system by reassigning payors to a different collection site. Occasionally, these changes are substantial enough that the system must be changed by dropping and/or adding sites.

- *Objectives* - The purpose of a lockbox study is to determine the optimal number and location of lockbox collecting points based on a representative sample of customer remittances. The objective is to minimize combined mail, processing and check clearing float. Lockbox studies use remittance data (customer remittance envelopes, photocopies of checks, and bank statements) to compile the following information for analysis:

  * location of remitting customers

  * geographic concentration of remitting customers

Exhibit 6-5

*Example of Lockbox
Cost Benefit Analysis*

This exhibit shows the lockbox savings and associated costs for a company with $108,000,000 annual sales ($9,000,000 per month). Each of the items is assumed to be a batch of checks with average size of $9,000; the annual volume of checks is 12,000. The company's annual opportunity cost is nine percent. The company's internal check processing cost assuming no lockbox is $.25 per item. The lockbox processor charges $10,000 per year plus a processing cost of $.50 per item.

Without Lockbox

Batch	Dollar Amount		Calendar Days of Collection Float Without Lockbox		Total Dollar-Days
1	$1,500,000	X	4	=	$6,000,000
2	4,500,000	X	2	=	9,000,000
3	3,000,000	X	6	=	18,000,000

Total Deposits	$9,000,000	Total Float without Lockbox		$33,000,000

Divided by 30 calendar days =
Average Daily Float $ 1,100,000

Times Opportunity Cost/Investment Rate =
Annual Cost of Float (9%) $ 99,000

With Lockbox

Batch	Dollar Amount		Calendar Days of Collection Float With Lockbox		Total Dollar-Days
1	$1,500,000	X	3	=	$ 4,500,000
2	4,500,000	X	1	=	4,500,000
3	3,000,000	X	5	=	15,000,000

Total Deposits	$9,000,000	Total Float with Lockbox		$24,000,000

Divided by 30 calendar days =
Average Daily Float $ 800,000

Times Opportunity Cost/Investment Rate =
Annual Cost of Float (9%) $ 72,000

Annual Cost of Float Without Lockbox	$99,000
Annual Cost of Float With Lockbox	($72,000)
Lockbox Float Savings	$27,000
Fixed Lockbox Cost	($10,000)
Variable Lockbox Cost: 12,000 checks @ $0.50	($6,000)
Saving of Internal Lockbox Processing Cost:	
12,000 @ .25	$3,000
Net Dollar Benefit of Lockbox	$14,000

* location of customers with largest payments
* intercity mail times
* bank availability schedules
* difference between company and bank processing costs
* administrative costs associated with using lockboxes

- *Mail Time Studies* - Treasury consulting firms do periodic studies to compare mail times for various combinations of cities. These services generally report mail times between central city post offices for a uniform distribution of mailings throughout the week. If necessary, adjustments can be made for non-surveyed mail points and day-of-the-week mail experience.

  The results of mail time studies are combined with information from banks' availability schedules to compare both city-average and banks' availability statistics. Banks or consultants use this data in conjunction with analysis of a company's actual remittances to determine which cities or combinations of cities are the most effective collection sites.

- *Computer Analysis* - Two approaches used for computer analysis are exhaustive search and discrete search.

  * *Exhaustive Search* - In the exhaustive search approach, many combinations of one or more lockboxes are considered. This approach produces close to an optimal solution and can be attractive for a company with many banking relationships that is willing to consider many different combinations of cities.

  * *Discrete Search* - The discrete search approach examines a smaller number of more likely solutions.

- *Processing Cost* - A lockbox study should take into account not only float but the difference in processing costs between a company processing center and a lockbox, and the price differences among lockbox processors.

- *Site Selection* - In doing a study, a firm will usually select no more than 10 to 20 potential sites based on the following criteria:

  * *Availability* - A lockbox in a Federal Reserve city or RCPC point generally gets faster availability than one in a Federal Reserve country point.

  * *Mail Center* - Important variables include the number of airline routes from other principal cities, the amount of mail volume relative to post office processing capacity, the degree of post office automation and the proximity of the post office to the airport.

  * *Customer Base* - Lockboxes are usually best located near high concentrations of customers.

* *Service Quality* - Processors may be pre-screened for service quality before they are included in a study.

9. **Lockbox Processor Selection** - In selecting individual lockbox processors, companies try to assess lockbox processing capabilities, check processing procedures, availability schedules, data transmission capabilities, deposit and balance reporting capabilities, and city postal service processing capabilities. Other factors may include capabilities to process a company's wholesale ACH payments as the number of transactions increases in the future.

    * *City and Processor Selection* - A company may first select lockbox cities based on a lockbox study, and then select processors within those cities, but there are other factors to consider that could modify the decision. Some processors may try to demonstrate features such as processing time and availability schedules that are better than the average for their cities and win customers from cities with marginally better mail times.

    * *Relationship Banks* - Having a lockbox at a bank where there is an existing relationship may allow the company to strengthen that relationship. Protecting access to credit facilities and making better use of operating balances for bank compensation are two examples. An existing relationship may give an advantage where there are small differences in the study.

10. **How Lockbox Service Features Vary** - In selecting or reevaluating a lockbox processor, a cash manager should determine how the lockbox operation meets the company's particular needs. Meeting a company's requirements is a more important characteristic than the technology used. The company should consider the following service features in evaluating each processor:

    * *Mail Time Performance* - As mentioned earlier, mail time performance varies considerably among cities for reasons such as total mail volume, post office proximity to the airport and the processor, post office processing capabilities and airline routes serving the city. A post office that processes mail 24 hours per day, sorts bar-coded envelopes automatically, reads non-bar-coded envelopes with OCR equipment and makes an individual ZIP code available to a single lockbox processor may be a more desirable site.

    * *Unique Zip Codes* - Many processors offering lockbox services have a unique zip code for lockbox remittances. Depending on the capability for fine sorting, this feature may speed processing of incoming mail by eliminating one post office sort and may save several hours of mail and processing float.

    * *Deposit Deadlines* - Incoming lockbox work should be processed expeditiously so that deposit deadlines are met and the best possible availability achieved. Related service features include frequent mail pick-ups and ample peak-time staffing when the bulk of the mail is received. These features are helpful to the extent that they help the lockbox operation

meet critical clearing deadlines. As deadlines approach, an effective lockbox operation should scan work for large-dollar items. Sometimes, the number of deposits per day is a matter of negotiation, and it is up to the company to decide whether the cost of more frequent deposits is justified by the check volume and potential improvement in availability.

- *Availability* - Banks may offer several availability schedules. The company should be aware of which availability schedule is applicable. A better availability schedule may be offered for a premium price or when it is merited by overall relationship profitability. The availability a company will receive from a bank does not necessarily agree with the independent studies done on the city and the bank.

  Some banks assign availability in the lockbox area, but regardless of where it is assigned the company may bear the risk of as-of adjustments or fractional availability if the bank incurs a float loss in clearing a check. Some banks guarantee availability to the company even if there is a delay in the transit area. A bank that guarantees availability may perform better than another bank that offers a better availability schedule but charges back any float losses.

- *End-Point Analysis* - An end-point analysis, in which all checks drawn on banks in selected cities are broken down by days of float, is one effective way to see how good a bank's actual availability is.

- *Direct Sends* - Direct sends improve the availability of funds. A detailed knowledge of the bank's direct send program helps a company understand the availability schedule.

- *Ledger Cut-Off Time* - The cut-off time for giving ledger credit on the current day for a check deposited on that day can vary from mid-afternoon until well into the evening. Generally, the later the ledger cut-off time the better it is for the depositing company as more checks can be received and processed through a lockbox. In evaluating lockbox banks, it is important to look at the total collection time rather than just availability. The ledger cut-off can influence the availability received but total collection time may not change. The ledger cut-off must be considered in conjunction with the availability schedule.

  For example, a check with one-day availability before the ledger cut-off may have zero-day availability if processed right after the ledger cut-off. In this case, there is no difference in total collection time. A check might also be available in one day before and after the ledger cut-off. In this case, there will be an increase of one day in the total collection time if the check is not processed before the cut-off time. It is important to understand the relationship between a bank's ledger cut-off, its availability schedule and the time of day the lockbox is processed.

- *Electronic Lockbox* - Banks provide electronic lockboxes for companies to receive payments from their customers by wire transfer or through the ACH. As companies start to receive an increased volume of electronic payments, they may want a consolidated report of ACH, wire transfer and lockbox receipts in the same format. A number of banks are equipped to transmit information in the BAI and ANSI formats, as well as their own proprietary formats. Hard copies of the reports may also be available.

- *Customer Service* - The overall quality of service and responsiveness to a company's inquiries is as important as mail time and availability performance. A number of processors have dedicated customer service representatives and guaranteed response times for answering inquiries. A company must evaluate the ability of a processor to serve its particular needs.

11. **Lockbox Networks** - Lockbox networks are collection systems that offer multiple locations to receive customer remittances through one organization such as a single multi-site bank, a consortium of banks, a non-bank processor, or a joint venture between a bank and a non-bank processor.

- *Advantages* - Potential advantages are the convenience of dealing with one vendor combined with the float reduction benefits of a configuration of lockbox locations.

- *Disadvantages* - Disadvantages of the multibank networks are that the service provided by a collecting bank or collecting point within the network may not be as good as the service a processor could provide when dealing with a company directly. There may be an extra step in solving operational problems at an individual collection site. Several consortia have disbanded, but some individual banks are offering their own internal lockbox networks through multi-state processing centers, their own multi-state bank networks or through a mail intercept network. The mail intercept network involves using post office boxes in multiple cities and then intercepting the mail and sending it by courier to a central processing site.

12. **UCC 3 and UCC 4 Revisions** - Recent revisions to UCC 3 and UCC 4 address attempts by payors to settle disputed invoices with partial check payments and a handwritten notation "paid in full". Until recently, it was the interpretation of the UCC that a payee accepted the partial payment as full settlement of the disputed amount by depositing the check. That has caused a problem when checks have been received and deposited by bank lockboxes. Under the revisions, the seller/payee may alleviate the problem by clearly indicating on the invoice a separate address for sending correspondence relating to disputed amounts. The inadvertent acceptance of a partial payment must be discovered and the funds returned to the payor within a reasonable time period, not to exceed 90 days.

VI. Over-the-Counter/Field Deposit Systems

With over-the-counter/field deposit systems, funds are received and deposited by local operating units in the form of cash, checks, or credit card vouchers. Field units include local offices, stores and restaurants. An important decision is the selection of banks for deposits made by field units. These banks are called deposit or collection banks. The following factors should be considered in the selection of deposit banks:

A. Location

A deposit bank close to the field unit offers convenience and increased cash handling security for the local field manager.

B. Branch Banking

Where regional or statewide branching is available, collections may be simplified by using branches of the same bank. This reduces the company's administrative and cash concentration costs, though the company may lose some flexibility in selecting convenient deposit bank locations and incurs a risk in relying on only one bank.

C. Compensation

The compensation of field banks, whether by fees or balances, should be consistent with the company's compensation policies for all of its banks. The company should be sure that field banks are fairly compensated regardless of their account analysis capabilities.

D. Deposit Reconciliation Services

A bank with multiple branches may offer deposit reconciliation services, also called branch consolidation services, which provide for the following:

1. Deposits from multiple branches or stores are credited to the corporation's primary account with a bank, which may be a regional or main concentration account.

2. MICR-encoded deposit tickets identify each branch or store and enable the bank to produce a report of deposits by branch or store on a daily, weekly or monthly basis.

E. Preprocessing Check Deposits

A bank may charge a company less and offer better availability for checks that are pre-encoded with the amount on the MICR line before they are deposited.

F. Cash Processing

A retailer that accepts cash has two alternatives for making cash deposits:

1. **Branch Deposits** - An employee of the company's branch or store can take cash to a nearby bank or bank branch for deposit. When the amounts are large, there is a security risk in this method and an armored carrier may be used.

2. **Centralized Cash Processing** - With centralized cash processing, an armored carrier is used to pick up cash from the company's locations and deliver it to the bank. This method is most common for large amounts because it reduces security risks. Use of armored carriers may result in cash being held overnight at the carrier facility before deposit.

    Companies can save fees by putting bills of the same denomination in straps, by putting each denomination of coin in standard rolls, or by filling

Fed standard bags with loose coins of a particular denomination in similar standard, defined amounts. If the cash is delivered in mixed denominations, the bank may charge extra for verification.

Banks may charge for these services in different ways such as the amount of time required to verify the deposit, the dollar amount of the deposit, or the number of straps or bills and deposits processed.

VII. Electronic Collection Systems

Electronic corporate-to-corporate payment methods include wire transfers and ACH transactions.

A. Wire Transfers

Wire transfers are used for large-dollar payments when speed and finality are important, and the cost is considered relatively minor given the dollar amount.

B. ACH Corporate-to-Corporate Payments

A company can pay a bill through the ACH network provided that the originating and receiving banks have ACH capabilities. Companies generally do not start to pay by ACH before discussing with their trading partners whether that method is acceptable and which ACH payment format is appropriate. Debits as well as credits can be originated.

1. **Applications** - Though most bills are paid by check, companies may collect a portion of their payments by ACH. A number of companies have initiated comprehensive programs to originate payments through the ACH.

   - *Federal Government* - The U.S. Treasury Department's Vendor Express program is used to pay government vendors electronically. The Department of Defense also pays its vendors electronically.

   - *Automobile Suppliers* - Many suppliers to automobile companies are receiving payments through the ACH as part of a more comprehensive EDI program, including purchase orders and invoices.

   - *Dealers with Floor Plans* - Automobile, truck, farm equipment suppliers and floor plan lenders have utilized the ACH network extensively to debit dealers. A floor plan is a loan to a dealer to finance inventory which is paid back when the financed item is sold.

   - *Debit Programs* - Companies can also collect funds by debiting their customers' accounts. This is typically done in two ways. These are:

     * On a specific day, an ACH debit is originated for the amount of money owed. This is prearranged with the customer, who therefore knows the amount and date of the debit beforehand.

     * On the day a company wants to pay a bill, it notifies its supplier of the amount it wants to pay. The supplier originates an ACH debit against its customer's account. This customer-initiated entry is pre-

arranged, giving the company whose account is being debited control over the process.

2. **Advantages** - Potential benefits of ACH corporate-to-corporate payments for the payee include:

- *Float* - Reduction of collection float

- *Cost* - Reduction of receivables processing cost; lower overall cost compared to either a lockbox or wire transfers

- *Forecasting* - Improved cash flow forecasting

3. **Disadvantages** - Despite possible cost savings opportunities in the long run, there are still many potential deterrents to the use of ACH corporate trade payments. These include:

- *Trading Partner Negotiation* - The payor (buyer) and the payee (seller) must agree to make the switch.

- *Float* - When a company starts to receive payments electronically, there must be agreement on (1) when the effective use of funds is being transferred under the existing system and (2) what the settlement date of the ACH transaction should be. For example, the payor may currently pay bills by check 25 calendar days after the invoice date and may on average be debited four days after mailing the check. The payee may or may not receive availability at the same time the payor is debited. The payor and the payee need to negotiate a settlement time for an ACH transaction that puts each party in approximately the same economic position as when checks were used to settle invoices.

- *ACH Formats* - Several different formats are currently used for corporate-to-corporate payments, as described in Chapter 4, The Payments System.

- *Set-Up Costs* - Preparation to receive ACH corporate-to-corporate payments can be time consuming and requires an investment in software and communications equipment.

- *Control* - A company may be reluctant to give someone outside the company the authority to debit its account.

4. **Preparation** - A company preparing to receive ACH corporate-to-corporate payments for the first time should take the following steps:

- *ACH Formats* - Review ACH payment formats with the payor. Take advantage of descriptive literature and other educational tools provided by the payor.

- *Bank Capabilities* - Discuss ACH receiving and translating capabilities with the bank where payments will be received.

- *Payment-Related Information* - Consider alternative ways that are available to receive payment-related information. Compare the capabilities and costs of banks and value-added networks (VANs) to transmit full details related to the payment. A company may want to consider buying translation software to enable automated receipt of ACH remittance information to update its accounts receivable system. There is still debate about the preferable alternative. Some favor sending the payment and payment information together through a bank while others favor sending the payment through a bank and the payment information through a VAN. This is covered in detail in Chapter 9, Information Management.

C. Preauthorized Payments

Preauthorized debits (PADs) are a payment method in which the payor approves in advance the transfer of funds from the payor's bank account to the payee's bank account. Preauthorized payments can be made through the ACH, or if the payee's bank is not a member of the ACH, by preauthorized checks (PACs). Consumer payments are governed by Federal Reserve Regulation E while NACHA rules apply to corporate-to-corporate payments.

These payments are usually made the same time each month but a variable schedule is possible. Notice of the withdrawal is sent to the customer ten days prior to the transfer of funds. If the customer does not have sufficient funds, the transaction can be returned through the ACH.

1. **Applications** - Common applications for preauthorized payments include the following:

   - insurance payments
   - utility payments
   - mortgage payments
   - installment loan payments
   - cable bills
   - association dues
   - health club dues
   - distributor/dealer payments
   - equipment lease payments.

2. **Advantages** - The benefits of preauthorized payments to the corporate payee include the following:

   - Elimination of mail float
   - Elimination of invoicing
   - Reduced processing float because deposits need not be prepared
   - Elimination of availability float because of immediate availability on settlement day
   - Fewer delinquent payments

- Reduced tendency of customers to change vendors or terminate services once preauthorized debits have been implemented.

3. **Disadvantages** - Potential deterrents to the use of preauthorized payments include the following:

- Cost and time required for consumer education

- Reluctance by some individuals to have their accounts debited by another party

- Bill sent electronically cannot be used to carry advertising. Some companies use this type of advertising to cross-sell and some earn revenues advertising for others.

- Often the statement cannot be eliminated even if an ACH debit is used because of regulatory or marketing considerations.

- Initial time and effort are required to set up each customer's standard monthly payment instructions, including the correct bank transit routing number and customer account number.

VIII. Other Collection Systems

A. Net Settlement Systems

In some industries such as airlines, oil and chemicals, companies make exchanges and buy and sell from each other. Airline A accepts a ticket from Airline B in exchange for a passenger making a change in reservations. Through a clearing system, it returns the ticket and is reimbursed by the airline that originally wrote the ticket. Oil Company A sells some of its supply on the east coast to Oil Company B while buying from the same company to cover for a shortage on the west coast. These industries have clearing systems that process the transaction information and allow participants to make periodic net settlements with each other.

B. Retail Collection Systems

1. **Credit Cards** - Credit cards are processed both manually as well as electronically.

- *Manual Processing* - There are basically two ways manual credit card vouchers can be deposited:

  * They can be mailed into the merchant bank/ processor, which credits the merchant's deposit account one or two days after the vouchers are received.

  * A merchant can take vouchers/tickets to a bank and make a deposit over the counter. The bank, at its discretion, may treat these deposits as cash or grant them zero, one, two or three days availability.

    In both cases, the merchant is given the face value of all tickets deposited. At the end of the month, the merchant bank/processor deducts a discount and other charges from the merchant's account. Availability and the discount rate are related pricing decisions by the merchant bank/processor. Other fees include terminal rentals, supplies, and authorization charges. Throughout the month, chargebacks (returned charges) and adjustments (addition errors) are made to the merchant's account.

- *Electronic Processing* - Availability of funds is typically one or two days. The charges are handled in the same fashion as described for manual processing. Credit card machines, PCs and various types of electronic cash registers are used to capture the information electronically.

- *Authorizations and Chargebacks* - A credit card payment is not guaranteed, even when authorized. An authorization indicates that the cardholder has available credit but it does not indicate that the right person is using the card. Consequently, it is possible for a merchant to receive a charge back as long as six months after funds have been received. When fraud occurs, the time may be even longer. Signature verification is necessary to determine if the right person is using the card.

2. **Automated Teller Machine (ATM) Networks** - Vendors that deal with a large number of retail customers can make arrangements with banks for bills to be paid at ATMs. The payment is transferred manually or electronically from the customer's account to the vendor's account at the time of sale, or in the case of a utility, when the customer decides to pay the monthly bill.

3. **Telephone Banking** - Vendors can make arrangements with banks that allow retail customers to call the bank and have their accounts debited to pay the vendors.

4. **Debit Cards** - A customer may be charged directly with a debit card. Debit cards settle in different ways. These are:

   - *On-Line* - A Personal Identification Number (PIN) is required to initiate the transaction. Positive authorization is received from the cardholder's bank. The merchant receives zero to two days availability. Funds are guaranteed.

   - *Off-Line* - There are two types of off-line programs:

     * *National Association Debit Cards.* Visa and Mastercard debit card products work like credit cards except that the transactions post to DDA accounts as debits rather than to credit card accounts. Availability is usually two days.

     * *Proprietary Cards.* Settlement for proprietary cards is through the ACH. The debit card is a substitute for a check. Several oil and grocery store companies are using this product

5. **Agents** - Retailers and financial institutions may act as agents for collecting monthly payments related to service providers such as telephone and utility companies.

Questions

The chapter questions are to test the information in the text and are not examples of CCM examination questions nor are they in the examination format.

Answers can be found at the back of the book on p. 320.

1. What are the major objectives in establishing a collection system?

2. What are the three major collection methods?

3. Which payment instrument is the fastest and most secure?

4. What elements compose collection float?

5. What determines availability float?

6. A firm has provided the following information:

Batch	Dollar Amount	Calendar Days of Float	Dollar-Day of Float
1	$100,000	3	$ 300,000
2	$350,000	4	$1,400,000
3	$210,000	2	$ 420,000
			$2,120,000

  If the firm's opportunity cost is 7% and there are 30 calendar days in the month, what is the annual cost of float?

7. What determines the selection of a mail payment processing system?

8. What are the major advantages of a lockbox?

Questions (Continued)

9. What is the difference between a wholesale and a retail lockbox?

10. The firm in Question 6 is considering using a lockbox, which would reduce float as follows:

Batch	Dollar Amt.	Calendar Days of Float	Dollar Days of Float
1	$100,000	2	$ 100,000
2	$350,000	2	$ 700,000
3	$210,000	1	$ 210,000
			$1,010,000

    The lockbox processor will charge $1,000 per year and a processing cost of $.30 per item. The current internal processing cost is $.20 per item. The annual volume of checks is 6,000. If the annual float cost without the use of a lockbox is $4,947 (see Question 6), is a lockbox appropriate for this firm?

11. What is the purpose of lockbox studies?

12. What is an electronic lockbox?

13. What is an over-the-counter/field deposit collection system?

14. What is a pre-authorized debit (PAD)?

15. What system would benefit firms in the same industry that buy and sell from each other on a regular basis?

16. What are the two types of computer analysis used in lockbox studies?

Cash Concentration ■

Chapter 7

Overview

This chapter discusses why companies concentrate cash, the objectives of a cash concentration system, the principal funds transfer mechanisms for concentrating funds, and how cost is minimized in a cash concentration system.

Learning Objectives

Upon completion of this chapter and related study questions, the reader should be able to do the following.

1. Explain why companies concentrate cash.

2. Discuss the objectives of a cash concentration system.

3. Explain the advantages and disadvantages of the principal funds transfer mechanisms used in cash concentration.

4. Explain how information flows in a cash concentration system.

5. Outline the cost components of a cash concentration system.

6. Explain how companies minimize cost in a cash concentration system.

7. Understand how to reduce risk and increase control in a cash concentration system.

Outline

I. **Why Companies Concentrate Cash**

II. **Objectives of a Cash Concentration System**
   A. Simplify Cash Management
   B. Improve Control
   C. Pool Funds
   D. Minimize Excess Balances
   E. Reduce Transfer Expense

III. **Types of Cash Concentration Systems**
   A. Over-the-Counter/Field Banking Systems
   B. Lockbox Banking Systems

IV. **Funds Transfer Alternatives**
   A. Electronic Depository Transfers (EDTs)
   B. Wire Transfers
   C. Depository Transfer Checks (DTCs)

V. **Cash Concentration Cost Components**
   A. Excess Bank Balances
   B. Transfer Charges
   C. Administrative Costs
   D. Dual Balances

VI. **Techniques to Reduce Cash Concentration System Costs**
   A. Improving Transfer Timing
   B. Reducing Transfer Costs
   C. Comparing Transfer Methods

VII. **Risks and Controls**
   A. Punctuality
   B. Fraud
   C. Bank Overdraft
   D. Bank Failure

I. Why Companies Concentrate Cash

Cash Concentration is the movement of funds from outlying depository locations to a central bank account, known as a concentration account, where it can be utilized and managed most effectively.

One bank account and one point for collecting payments may be sufficient for a smaller company, but not for a larger company. Larger companies may have multiple bank relationships and cash collection points for many reasons, including multiple manufacturing plants, stores, sales offices, lockboxes, and divisions and subsidiaries.

II. Objectives of a Cash Concentration System

The treasury function should design its corporate cash concentration system to accomplish the following:

A. Simplify Cash Management

Enable the cash manager to focus on fewer balances in the day-to-day management of corporate liquidity.

B. Improve Control

Place control of funds in the hands of key financial managers. Separate deposit gathering from disbursement for control, tracking and forecasting. Provide an audit trail for incoming deposits.

C. Pool Funds

By pooling cash from multiple accounts, the firm can buy larger blocks of short-term securities which tend to earn higher yields. Funds may also be used to reduce debt.

D. Minimize Excess Balances

Minimize excess balances in the company's banking network.

E. Reduce Transfer Expense

Reduce the expense of transferring funds from outlying banks to the concentration account(s).

III. Types of Cash Concentration Systems

There are basically two types of cash concentration systems, over-the-counter/field banking systems and lockbox banking systems.

A. Over-the-Counter/Field Banking Systems

Some companies receive payments from customers in a number of locations. Examples include companies with regional sales offices and retailers.

Companies deposit cash and checks received over the counter in field banks. Although field banking systems vary, most have the following features:

1. **Multiple Banks** - A geographically dispersed firm may use many banks because of the need to have a convenient local depository for each unit.

2. **Local Banks** - A field banking system may include local community banks as well as larger regional and money center banks.

3. **Limited Need for Daily Deposit and Balance Information** - Because sales and deposit information is often sent to the headquarters and concentration bank by the company's field units, the headquarters may require fewer deposit and balance reporting services from field banks than from a concentration bank. Generally, field offices do not use field banks extensively for cash management services.

4. **Local Deposits** - Coin-and-currency, depository and funds transfer services are primary functions for field banks. Deposits consist mainly of cash and checks. Checks are often drawn on nearby banks. Currency is usually given immediate availability. Local checks may take one day to clear; on-us items may clear faster. Community banks may not make a distinction between ledger and collected balances.

B. Lockbox Banking Systems

In a lockbox banking system, the company collects through one or more lockboxes and transfers available funds to the concentration bank. A company may have several lockboxes to optimize collection float, and may also use different lockboxes for its subsidiaries. Though lockbox systems vary, most have the following characteristics:

1. **Relatively Few Banks** - The trend for most companies has been toward the use of fewer lockbox banks in recent years.

2. **Corporate Services** - Lockbox banks tend to be regional or money-center banks. Standard capabilities include daily reporting of transaction details and ledger and collected balances, and moving funds by wire transfer or ACH. Often these banks provide the company with credit facilities and a variety of services.

3. **Account Analysis and Compensation** - Lockbox banks usually provide account analyses for credit and other services. Compensation for these services may be in fees, balances or a combination of fees and balances.

4. **Delayed Availability** - Because lockbox banking systems involve check deposits, a portion of a company's daily deposit normally has delayed availability. The delay is generally one or two days from the day of deposit.

5. **Electronic Payments** - Corporate-to-corporate payments through the ACH are growing as the EDI movement gains momentum. While electronic payments are not likely to reduce the need for field banking or lockbox banking systems many companies can expect to receive a portion of their corporate-to-corporate payments through the ACH.

With electronic payments, a company's bank can be located anywhere, as the remittance data do not have to be transported physically to a bank or to the company's offices. This will reduce the need to make extensive cash concentration transfers.

A typical corporate concentration system, incorporating both a field banking system and a lockbox banking system, is illustrated in Exhibit 7-1.

7-1

Example of a Concentration System

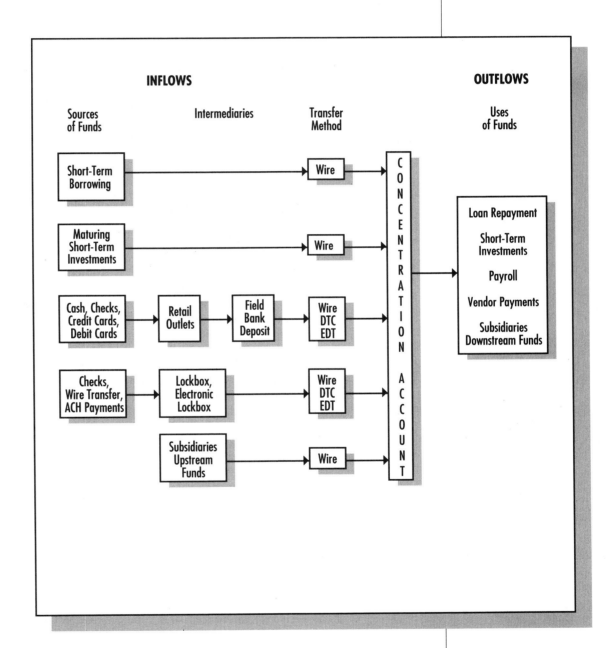

IV. Funds Transfer Alternatives

The most frequently used mechanisms for concentration are electronic depository transfers (EDTs), wire transfers and depository transfer checks (DTCs).

A. Electronic Depository Transfers (EDTs)

An electronic depository transfer (EDT) is an ACH transaction used for concentration. It is the most common method used today.

1. **Concentration Payment Origination** - EDTs can be originated by field offices and field banks or they can be originated by a headquarters office or concentration bank. A field office could provide a debit authorization to a field bank and regularly notify headquarters of the amount to be transferred from the field bank, or notify the concentration bank of the amount to be transferred. Some large retail networks, fast food chains, for example, transmit information on cash receipts along with other necessary management information from point-of-sale (POS) terminals to headquarters. The headquarters then transmits ACH debit instructions to the concentration bank.

2. **Notifying the Concentration Bank** - There are several ways that the field unit or lockbox bank can send deposit information to the concentration bank, including voice, touch tone phone and, personal computer.

   - *Third-Party Vendor* - Several firms specialize in gathering deposit information from field units. Deposit data may be transmitted to both the concentration bank for EDT preparation and firm headquarters for follow-up of non-reporting units. In some cases, deposit data are sent to headquarters, which decides on EDT amounts. Transfer instructions are then sent to the concentration bank, which originates the EDT.

   - *Through Headquarters* - In some companies, managers call headquarters directly or convey the deposit data to a headquarters computer via a remote terminal. Deposit data are then relayed to the concentration bank by headquarters.

   - *Notifying the Concentration Bank Directly* - Some banks are able to receive deposit reports directly from field units or lockbox banks. EDTs are prepared from these reports.

3. **ACH Format** - EDTs are transmitted in the CCD format.

4. **Advantages**

   - *Cost* - EDTs normally cost less than depository transfer checks (DTCs), particularly when there are a large number of transfers. Pricing generally includes a charge per transfer, and may include a charge for each transmission.

   - *Settlement* - There is uniform one-day settlement.

5. **Disadvantages** - Not all banks are members of the ACH system. As a result, a few transfers may have to be made by depository transfer check (DTC).

B. Wire Transfers

Wire transfers are an alternative for concentrating large amounts because funds can be transferred with same-day value and finality.

1. **Instructions to Wire Funds** - Either the field manager or the headquarters staff may request the deposit bank to wire funds into the concentration bank.

    In some cases, the field or lockbox bank has standing instructions to transfer funds in excess of a specified balance on a periodic basis. Standing transfer instructions can also be used for EDTs and DTCs.

    Headquarters may send transfer instructions to the concentration bank to wire in funds from a field or lockbox bank. This is known as a drawdown wire. The company concentrating the funds gives standing instructions to the lockbox or field bank authorizing transfers initiated by the concentration bank.

2. **Deposit Information** - Deposit information that is related to the wire transfer can flow to headquarters through deposit reports, telephone or data transmission.

3. **Advantages** - Wires provide immediate availability and help reduce excess balances at deposit banks. They are typically used when large amounts of immediately available funds are deposited in lockbox or field banks.

4. **Disadvantages** - Wires are the most expensive funds transfer mechanism.

C. Depository Transfer Checks (DTCs)

A depository transfer check (DTC) is an instrument used by a company to transfer funds from one of its outlying depository locations to its concentration account. It is an unsigned, restricted-payee instrument payable only to the bank of deposit for credit to a specific company account. Instead of writing and depositing checks to concentrate funds, the corporate headquarters or field office instructs the concentration bank to prepare DTCs drawn on field banks for deposit into the concentration account. After DTCs are deposited, they are cleared back to field/drawee banks in the same manner as regular checks. Availability is one or two days.

1. **Mail DTC** - The field office makes a deposit into the field bank and at the same time prepares a DTC drawn on that bank, often in the amount of the deposit. The DTC is mailed to the concentration bank which clears it back to the depository bank. Mail DTCs are used primarily for field banking systems with small deposits.

    - *Advantages*
        * *Simplicity* - The DTC is essentially the deposit report, and no other report of deposit-related information need be made to the corporate headquarters.
        * *Low cost* - Administrative and transfer costs are low compared to wire transfers, though not as low as for EDTs.

- *Disadvantages*

  * Accumulation of balances. Balances accumulate in field banking accounts because of the time required for the DTC to be mailed and cleared back to the field bank.

  * Control. There is no centralized control of field managers or of the initiation of the transfer of funds.

  * Limited Availability. Some checks have two-day availability.

2. **Centrally Initiated DTC** - Field deposits are made at a local bank. The methods for notifying the concentration bank are the same as used for EDTs. The concentration bank prepares the DTC, deposits it into the firm's account, grants availability and clears the check back to the bank of deposit.

   - *Advantages*

     * *Speed* - No mail time component.

     * *Control* - There is central control of the amount and timing of the transfer and some control over field managers.

     * *Low Cost* - Relatively inexpensive compared to wire transfers.

     * *Lower Balances* - Lower excess balances than mailed DTCs.

   - *Disadvantages*

     * *Availability* - Centrally-initiated DTCs do not offer immediately available funds as do wire transfers. Some DTCs will be available in two days.

     * *Cost* - They are more expensive than mailed DTCs and require a system to gather and transmit deposit information.

   Exhibit 7-2 is an example of EDT and DTC clearing.

V. Cash Concentration Cost Components

A. Excess Bank Balances

Balances are said to be in excess when the average collected balance in an account is above the level that the bank requires for compensation or the level that the company has chosen to have at the bank. The calculation of excess balances is found in Chapter 14, Bank Relationship Management.

1. **Determining Required Balances**

   - *Account Analysis* - Most large banks provide a monthly account analysis showing the price of each service used, the volume of activity and the compensation required. Companies have the flexibility to compensate the bank in balances, fees, or a combination of the two.

Exhibit 7-2

Example of EDT and DTC Clearing

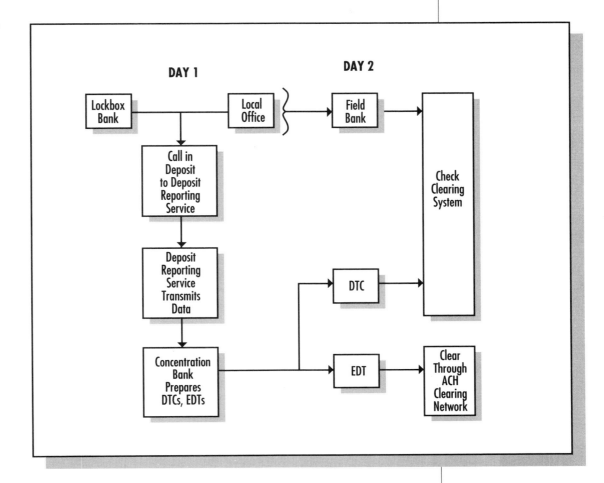

- *Estimates for Field Banks* - Some small field banks may not have the capability to provide the type of account analysis described earlier. Therefore, the firm may be left to determine a fair compensating balance. Using estimated per-item service costs, average volume and a reasonable earnings credit rate, the firm can compute a target compensating balance for the field bank.

2. **How Excess Balances Arise**

- *Deposit Reporting Delays* - Deposit reports by field units may be delayed by local management or the deposit information gathering system. Excess balances may result from delayed concentration transfers.

- *Clearing Delays* - If concentration is done with EDTs or DTCs, there can be one or more days of float between transfer initiation and clearing or settlement. When immediately available funds are deposited, or when checks deposited in field or lockbox banks clear before the concentration transfers clear back to the deposit account, excess balances may be created.

- *Transfer Initiation Delays* - The firm or the firm's concentration bank may be delayed in preparing transfers. For example, if an EDT is not originated in time to meet the appropriate cutoff, settlement will be delayed an extra day.

B. Transfer Charges

In concentration systems, there are various transfer costs associated with the banking system and reporting services. These services include:

1. **Deposit Bank Charges** - The deposit bank charges for depositing funds, outgoing wires, EDT and DTC clearings, deposit reports, account maintenance fees and overdrafts.

2. **Concentration Bank Charges** - The concentration bank charges for receiving wires, originating and depositing EDTs and DTCs, for receiving and reporting deposit information and for account maintenance.

3. **Third-Party Vendor Charges** - The firm may use vendors to assist in concentration. Those vendors charge for collecting deposit information from field units or lockbox banks and for transmitting data to the concentration bank and/or company.

C. Administrative Costs

1. **Managing Deposit Reporting** - Receiving and monitoring daily deposit reports from field managers and lockbox and concentration banks, is a major administrative responsibility.

2. **Cash Transfer Scheduling** - Deciding when and how much to transfer is called cash transfer scheduling. Often the firm's policy is to transfer the amount of the deposit every day, and cash transfer scheduling is a routine decision.

3. **Overdrafts** - Cash concentration systems have occasional overdrafts caused by misdirected transfers, returned items, or missed deposit deadlines. Often, a check deposited at a field or lockbox bank is returned after the amount was included in the concentration transfer. A field office may reimburse a field bank for a returned item, or more likely, reduce the next concentration transfer by the amount of the return item.

D. Dual Balances

Dual balances involve available balances which exist simultaneously in two banks. They occur when availability is granted by the depositing bank before a check is cleared at the payor's bank.

The magnitude of dual balances has diminished since the Federal Reserve was mandated by the Depository Institutions Deregulation and Monetary Control Act (DIDMCA) in 1980 to reduce float in the banking system.

VI. Techniques to Reduce Concentration System Costs

A. Improving Transfer Timing

Excess balances can be reduced by removing information delays, anticipating deposits and by using a faster transfer mechanism.

1. **Removing Information Delays** - There are sometimes delays in informing the concentration bank of required transfers. To overcome those delays, a company may do the following:

   - *Timely Reports* - Require timely reports from field managers. Banks offer reporting services which help monitor non-reporting locations as well as the timeliness of reporting locations.

   - *Cutoff Times* - Ensure concentration bank cutoff times are met. Transfer reports must be timed to meet the concentration bank's schedule to avoid adding extra float to the process.

2. **Anticipating Deposits**

   Anticipation is initiating a transfer before funds become available at the deposit bank. Given the possibility of abuses of this technique or of occasional, accidental overdrafts, it should not be practiced unless there is written agreement with the banks involved. There are two forms of anticipation. These are:

   - *Availability Anticipation* - In this form, the transfer is initiated on the basis of deposit information. Deposits become collected balances after a time delay. For example, a field manager reports a Monday deposit of $100,000 in checks. A $100,000 ACH transfer is originated on Monday with one-day settlement. There is little risk of ledger overdraft with this method because the ledger balance is known with virtual certainty when the transfer is initiated. However, there is a risk of drawing into uncollected funds in the account since the collected balance is not known with certainty.

   - *Deposit Anticipation* - In this form, the transfer is initiated on the basis of expected deposits that have not yet been reported. These techniques are often used by retailers. For example, a field bank is expected to receive $15,000 in cash on Monday morning from weekend sales. A $15,000 ACH transfer from the field bank to the concentration bank is originated on Friday with Monday settlement. It will clear on Monday when the field deposit is made. This form of anticipation is more risky because there is no guarantee that the full $15,000 will be deposited. Use of deposit anticipation requires a good forecasting system. Administrative time is required to forecast daily receipts and reconcile transfers to deposits.

3. **Using Faster Mechanisms** - The use of wire transfers results in immediately available funds while EDTs or DTCs are available only after a one- or two-day time delay. In many cases, EDTs may become available more quickly than DTCs. Wire transfers are more expensive.

B. Reducing Transfer Costs

There are basically two ways to reduce transfer costs: to transfer less often and to use less expensive transfer mechanisms.

1. **Transfer Timing**

    - *Less than Daily* - Daily transfers are the norm; firms that receive deposit information daily often assume that transfers should also occur daily. This may be unnecessary for banks with small daily deposits.

        * *Average Daily Deposit Less than Target* - If the target balance is $50,000 and the daily deposit is $10,000, then transferring once a week or even less often may be sufficient. An explanation of how daily opportunity costs are calculated and how they relate to the cost of transferring funds is found later in this section.

        * *Deposits Grouped Toward Certain Days of the Week* - If deposits are made primarily on certain days of the week, for example, on Monday, then it is possible to transfer less often than daily.

    - *Balance Averaging* - Banks compute monthly average collected balances for compensation purposes. Banks rarely require minimum collected balances from corporate customers though they may charge for overnight collected as well as ledger overdrafts. It is possible to allow the firm's collected balances to fluctuate around the target as long as the target is met on average. Balance averaging is essential in reducing costs in concentration systems because it allows:

        * Reduction in the number of transfers and related transfer costs.

        * Initiation of larger transfers on critical days.

        * Reduction in excess balances through anticipation. Large weekend transfers, for example, may clear on Monday and drop the deposit bank balance below the target.

2. **Transfer Mechanisms**

    - *EDT versus Wire Transfer* - In some of the company's accounts, deposits may be mostly checks with delayed availability, for example lockbox deposits. The company could be just as efficient in initiating a less expensive mechanism such as an EDT or DTC on the day of deposit as it would in initiating a wire transfer on the day funds become available.

    - *Repetitive Wire Transfers* - Repetitive wire transfers are usually less expensive than manual, non-repetitive transfers, and can therefore reduce concentration costs.

3. **Target and Threshold Concentration** - A company can manage its balance level in field banks with a system of either target or threshold balances. Many bank concentration systems offer the headquarters the flexibility to change the amounts reported by field units.

    - *Target Concentration* - With target concentration, a target balance is set and all funds above that balance level are transferred to the concentration bank. This system maintains balances at the desired level, but could involve transfers as often as every day.

- *Threshold Concentration* - With threshold concentration, balances are allowed to build up to a predetermined level, and then most or all of the funds are transferred to the concentration bank. This method helps minimize the number of transfers required. The cash manager can watch the average balances that result from this system over time and make necessary adjustments.

4. **Deposit Reconciliation Services** - A bank with multiple branches may offer deposit reconciliation services, which provide for the following:

- Deposits from multiple branches or stores are credited to the company's primary account with the bank, which may be a regional or main concentration account. This reduces the number of transfers and bank accounts that must be maintained.

- MICR-encoded deposit tickets identify each branch or store and enable the bank to produce a report of deposits by branch or store on a daily, weekly, or monthly basis.

5. **Timely Local Deposits** - Ensuring that deposits are made in field banks in order to receive same-day ledger credit accelerates the availability of funds and reduces expenses related to potential overdrafts.

C. Comparing Transfer Methods

In determining whether to use an EDT, a DTC, or a wire transfer to concentrate funds, it is important to find the value of the accelerated funds. By comparing this value to the cost of the transfer mechanism, the appropriate transfer mechanism can be decided.

For example, assume the following:

1. Total costs for an EDT are $1.00.

2. Total costs for a wire transfer are $20.00.

3. Available funds for transfer are $100,000.

4. The opportunity cost of funds is 10%.

5. A wire transfer accelerates funds one day faster than an EDT.

Funds Value = Available Funds x Days Accelerated x Opportunity cost

$$= \$100,000 \times 1 \times .10/365$$

$$= \$27.40$$

Because the funds value, $27.40, exceeds the incremental cost of a wire transfer, $19.00 ($20.00 -$1.00), it is advantageous for the firm to wire transfer the funds rather than to use an EDT.

Another way of looking at this situation is to determine the minimum wire transfer required to break even. This can be determined as follows:

$$\text{Minimum Transfer} = \frac{\text{Wire Cost - EDT Cost}}{\text{Days Accelerated x Opportunity Cost}}$$

$$= \frac{\$20.00 - \$1.00}{1 \times .10/365}$$

$$= \$69,350$$

As long as the wire transfer amount is larger than $69,350, the additional cost is justified.

VII. Risks and Controls

A. Punctuality

The primary operational risk of a concentration system requiring daily deposits and calling in by field offices, customers and third-party vendors is the failure of field office personnel to make calls and report accurately by the concentration bank's clearing deadline. Banks offer reports that allow companies to monitor deposit reporting.

B. Fraud

When field office personnel are not subject to daily supervision, some types of fraud may be more likely, and such fraud may go undetected for a period of days and even weeks. For example, an amount reported may not be deposited. Preventive measures include the following:

1. Having more than one type of report from field offices, for instance a sales report and separate cash concentration report, requiring different reports to be prepared by different people, and reviewing the reports promptly each day.

2. Conducting surprise audits of field offices if the company is particularly concerned about potential fraud.

3. Instructing banks to allow no overdrafts and to return the item, or to call with overdrafts.

4. Requiring daily reporting and follow-up by headquarters.

C. Bank Overdraft

The failure to make a single transfer from a deposit bank to a concentration bank could be sufficient to cause overdrafts at the concentration bank.

D. Bank Failure

Field deposit systems typically have many banks and the company may be at risk if an institution fails. A prompt concentration system limits this risk. The cash manager needs to be continually aware of the creditworthiness of each bank.

Questions

The chapter questions are to test the information in the text and are not examples of CCM examination questions nor are they in the examination format.

Answers can be found at the back of the book on p. 322.

1. What are the objectives of a cash concentration system?

2. What are the two major types of concentration systems?

3. What is EDT?

4. What other electronic alternative is available for concentration other than an EDT?

5. What is a depository transfer check (DTC)?

6. What are the major cost components of a cash concentration system?

7. What can cause excess balances?

8. What is anticipation?

9. What is threshold concentration?

10. A firm provides the following information:
    - EDT costs total $1.00
    - Wire transfer costs are $22.00
    - A wire accelerates availability one day
    - Opportunity cost of funds is 8%

    What is the minimum wire transfer required to break even?

Questions (Continued)

11. What are some ways fraud may be prevented in a concentration system?

12. Why is the pooling of funds a valuable objective of cash concentration?

Disbursements

Chapter 8

Overview

This chapter discusses the objectives of a disbursement system, the principal methods used for disbursements, and the role of commercial banks in the disbursement process.

Learning Objectives

Upon completion of this chapter and the related study questions, the reader should be able to do the following:

1. Discuss the objectives of a disbursement system.

2. Describe how corporate disbursement activities are organized.

3. Discuss the components and calculation of disbursement-float.

4. Explain how imprest accounts, zero balance accounts, payable through drafts and multiple drawee checks are used.

5. Explain the objectives, mechanics and performance criteria for controlled disbursement services.

6. Describe reconciliation, positive pay and check retention services.

Outline

I. Disbursement System Objectives

A. Cost Reduction

B. Information

C. Payee Relationships

D. Control and Fraud Prevention

E. Disbursement Float

II. Disbursement Organization

A. Centralization versus Decentralization

B. Control and Fraud Prevention

III. Disbursement Float

A. Mail Float

B. Processing Float

C. Clearing Float

IV. Selecting Disbursement Sites

A. Disbursement Networks

B. Remote Disbursement

C. Compliance with Trade Terms

V. Bank Products for Disbursement

A. Zero Balance Accounts (ZBAs)

B. Payable Through Drafts (PTDs)

C. Electronic Payable Through Drafts

D. Multiple Drawee Checks

E. Imprest Accounts

Outline (Continued)

VI. Forecasting and Funding Disbursement Accounts

VII. Controlled Disbursement
- A. Description
- B. Payor Bank Services
- C. Discrepancies After Notification
- D. Funding Controlled Disbursement Accounts
- E. Credit Risk
- F. How to Select a Controlled Disbursement Bank

VIII. Account Reconciliation and Check Retention Services
- A. Sort Only
- B. Partial Reconciliation
- C. Full Reconciliation
- D. Positive Pay
- E. Stop Payments
- F. Check Inquiry
- G. Check Retention (Check Safekeeping)
- H. High-Order Prefix (Divisional Sort)

IX. Electronic Disbursement Methods

X. Special Types of Disbursements
- A. Freight Payments
- B. Tax Payments

I. Disbursement System Objectives

A. Cost Reduction

An important objective of a disbursement system is to reduce a company's net cost of making payments to its suppliers, employees, and stockholders. These costs include:

1. **Opportunity Costs** - Opportunity costs include the following:

    -   The cost of excess borrowing or lost investment income when idle balances exist in disbursement accounts.

    -   The costs of payment mistiming, which include:

        *   The costs of paying bills late, such as lost discounts, ill will and other related costs, and

        *   The opportunity costs of paying bills early, such as interest income lost or extra interest expense incurred.

2. **Transfer Costs** - Transfer costs include the costs of transferring funds from depository and concentration accounts, or of transferring investments to the bank accounts from which disbursements are made.

3. **Overdraft Costs** - Overdraft costs include the monetary costs of overdrawing disbursement accounts as well as possible damage to the banking relationship.

B. Information

This is the process of producing timely information about the status of disbursement accounts and disbursement float positions, so that the company can manage its cash position.

C. Payee Relationships

It is important that good relationships are maintained between vendors and other payees.

D. Control and Fraud Prevention

This helps to maintain safeguards through the establishment of authority, responsibilities, and separation of duties.

E. Disbursement Float

Manage disbursement float in light of company objectives and policies.

II. Disbursement Organization

A. Centralization versus Decentralization

Disbursement systems may be centralized or decentralized. The advantages and disadvantages of each are as follows:

1. **Centralized Check Issuance** - In this type of system, headquarters controls disbursement accounts and is responsible for check writing and account reconciliation.

   - *Advantages:*

     * Bank and internal costs may be reduced.

     * Idle cash at local banks is minimized; excess cash is concentrated and available for investment or loan repayment.

     * Payment of bills can be scheduled to coordinate with the cash inflows of the firm.

     * Information about a company's cash position can be obtained easily and quickly.

     * As fewer individuals have access to the system, there is less likelihood of unauthorized disbursements.

   - *Disadvantages:*

     * Payments to suppliers may be delayed and the organization may miss a discount because invoices must be sent to a central location for processing.

     * Disbursement float may increase and payees may perceive that it is being increased at their expense.

     * Problem resolution requires coordination between headquarters and field offices.

2. **Decentralized Check Issuance** - Checks may be drawn on a local disbursement bank or a disbursement bank used by the headquarters office.

   - Checks Written on a Local Disbursement Bank - In this type of system, check writing and account reconciliation are performed at the local level.

   - *Advantages:*

     * In large, decentralized corporations, it may be more efficient for the local manager to have control over disbursement activities.

     * Relationships with payees may be better because checks are drawn on local banks and the local manager can resolve payment disputes more easily.

- *Disadvantages:*

  * Idle balances in numerous disbursement accounts may result in significant excess balances for the company as a whole.

  * Disbursement float may be lower when local disbursements are made to local vendors.

  * Information about a company's day-to-day aggregate cash position may be more difficult to obtain. More company accounts may need to be monitored.

  * There may be a greater likelihood of unauthorized disbursements because more people have access to the system.

  * There may be additional transfer costs for funding local disbursement accounts.

3. **Local Checks Written on a Centralized Disbursement Bank** - Check writing and account reconciliation are performed at the local level, but headquarters is responsible for choosing disbursement banks and funding disbursement accounts.

   - *Advantages:*

     * Minimizes the number of bank relationships.

     * Reduces excess balances in field locations.

     * Allows more opportunity for volume discounts on disbursement bank charges.

     * Allows local manager autonomy.

     * Allows local control of payment timing.

     * Improves vendor relationships.

   - *Disadvantages:*

     * Provides less control over when checks are written; headquarters does not know what checks will clear and when.

     * Results in higher administrative costs.

     * Requires use of a non-local bank on checks sent to local vendors.

B. Control and Fraud Prevention

Control and fraud prevention measures include the following:

1. Formal, written establishment of approval authority and procedures for each type of disbursement.

2. Separation of functional authority for collection and disbursement.

3. Separation of expense approval, check-signing authority and account reconciliation.

4. Use of checks that are difficult to reproduce.

5. Storing checks in a secure area with limited access.

6. Use of Positive Pay, a service that matches check serial numbers and dollar amounts to a database to determine the checks to be paid. This is described later in this section.

7. Setting a specific dollar amount limit for each type of account. Checks issued above this limit are returned to the depositor as unauthorized.

III. Disbursement Float

Disbursement float results from the delay between the time when a payor mails the check and the time when the funds are debited from the payor's account. The time has the following components:

A. Mail Float

Mail float is the delay between the time a check is mailed and the date the check is received by the payee or at the processing site.

B. Processing Float

Processing float is the delay between the time the payee or processing site receives the check and the time the check is deposited

C. Clearing Float

Clearing float is the delay between the time the check is deposited and the time it is presented to the payor's bank for payment. It has two components:

1. **Availability Float** - The delay between the time a check is deposited and the time the firm's account is credited with collected funds.

2. **Clearing Slippage Float** - The difference between the time the payee receives collected funds and the time the payor's account is debited.

    The components of disbursement float are illustrated in Exhibit 8-1.

IV. Selecting Disbursement Sites

In principle, selecting a system of disbursement sites can follow the same logic as used in selecting a lockbox system, except that longer float times are viewed favorably. Potential disbursement banks can be identified based on existing relationships, good float and/or control characteristics, quality of service, service features and cost.

A disbursement study can be conducted based on standard clearing times from current published studies and the actual dollar amounts sent to each geographic location. These studies are used to quantify the float generated by various disbursement points.

Exhibit 8-1

*Components of
Disbursement Float*

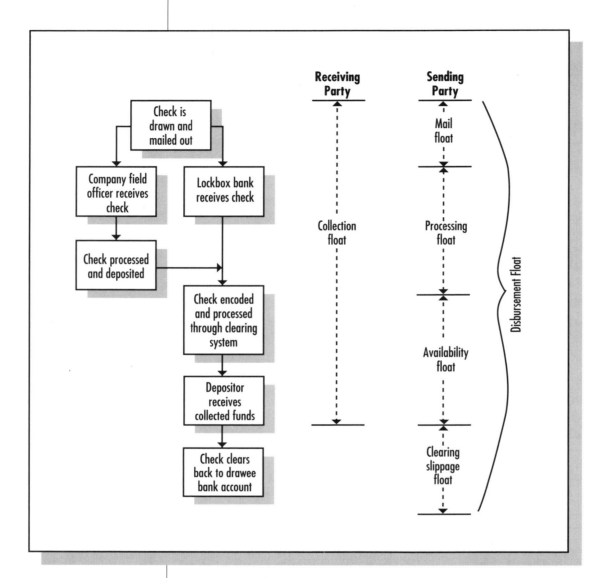

A. Disbursement Networks

Disbursement networks are systems of check mailing locations and drawee banks based on disbursement studies and designed to maximize disbursement float. Disbursement networks are not widely used. The cost and control benefits of making disbursements from just one or two banks often outweigh the float benefits of using a greater number of banks.

B. Remote Disbursement

Remote Disbursement is a method that is designed to delay the collection and final settlement of checks by using bank locations with longer clearing times. The Federal Reserve considers this practice to be an attempt to avoid more efficient payment arrangements for the purpose of gaining disbursement float.

In 1980, mandated by the Monetary Control Act (DIDMCA), the Fed began a program to reduce check clearing float in the banking system. The reduction of float, coupled with moderation of interest rates in the mid 1980s, made remote disbursement less effective.

C.   Compliance with Trade Terms

Lengthening mail float does not benefit the company unless it is given credit for having paid the bill on the postmark date. The postmark date may settle a technical dispute, but in today's environment a vendor might view a substantial delay in receiving good funds as a late payment.

V.   Bank Products for Disbursement

A.   Zero Balance Accounts (ZBAs)

1.   A zero balance account (ZBA) is a disbursement account on which checks are written, even though the balances in the accounts are maintained at zero. Checks debited to a ZBA for payment are covered by a transfer of funds from a master account located in the same bank. Funding of the ZBA account is automatic and involves only an accounting entry by the bank.

   Depending on bank system capabilities, ZBAs may be multi-tiered to conform to the organization's structure. Debits and transfers are posted to each account, and zeroing entries are made through the respective tiers at the end of each day.

2.   Credits and debits are posted just before the close of business, when a credit from the master account is posted to bring the balance back to zero. If credits in the ZBA exceed debits, the ZBA will be debited and a credit made to the master account.

3.   ZBAs may be used to allow companies with multiple divisions and subsidiaries to write checks on separate accounts and to segregate different types of payments such as payrolls, dividends and accounts payable. The cash manager can control the balances and funding of a master account and its associated ZBAs as if they were all one large account. This reduces idle balances and the need for multiple transfers.

B.   Payable Through Drafts (PTDs)

A payable through draft (PTD) is a payment instrument resembling a check that is drawn against the payor, not the bank, and on which the payor has a period of time in which to honor or refuse payment. Although for most, this is four to eight hours, it may be as long as twenty-four hours with certain banks.

The purpose of PTDs is to allow the paying company a period of time to approve payment. The deadline under Federal Reserve Regulation CC for approval or rejection of a PTD is the same as for a check. PTDs are frequently used for insurance claims and other field office disbursements that require final headquarters approval. They give the company time to ensure that all terms have been met or expenditures authorized.

C. Electronic Payable Through Drafts

Electronic payable through drafts are ACH debits to a company's account in which the company is notified in time to pay or reject each item. They are used for similar purposes as paper payable through drafts.

D. Multiple Drawee Checks

Multiple drawee checks, also known as **payable-if-desired (PID)** checks, are checks that can be presented for payment at a bank other than the drawee bank. Both bank names appear on the check.

1. **Applications** - Examples include payroll in states that require employees to be paid by checks payable in the state, payroll for employees on assignments away from the company office, and dividend checks.

2. **Banking Arrangements** - Balances are usually maintained at the alternate payment bank to compensate it for cashing multiple drawee checks. The alternate bank will require indemnity from the paying company for any loss relating to those checks.

E. Imprest Accounts

An imprest account is an account maintained at a prescribed level for a particular purpose or activity, and periodically replenished to the prescribed level. For example, a field office may have an imprest account for local disbursements with a balance sufficient for one or two months' expenses. Based on an established time frame or level of imprest account balances, the office submits expenses to headquarters for approval, and headquarters reimburses the imprest account.

VI. Forecasting and Funding Disbursement Accounts

The cash manager needs to be sure that disbursement accounts are funded to pay checks presented but do not have excess non-earning balances.

One of the most basic methods of managing a disbursement account is through **staggered** or **delayed funding**. This approach uses a forecast or formula for transferring funds to the disbursement account. The amount is usually based on historical clearing patterns. Statistical models such as regression and time series analyses are often useful in preparing such forecasts. They are described in Chapter 10, Forecasting.

VII. Controlled Disbursement

Another method used to minimize balances in disbursement accounts is controlled disbursement.

A. Description

1. Controlled disbursement is a bank service that provides same-day notification, usually by early or mid-morning, of the dollar amount of checks that will clear against the controlled disbursement account that day. The disbursement bank must receive its final cash letter of the day from the local Fed early in the morning so that the checks can be sorted and the company notified of its funding requirement. Payor bank services, described in Section B, are often used to aid in this process.

2. Companies generally find better rates for short-term investments early in the morning; consequently, they require check clearing information as early as possible.

3. In 1984, the Fed started the high dollar group sort (HDGS) program. Under that program, the local Reserve Bank makes a second daily presentment to drawee banks to which more than $10 million is presented from banks outside their Fed district. This program has had a significant impact on controlled disbursement.

B. Payor Bank Services

1. Payor Bank Services is an information service in which the Federal Reserve electronically notifies controlled disbursement banks early in the morning of all checks that will be presented that day. There are typically two notifications: the first early in the morning, and the second no earlier than 9:30 A.M., Eastern Time. Banks are then prepared to notify customers after an appropriate processing time.

2. Fed banks and branches are not uniform in their ability to provide Payor Bank Services.

C. Discrepancies After Notification

1. There is risk of presentment after the morning notification. A check missed by the Fed in the Payor Bank Services notification but discovered the same morning will be presented that day. There is also the slight possibility that a check will be presented over-the-counter, through the bank's branch network, or in a direct send from another bank. Companies make every effort to select controlled disbursement banks where such events are unlikely.

2. Some banks offer a controlled disbursement option to prevent the problems caused by late presentments. The bank guarantees that the final presentment amount will be equal to the morning notification, and makes whatever adjustments are required to the account the next day.

D. Funding Controlled Disbursement Accounts

1. A controlled disbursement account is normally funded from a corporate concentration account. The account can be funded either by the corporate customer or the bank. The transfer is usually on a same-day basis.

2. If concentration and controlled disbursement accounts are in unaffiliated banks, a wire transfer or the ACH can be used for funding. For applications that are not wire transfers, credit approval may be required, and maintenance of a balance equal to one day's clearing maintained.

E. Credit Risk

Controlled disbursement poses credit risk for the bank, with important implications for the company.

1. When the bank on which checks are actually drawn is funded on a same-day basis with a wire transfer or from another account at the same bank, there is very little credit exposure because the bank can return any checks if funds are not sufficient.

2. There are two situations in which a bank has credit exposure. These are:

- With delayed funding, there is risk that the EDT or DTC may be returned by the bank on which these items are drawn. By the time the returned EDT or DTC reaches the disbursement bank, it may be too late to return any disbursement checks being funded by the EDT or DTC. The disbursement bank is owed funds and becomes a creditor of the company.

- With the use of an affiliated bank for disbursing with funding through the parent bank, there is no problem if the affiliate bank is funded directly on a same-day basis by a wire transfer. However, if the company funds the parent bank and the parent bank automatically funds the affiliate with immediate funds, there is a problem. Since the affiliate bank does not have an overdrawn account, it cannot legally refuse to pay the checks even though there may be an overdraft at the parent bank.

  Such risks make it very likely that a bank will undertake a credit review of a company that wants to use its controlled disbursement service. A formal credit facility may be required. Companies with credit problems may find it difficult to use this service unless same-day wire transfer funding is used at the bank on which checks are drawn. When an affiliate bank is used, an agreement may be required that allows checks to be returned if sufficient funds are not available at the parent bank.

F. How to Select a Controlled Disbursement Bank

In addition to overall relationship considerations, there are a number of service considerations which should be evaluated in the selection of a controlled disbursement bank. Disbursement float remains important for the company, but in recent years other considerations have become relatively more important. They include:

1. **Timeliness of Reporting** - This is important because the company wants to make investing or borrowing decisions as early as possible.

2. **Processing Accuracy** - Processing errors can result in over- or underfunding of the disbursement account.

3. **Volume Capacity** - Capacity should be sufficient, so that reporting deadlines can be met.

4. **Reporting Detail and Reconciliation Services** - Reports should contain adequate detail and be timely enough to meet the company's information needs.

5. **Cost** - Service pricing should reflect fair and reasonable compensation.

6. **Customer Service Support** - Bank customer service staff should provide prompt and knowledgeable responses to the company's requests.

VIII. Account Reconciliation and Check Retention Services

Banks provide account reconciliation services to meet companies' information and control requirements. The following services are available:

A. Sort Only

The bank sorts the checks by check serial number.

B. Partial Reconciliation

The bank lists all checks paid in numerical order by check serial number, or date paid. For each item, the paid report shows the check serial number, dollar amount, and date paid. The listing is available in hard copy and/or electronic form.

C. Full Reconciliation

The company supplies an electronic file of checks issued and the bank matches checks paid against the file. The bank supplies a listing, either in hard copy and/or electronic form, of checks paid and outstanding in check serial number order.

D. Positive Pay

Positive Pay is used for fraud control. With this system, the company transmits a file of checks soon after issuance to the bank. The bank matches check serial numbers and dollar amounts and pays only those checks that match.

E. Stop Payments

Stop Payments can be initiated by the company either by voice, electronically or in writing. Written confirmation may be required by the bank for telephone instructions.

F. Check Inquiry

The customer can check, electronically, to determine the status of checks written.

G. Check Retention (Check Safekeeping)

A bank retains paid checks for periods that typically range from one to six months. Microfilm records are usually maintained for seven years. Copies of checks can be obtained when needed.

H. High-Order Prefix (Divisional Sort)

This service allows a single account to be used by a company with multiple units. Codes identifying the various units are included in the check serial numbers. Reports are available showing unit subtotals.

IX. Electronic Disbursement Methods

Electronic disbursements via Fedwire and ACH are used for payments from corporations to individuals, from individuals to corporations, and from corporations to corporations. The item volume of such payments is low compared to checks, but is expected to increase because of the declining value of float, and the increasing emphasis on expense control.

For additional information on disbursements for consumers and/or corporate-to-corporate payments, refer to Chapter 4, The Payments System, and Chapter 9, Information Systems.

X. Special Types of Disbursements

A. Freight Payments

A few banks and third parties offer a specialized payment service in which freight payment specialists pay all of a shipper's freight bills, audit bills for possible overcharges and duplicate payments, and provide reports that help the company compare costs for different routes and carriers.

B. Tax Payments

1. **Federal Tax Deposit System** - This system collects and accounts for taxes withheld by employers from individuals' salaries and wages as well as corporate business and excise taxes.

   To make a tax payment, a company debits its account or instructs a designated bank to debit its account. Either the company or the bank prepares a Federal Tax Deposit (FTD) coupon (Form 8109) indicating the dollar amount, tax period, and type of tax payment. The financial institution sends a copy of the Advice of Credit to its local Federal Reserve Bank, and credits the Treasury's account at the financial institution. Based on the Advice of Credit, the Federal Reserve Bank debits the reserve account of the bank.

2. **State Tax Payments** - Historically, states have had payment facilities through banks similar to the federal tax arrangements described earlier. Many states have implemented programs requiring companies to remit taxes electronically. This may be done with an ACH credit, ACH debit or wire transfer. TXP is the standard payment format for state tax payments via the ACH.

Questions

The chapter questions are to test the information in the text and are not examples of CCM examination questions nor are they in the examination format.

Answers can be found at the back of the book on p. 323.

1. What are the major objectives of a cash disbursement system?

2. How may disbursement systems be organized?

3. What are the components of disbursement float?

4. What is remote disbursement?

5. What is a zero balance account (ZBA)?

6. What is a multiple drawee check?

7. Is controlled disbursement the same as remote disbursement?

8. Who provides payor bank services?

9. What factors should be examined in the selection of a controlled disbursement bank?

10. What is Positive Pay?

11. What is sort only account reconciliation?

Information Management

Chapter 9

Overview

This chapter deals with the tools used by cash managers to handle information and explains how these tools fit into the overall framework of treasury management. It covers automated treasury systems and information management. It also discusses obtaining and handling information, implementing a treasury management information system, and includes an introduction to electronic data interchange (EDI).

Learning Objectives

Upon completion of this chapter and the related study questions, the reader should be able to do the following:

1. Understand the objectives of treasury management information systems.

2. Understand how information flows in the treasury function.

3. Describe the hardware and software in a treasury management information system.

4. Describe how information is managed in a treasury management information system.

5. Discuss the benefits and basic functions of electronic data interchange (EDI).

Outline

I.   **Objectives of a Treasury Management Information System (TMIS)**

II. **Treasury Management Information Systems**
   A.   Components
   B.   Capabilities
   C.   Advantages

III. **Information Management**
   A.   Monitoring External Information
   B.   Monitoring Internal Information
   C.   Transaction Initiation

IV. **Software and Information Management**
   A.   Types of Software
   B.   Obtaining and Developing Software
   C.   Information Security

V.   **Electronic Data Interchange (EDI)**
   A.   Origins
   B.   Potential EDI Benefits
   C.   Strategic Incentives versus Quantified Payback
   D.   Potential to Replace Paper Forms and Check Payments
   E.   Implementation
   F.   Audit and Control
   G.   EDI in the Business Transaction Cycle
   H.   The ANSI X12 Data Interchange Standards

I.   Objectives of a Treasury Management Information System (TMIS)

The cash manager operates in an environment in which information is becoming more important and more readily available. In such an environment, automated data access, storage and handling become increasingly necessary.

Poor data management or lack of timely information can impede sound financial decision- making and cause idle balances, overdrafts, overcompensation of banks, missed investment opportunities, and unnecessary borrowing.

The objectives of a treasury management information system include:

- Collecting information such as bank balances and transactions, investment rates and foreign exchange rates.

- Organizing information in a format suitable to the user's needs.

- Providing tools for the analysis of information.

- Supporting treasury decisions concerning movement of funds, short-term investment and borrowing.

- Initiating transactions such as wire transfers and Automated Clearing House (ACH) transactions.

Information management is essential for treasury management. A well-designed treasury management information system improves the performance of the full range of treasury and cash management activities including data collection and analysis, movement of funds and management of bank relationships. The type and quantity of information needed, as well as the corporate structure, define the requirements for a company's treasury management information systems (TMIS).

II.   Treasury Management Information Systems

Treasury Management Information Systems (TMIS) are configurations of hardware, software and information sources designed to assist the cash manager by collecting and formatting information and doing routine calculations. They accomplish tasks that would otherwise have to be done manually.

A.   Components

The components of a treasury management information system include:

1.   **Hardware**

- *Personal Computer (PC)* - A treasury management information system usually consists of a PC and software used to perform treasury management operations.

- *Minicomputers and Mainframes* - Companies may have cash management needs that exceed the capacity of a PC and use large-scale computers for selected treasury management functions. These computers are effective for data storage and manipulation. The minicomputer or mainframe computer is often accessed via a remote terminal or PC.

- *Telephone/Audio* - Some reporting systems offer audio response, which permits the caller to obtain balance reports by telephone. This method usually provides less detailed information than computer-to-computer transmission, and may be more expensive.

2. **Software** - Software is the set of instructions that allows computer hardware to process data and perform a variety of tasks. Software applications used for treasury management are discussed in Section IV of this chapter. The following are some of the basic tasks performed:

- Receiving and sending data electronically

- Reformatting data

- Performing calculations

- Initiating transactions

- Generating reports

3. **Peripherals** - Peripherals are additional pieces of equipment connected to the computer to enhance its capabilities. Common peripherals include:

- *Printers and Plotters -* Produce hard copy of reports and graphs.

- *Modems -* Allow the computer to send and receive information over communication lines.

- *Networks -* Link together one or more microcomputers to a set of peripheral devices in a local area network.

4. **Information** - Information is the final component of a treasury management information system.

- The types of information range from daily account activity, to banking relationship data, and long-term cash forecasting.

- Sources of information range from internal, to banks, to commercial information services.

B. Capabilities

1. **Daily Activities** - Treasury management information systems are used for daily activities including:

- Collecting information on bank account activity

- Determining the company's cash position

- Verifying banking activity

- Initiating transactions.

2. **Decision Support** - Treasury management information systems are also used for decision support in a number of areas of corporate finance, including:

- Short-term cash flow forecasting

- Long-term financial planning and forecasting

- Analyzing historical financial data for performance evaluation and trends

- Investment yield analysis

- Monitoring bank relationships and compensation

3. **Accounting Support** - TMIS may also interface with corporate accounting systems. This involves tracking investments and borrowing, calculating interest income and expense accruals, and booking and tracking deposits, clearings and transfers. Some systems provide a general ledger interface to automate journal entries.

C. Advantages

A TMIS provides the following advantages:

1. **Access to Information** - The TMIS can also increase the access to, and the availability of data and promote the integration of information throughout an organization.

2. **Productivity Improvement** - TMIS can significantly reduce the amount of time spent to gather data and perform routine calculations, giving the cash manager more time to become active in financial decision-making and corporate finance.

3. **Maintenance of Bank Relationship Data** - With a TMIS, a company can identify discrepancies between internal and bank-generated information quickly.

4. **Increased Security** - A TMIS may provide enhanced security by controlling access to information and reducing unauthorized transactions.

III. Information Management

Cash management activities and decisions are based on information from a variety of sources, both internal and external to the company. This data may be available as previous-day information, current-day information or both.

A. Monitoring External Information

The daily cash management monitoring effort includes gathering information from external sources about collections, check clearings and the company's cash position. The data about bank account balances and account activity are the basic information blocks that support the cash manager's subsequent activities and decisions, and should be entered into the system as soon as available.

1. **Previous-Day and Historical Information** - This usually consists of the following kinds of data:

- *Balance and Transaction Reports* - Information on current ledger and collected balances, deposits subject to one- and two-day availability and adjustments as well as detail debits and credits. Average balances and a balance history may also be reported.

- *Borrowing and/or Investment Activity* - Summaries of investment purchases and sales, as well as debt issuance and retirement.

- *International Transactions* - Offshore account balances, debits and credits, wire transfers, draft activity, letters of credit and foreign exchange transactions.

- *Custody* - Safekeeping inventories and approaching maturities.

- *Stop Payments and Check Inquiry* - Verification of stop payment requests and status of checks written.

2. **Same-Day Information.** Includes the following:

- *Controlled Disbursement* - Check clearings to be funded.

- *Lockbox Deposits* - Including a float breakdown of deposits.

- *ACH Transactions* - Debits, credits, EDTs

- *Wire Transfers* - Both incoming and outgoing

- *Money Market and Foreign Exchange Rates*

- *Concentration Reports* - EDT activity and exception reports, such as identifying sending locations that have not reported daily deposits. This information may also be available on previous-day reports.

3. **Multi-Bank Balance Reporting Systems** - Reports for all banks reporting to a service can be combined so that the cash manager receives one consolidated report instead of several individual reports. Typically, one bank or a third-party vendor consolidates the information. Data exchange is the most common mechanism used to move this information between banks.

4. **Account Analysis** - A treasury management information system can help with the verification of account analyses and highlight major differences. Electronic receipt of account analyses is preferred for this application. Account analysis is discussed in detail in Chapter 14, Bank Relationship Management.

5. **Commercial Reporting Services** - Commercial reporting services provide information about money market and foreign exchange rates and financial news. This information is either real-time or is updated frequently throughout the day.

6. **Financial Data Bases** - Financial data bases are information services available to the public for a fee. Although they are updated daily, they are used primarily for historical financial and business analysis.

7. **Formats** - The most common format for bank data exchange is the Bank Administration Institute (BAI) standard, which was developed by the Bank Administration Institute. Many banks can deliver data to their corporate customers in the BAI format, which can be loaded easily into treasury system data bases. However, all BAI formats are not the same; the "standard" left much discretion to each user, and, as a result, many variations have been created. ANSI has also addressed this question, and the TMA and BAI have announced joint plans to develop and maintain one standard.

B. Monitoring Internal Information

In addition to the external information outlined earlier, the treasury manager uses information on important financial activity from other parts of the company. Data should be captured at their sources, e.g., balances, check clearings and lockbox activity from the banks, checks written from company sources or investments from the investment manager. Examples include:

1. Accounts payable, payroll and tax disbursements

2. Payments received over the counter and credit sales

3. Other transactions such as dividend payments, pension payments, and stock repurchases

C. Transaction Initiation

In addition to accessing information, a TMIS can be used to initiate transactions. Among the transactions that can be initiated are:

1. **Funds Transfers** - Funds transfers may be used to concentrate cash, to fund disbursement accounts, to repay borrowings and to invest in short-term securities.

2. **Other Transactions** - Banks offer facilities to initiate a variety of transactions electronically including:

   - Short-term investments

   - Letter of credit applications

   - Line drawdowns

   - ACH debits and credits

   - Stop payments

   - State and federal tax payments

   - Foreign exchange transactions

IV. Software and Information Management

A computer cannot operate without specific instructions or programming, i.e., software. Banks and specialized vendors that have developed interrelated cash management software often refer to individual components as modules, for example, the balance reporting module or the investment module.

A. Types of Software

Several basic types of computer programs are used for treasury management. These are:

1. **Spreadsheets** - Spreadsheet software allows data to be input, arranged and analyzed. It is probably the most popular application for treasury management.

2. **Data Base Management** - Data base management software organizes the way data is stored and retrieved in the computer. It allows data to be identified and stored efficiently in individual units for later use in any combination and in any order.

3. **Communications** - Communications software enables a computer to send data to, and receive data from other telecommunications devices and provides error checking of data transfer. A parsing capability is a software feature that enables a PC to recognize the units of data so that they can be extracted from the transmission and stored in a data base. It is used in conjunction with a modem.

   An autodial feature allows an unattended computer to initiate telephone communications at a prearranged time. It has the ability to call back when a busy signal is encountered or a transmission is interrupted. The autodial function has the advantage of being able to call early in the morning so that information is ready and waiting when the user arrives.

4. **Treasury Applications** - Integrated TMIS are available from select banks and third-party vendors. These systems include modules for specific treasury functions and may automatically integrate the data into a treasury data base. To supplement an integrated TMIS, a company may use bank-specific software to initiate transactions such as wire transfers, ACH transfers, investment purchases and letters of credit. Some of the common modules available in an integrated TMIS are:

   - *Account Analysis Modules* - These modules examine bank account analyses to verify prices, volumes and balances, and perform comparative assessments among banks.

   - *Bank Relationship Management Modules* - Bank relationship modules maintain pertinent data about individual accounts. These programs store information such as account name and number, services used, credit lines and terms, protocols and access time, signing authorities, and names and telephone numbers of bank representatives.

   - *Cash Position Worksheet Modules* - These are the heart of any cash management operation, and provide the user with a consolidated report of the company's cash balances. Such modules draw data from balance reporting systems, transfer modules, investment and borrowing systems, foreign exchange modules and other sources of bank transactions. Some worksheets can even be integrated with target balance modules to make recommended additions or deletions to major bank accounts.

   - *Cash Ledger Accounting Interface Modules* - These modules link the accounting and treasury functions. Some programs, where corporate policy and internal systems allow, assign general ledger codes to transaction information, and then transmit the information directly from one system into the other. Others prepare cash management information for the general ledger, but the information is re-entered into the accounting system.

- *Debt and Investment Applications* - Primarily used for tracking portfolios for management reporting.

  * They include all the relevant information such as name of security, dealer, price, interest rate, yield to maturity, and maturity date.

  * Rates can be updated at any time and then the value of a security or portfolio can be automatically recalculated.

  * Many also feed directly into the daily cash position worksheet at maturity.

- *Forecasting Modules* - Forecasting modules must be able to accept data from other modules such as cash position worksheets, account records, debt and investment maturity schedules, foreign exchange, and planned transfers.

- *International Transactions* - International functions are available on software for initiating foreign exchange transactions, transferring funds, obtaining financial information, modeling hedging transactions, and netting transactions among company subsidiaries. These functions are described in Chapter 15, International Cash Management.

- *Reconciliation* - Reconciliation modules are needed to verify that the transactions reported by the bank match the transactions recorded in the treasury data base. This is especially important when this data flows automatically into accounting records.

B. Obtaining and Developing Software

Cash management software can be licensed, purchased or developed internally.

1. Companies can license specially designed programs from banks or third-party vendors.

2. Companies can purchase off-the-shelf software such as spreadsheets or data base managers and adapt it to their treasury needs.

3. Companies can use in-house computing resources to design, write, test and implement their own software.

4. In-house development may be advantageous because it can be on the company's choice of hardware, can be applied to the specific need of its users, and is not dependent on outside suppliers.

5. Outside software is programmed to fit the needs of a wide variety of companies and offers continuing development and upgrading.

C. Information Security

Security of information is an important consideration regardless of the kind of treasury management information system a corporation has established. Violations of security can be manual, for example, altering information on a report or making an unauthorized transfer of funds. Violations can also be computerized, for example, using a computer to enter the automated corporate system and gain access to information or initiate transactions.

1. **Physical Security -** Physical security of equipment and data is important for all systems. Security includes basic safeguards, such as back-up computers, restricted access, appropriate and adequate information filing facilities, as well as window and door locks.

2. **Back-Up Storage -** All systems also require a separate, secure location for back-up storage of information. The treasury management system should provide data back-up aids that can be removed from the computer and stored in an off-site, secure location. There are five ways of saving data that can be restored or loaded back into the computer. These are:

   - *Floppy diskettes* - These are inexpensive, but copying is slow and time consuming.

   - *Tapes* - These are simple to operate, but require additional hardware and can be difficult to use to restore specific files.

   - *Removable hard disks* - These are fast, simple to operate, can easily restore simple files and can be used as alternate hard disks.

   - *Transmission to a mainframe* - This requires additional hardware and special software, and requires the assistance of the systems staff.

   - *Transmission via local area network (LAN)* to another micro or network point involves software and hardware which link together one or more microcomputers as well as a set of peripheral devices.

3. **Disaster Recovery -** Plans must be made to rebuild the TMIS and restore its functions quickly in the event of a disaster such as total destruction of the system or a similar disaster at one of the company's principal service banks. The plan should be tested regularly.

4. **Protection Against Viruses -** Computer viruses are commands within software which cause errors or other aberrations in the functioning of the system. Virus protection methods include:

   - Prohibit electronic mail on operating system.

   - Prohibit downloading from public bulletin boards.

   - Establish a program approval policy.

   - Buy software from reputable dealers.

   - Prohibit copied or pirated software.

   - Use virus-detection programs regularly.

5. **Controls -** Operations that are vulnerable to violations of security can be strengthened by instituting new procedures. Treasury tasks should be distributed so that no one with authority to transfer funds deals with a transaction in its entirety. Levels of responsibility that limit access to information should be established. Procedures should be instituted so that high-dollar transactions require multiple approvals before they are initiated.

6. **Audit Trails -** An audit trail is a necessary security measure for a computerized system. The system should generate a log of who has done what

and when. This is called event logging. It allows the tracking of unauthorized transactions. The system should also generate a record that will permit periodic substantiation of report balances and transaction activity.

7. **Written Policies** - A formal set of policies that spells out all procedures, security levels, the maintenance of codes, passwords and other restricted information should be established, implemented and enforced. Often such a policy provides for a security officer. The policy is only good if it is used.

8. **Security Procedures** - With more funds transfers being initiated through a TMIS, companies and banks are concerned about security of the payment information. Section 4A of the Uniform Commercial Code has been a key factor in this movement. The article requires that commercially reasonable security procedures be in place. Among the most common security procedures being used are the following:

   - *Personal Identification Number (PIN)* - This is a unique number assigned to an individual used to determine that this person is authorized to execute the transaction.

   - *Callback* - To ensure that a transaction is authorized, a bank calls back to a company after the transaction is entered but before it is executed. It is often used with wire transfers to third parties. The individual called should be someone other than the person initiating the transaction. Another form of callback involves a company signing on to a TMIS. The bank's system does not accept the connection but automatically redials the company's system.

   - *Encryption* - Encryption is a process which scrambles a message so that it cannot be read by someone who might intercept it. Messages are coded and so must be translated when received. Hardware and software are available for this purpose.

   - *Message Authentication* - Message authentication is a digital signature. It is used to protect the integrity of a message and ensure that it has not been tampered with. The sender calculates a message authentication code in a unique manner and transmits it with the message. The receiver duplicates the calculation and a match indicates the transaction is valid.

V. Electronic Data Interchange (EDI)

EDI is computer-to-computer communication for routine business transactions. With EDI, electronic transmission replaces paper documents throughout the business transaction cycle. Messages are coded in standard formats, and sent between the buyer's computer and the seller's computer, through publicly available data transmission networks, or by direct transmission.

A. Origins

EDI originated in corporate areas such as production, and purchasing. Newer inventory management techniques, such as just-in-time, have encouraged EDI development because they require more trading partner contact, which would be inefficient and time-consuming if not done electronically. Treasury has often been the last part of this development, automating the payment portion of the process. Financial EDI is the use of the various capabilities of EDI for corporate-to-corporate payments and the transmission of remittance advices related to the payment. Non-financial EDI involves transactions such as purchase orders and invoices.

Many companies have investigated or started to use EDI in some way, but implementation takes time. Even users with the most organized EDI projects are still carefully evaluating their experience with the first two or three transaction sets as they plan the next steps. A **transaction set** is the electronic equivalent of a paper business document. Transaction sets are formed using specific rules for formatting the information in the business document.

B. Potential EDI Benefits

EDI can provide the following advantages to the corporate user:

1. Improve a seller's response time to buyer orders.

2. Reduce clerical expense by eliminating the need for rekeying, filing, and retrieving paper-based information.

3. Reduce errors that result from copying and rekeying.

4. Decrease order lead time providing a reduction in inventory levels.

5. Reduce the delay in preparing and mailing reports such as invoices, and allow more accurate cash forecasting, and better inventory control.

6. Eliminate the uncertainty of mail and check clearing time, can also reduce related paperwork through electronic corporate-to-corporate trade payments.

C. Strategic Incentives versus Quantified Payback

EDI requires the involvement and support of top management. It is usually undertaken for strategic reasons, not because of a feasibility study showing a payback within two or three years. EDI involves many different exchanges between trading partners such as purchase orders, material release advices, receipt advices, and remittance advices. It is typically approached by implementing one or two transaction sets at a time. At the beginning of EDI implementation, it is almost impossible to project all of the costs and benefits.

D. Potential to Replace Paper Forms and Check Payments

Replacing paper forms and check payments is normally a long, gradual process. Maintaining dual systems, electronic and paper, is a necessity for most companies for a substantial period of time.

E. Implementation

Implementation is a deliberate process that must be undertaken a step at a time. Informal cooperation among departments is the primary way that EDI gets started within the company. The focal point within the corporation is often the systems function. Members of the systems staff may be designated as a resource for other company functions.

F. Audit and Control

EDI may be resisted because of the lack of a paper trail. However, papers can be stolen or lost. Through passwords, authentication, and encryption, electronic systems can offer equal if not greater protection than paper-based systems.

G. EDI in the Business Transaction Cycle

EDI simplifies and accelerates the entire business transaction cycle. Documents that have been traditionally sent between a buyer and seller in paper form are transmitted electronically. Electronic transmission saves mail time and eliminates the rekeying of data.

The information may be sent directly between the two trading partners or it may be sent through a third-party communications provider called a **value added network (VAN)**, which acts as an intermediary.

The information sent between the two companies is in **American National Standards Institute (ANSI)** formats. The formatted information is translated either by the companies' computers or by the VAN.

H. The ANSI X12 Data Interchange Standards

The American National Standards Institute (ANSI) is the recognized coordinator and clearing house for information on national and international standards. ANSI's Accredited Standards Committee X12 develops uniform standards for inter-industry electronic interchange of business transactions such as order placement and processing, shipping, invoicing, payment, and application of funds received.

1. **Content of the Standards**

   The ANSI X12 standards consist of the following:

   - *Transaction Set Standards* - Define the procedural format and data content requirements for specific business transactions. The following are some of the transaction sets developed to facilitate EDI:

     * *810 Invoice*

       This allows the user to convey invoice data from a seller to a buyer, such as unit price and quantities purchased and terms of sale.

     * *820 Payment Order/Remittance Advice*

       This transaction set has a dual purpose. It initiates a money transfer to a payee and/or provides the payee with information describing the purpose of the associated payment. The 820 allows multiple invoices to be paid in a single payment. It also includes the amount of discounts taken and other payment adjustments.

* *821 Financial Transaction Reporting*

This conveys transaction information to a payment originator to facilitate account reconciliation including payment number, date of settlement, and amount paid.

* *822 Customer Account Analysis*

This conveys detailed service charges, and balance and adjustment data to companies. It is designed primarily for transmission from a bank to its corporate clients. This transaction set can accommodate the Treasury Management Association (TMA) Standardized Account Analysis format.

* *823 Lockbox Transaction*

This conveys check deposit data from lockboxes including deposit totals, funds availability, and remittance detail.

* *997 Functional Acknowledgement*

This notifies a transaction originator that the transmitted transaction sets meet the format rules established by X12.

- *Data Dictionary* - Defines the precise content for data elements used in building transaction sets. Data elements are like words; they are the smallest unit in the X12 information structure.

- *Segment Dictionary* - Provides the definitions and formats of data segments used to build transaction sets. A data segment is a single line of information within a transaction set corresponding to a single line on a paper order form or invoice. It contains information such as quantity, description, and price.

- *Transmission Control Standards* - Define the formats required for sending the data.

2. **Translation and Communication** - The physical process of electronic data interchange requires translation of data from the sender's format to a mutually-agreed, machine-readable format, communication of that data through a medium acceptable to both companies' computers, and translation from the agreed format to the internal format of the receiver.

EDI communications can take place in several ways such as through physical delivery of disks or magnetic tapes, point-to-point, through the telephone system, and through third parties.

- *Physical Delivery* - Physical delivery is slow, subject to delay, and appropriate only in unusual situations such as those involving a sender and receiver with of high-volume, similar equipment, and located close to each other.

- *Point-to-Point Communication* - This may be a suitable method for trading partners with very high bilateral volume. For most companies, it is inconvenient because of the need to maintain communications equipment with compatible line speeds and protocols, and the need to coordinate transmission schedules.

- *Value Added Networks* - VANs eliminate most compatibility problems.

- *Communication and Translation Functions* - A number of other functions are accomplished either externally by the VANs or internally, depending on the user's size and EDI involvement. When these functions are done internally, software is either purchased off-the-shelf, enhanced by the vendor for the customer's needs, or developed internally. Those functions include:

    * Translation of company, industry, and standard formats.

    * Functional acknowledgment to the sender that the message has been received.

    * Compliance checking to ensure that all elements of the document are in the correct format and sequence.

    * Special editing to suit a user's needs such as ensuring that numbers fall within prescribed ranges.

    * Audit functions such as matching functional acknowledgments received against previously transmitted data, reports of all items received or sent, and reports of messages unacknowledged.

Questions

The chapter questions are to test the information in the text and are not examples of CCM examination questions nor are they in the examination format.

Answers can be found at the back of the book on p. 325.

1. What are the objectives of a treasury management information system (TMIS)?

2. What are the advantages of a TMIS?

3. What are the major types of external information that must be monitored?

4. What types of transactions may be initiated through a TMIS?

5. What types of modules are often found in treasury management software?

6. How can a company obtain cash management software?

7. What is a disaster recovery plan?

8. What are some of the security procedures used in connection with electronic funds transfers?

9. What is EDI?

10. What are some of the potential benefits of EDI?

11. What is a VAN?

12. What are transaction sets?

13. Why is translation required in EDI transactions?

14. What is some of the same-day external information that is monitored by a TMIS?

Forecasting Cash Flows

Chapter 10

Overview

This chapter describes the objectives of forecasting, the difference between short-, medium-, and long-term forecast horizons, and the principal techniques used for forecasting.

Learning Objectives

Upon completion of this chapter and the related study questions, the reader should be able to do the following:

1. Discuss the objectives of cash forecasting.

2. Discuss the distinction between short-, medium-, and long-term forecasting.

3. Explain steps in the forecasting process such as data selection, source selection, forecast method selection, and forecast validation and implementation.

4. Describe short-term forecasting techniques such as cash scheduling, and the related receipts and disbursements and distribution methods.

5. Describe long-term forecasting methods such as percentage-of-sales, adjusted net income, and pro forma financials.

6. Discuss issues relating to selection of medium-term forecasting techniques.

7. Discuss the application of statistical forecasting methods such as simple moving averages, and exponential smoothing.

Outline

I. **Objectives of Cash Forecasting**
    A. Liquidity Management
    B. Financial Control
    C. Strategic Objectives
    D. Capital Budgeting
    E. Minimizing Net Cost of Funds

II. **Cash Forecasting Horizons**
    A. Short-Term Forecasting
    B. Medium-Term Forecasting
    C. Long-Term Forecasting

III. **The Forecasting Process**
    A. Cash Flow Components
    B. Degree of Certainty
    C. Data Sources
    D. Data Organization
    E. Forecast Method Selection
    F. Forecast Validation

IV. **Short-Term Forecasting**
    A. Receipts and Disbursements Forecast
    B. Distribution Method

V. **Long-Term Forecasting**
    A. Pro-Forma Statements
    B. Adjusted Net Income

VI. **Medium-Term Forecasting**

VII. **Statistical Forecasting**
    A. Time Series Forecasting
    B. Regression Analysis

I. Objectives of Cash Forecasting

Forecasting cash flows is one of the more important tasks of the cash manager. **Cash forecasting** is the process of predicting cash flow for the purposes of liquidity management and financial control. Accurate forecasting provides management with necessary information for decision-making.

A. Liquidity Management

Forecasting the net cash position is essential in scheduling maturities of borrowings and investments as well as in anticipating borrowing requirements.

B. Financial Control

Predicted cash flows provide a standard of measurement and comparison for actual cash flows. Variance analysis can help identify insufficient cash movements, unacceptable inventory changes, delays in receivables collection, premature payments and other problems. Early detection of these problems allows corrective measures to be taken quickly and the negative consequences of these problems to be minimized.

C. Strategic Objectives

Cash forecasts are used to evaluate and develop the firm's strategic objectives and policies, relative to analyzing the company's future funding requirements.

D. Capital Budgeting

Forecasts of expenditures, revenues, and funding costs are required in evaluating potential projects.

E. Minimizing Net Cost of Funds

Decisions as to the utilization of available cash often involve conflicting goals and trade-offs. By concentrating on minimizing the net cost of funds, improvement in overall results can be achieved by:

1. Minimizing borrowing costs and excess bank balances.

2. Optimizing short-term investment income.

II. Cash Forecasting Horizons

A. Short-Term Forecasting

1. Short-term forecasts predict cash receipts and disbursements on a daily or weekly basis, typically for a 30-day horizon.

2. Short-term forecasts aid in scheduling cash concentration transfers for field and lockbox accounts, funding disbursement accounts and making short-term investing and borrowing decisions.

B. Medium-Term Forecasting

1. Medium-term forecasting is concerned with net cash positions from one month to a year. It focuses on the overall cash position rather than on daily position management.

2. Medium-term cash forecasts are typically in the form of monthly or quarterly estimates. They commonly use accrual-based operating budgets as their starting point to create the cash flow forecast. This forecast will require adjustment to reflect the timing of the actual cash flows.

3. Medium-term forecasting is used extensively in liquidity management decisions involving credit lines, commercial paper sales, credit and payables policies, and short-term investment portfolios.

C. Long-Term Forecasting

1. Long-term forecasts cover one or more years. They take into account the long-term sales and product objectives of the firm as well as its market environment.

2. Long-term forecasts are generally based on accounting projections of revenues, expenses, and changes in balance sheet items. Revenues and expenses are usually estimated on an accrual basis, with adjustments made to recognize the effects of changes in assets and liabilities on cash flow.

3. Long-term forecasts are used in financial planning and analysis. They are also used by financial institutions in credit evaluation.

III. The Forecasting Process

The methods used for cash forecasting are diverse. Computer spread sheets are used extensively in developing forecasts. Development of a particular forecast depends upon the forecasting horizon and the size, business and structure of the organization. It also depends on the availability of information and forecasting tools. A forecaster's understanding of the organization and its business environment play an important role in the forecasting process.

A. Cash Flow Components

The first step in cash flow forecasting is to divide cash flows into their major components. This is necessary because the factors determining the magnitude and timing of each cash flow component may influence the selection of the appropriate forecasting techniques.

It may be appropriate to split disbursements into categories such as interest payments, dividend payments, payroll, large-dollar vendor payments, and small-dollar vendor payments.

B. Degree of Certainty

It may also be possible to categorize cash flows by the degree of certainty attached to each component:

1. **Certain Flows -** For many companies, a significant number of cash flows are known in advance. Examples of certain cash flows include tax, interest, and royalty payments.

2. **Forecastable Flow -** Cash collections from credit sales are an example of a cash flow component that can be forecast with reasonable accuracy. The cash flow on a given day depends on factors such as the recent history of credit sales. A prediction of future cash flows can then be made on the basis of past observations.

3. **Less Predictable Cash Flows -** Some cash flows are more difficult to forecast accurately. Examples may include sales of a new product, temporary damage repairs pending settlement of insurance claims, or the cost of settling a strike.

C. Data Sources

It is important to identify the sources from which data may be gathered.

1. **Range of Sources -** Information is available from multiple sources including the company's banks, field managers, sales managers, and the accounts payable or accounts receivable departments.

   The identification of sources is affected by the degree of centralization or decentralization in the company's structure. In a decentralized company, local managers will usually have the most current financial data related to their operation. In a centralized company, there is less dependence on local sources.

2. **Reporting Requirements -** In order to ensure the usefulness of the data selected, it is essential that the data be precisely defined and accurately reported in a timely manner.

D. Data Organization

Data selection is an important step in forecasting cash flows. The choice involves the organization of available data to be included in the forecast.

In predicting cash flows from credit sales, data for the past three months or the past year could be used. Individual customer payment histories may be used, or information may be broken down by other categories such as credit rating, internal credit score, size, industry, or location. The cost of a more detailed analysis must be weighed against the expected improvement in the accuracy of the forecast.

E. Forecast Method Selection

1. **Data Relationships -** The relationship between the available data and the cash flow components to be forecast should be determined in order to select the appropriate forecasting method.

This determination can be done informally by viewing the data graphically, or a more formal analysis may seek to establish a statistical relationship.

Daily cash disbursements may be modeled as a function of recent invoices; monthly cash collections could be based on prior months' credit sales.

2. **Method Selection** - A forecasting method is selected after the relationship between the input data and the cash flow to be forecast is established. For example, a daily cash disbursement forecast suggests the specific identification and grouping by payables type for cash scheduling. The monthly cash collections example indicates the application of a statistical model to forecast when sales will result in cash receipts.

3. **Testing Relationships** - Sample input data is used to test the accuracy of the selected method. The result is a model used to forecast cash flows.

F. Forecast Validation

After developing a model, validation is required. This should be done on two levels.

1. **In-Sample Validation** - In-sample validation tests how well the model works using the historical data from which the model was developed. From this series of "forecasts" the differences are calculated between the actual and predicted values. The differences, residuals, indicate how accurately the model fits the past data.

2. **Out-of-Sample Validation** - Out-of-sample validation tests the accuracy of the model using data not involved in the model's estimation. For example, if three years of monthly data are available, the model can be estimated using the first 30 months of data. The model can then be used to predict the last six months. Residuals from the out-of-sample validation will generally be higher than the in-sample validation.

3. **Ongoing Validation** - Continuing feedback from projected versus actual comparisons allows continuous evaluation and refinement of the model.

IV. Short-Term Forecasting

An accurate short-term forecast is based on information relating to receipts and disbursements that will occur in the near future.

When used with the individual cash flow details, a number of methods help develop short-term cash projections. These are:

A. Receipts and Disbursements Forecast

This is a basic method used for short-term cash forecasting. The receipts and disbursements forecast begins with the creation of separate schedules of cash receipts and cash disbursements. Both schedules are prepared on a cash basis.

1. **Receipts Schedule** - Receipts schedule consists of a projection of collections from customers (cash sales or payments on accounts receivable) and unearned income such as interest or dividends received from investments. Proceeds from the sale of assets would also be included.

2. **Disbursements Schedule -** A disbursements schedule involves a forecast of purchases and other outflows like payroll, taxes, interest, dividends, rent and payments of principal.

The forecast itself (see Exhibit 10-1) combines the two schedules and a decision about the minimum cash balance the firm would be comfortable holding during the forecast period.

In Exhibit 10-1, the firm has determined its minimum cash requirements to be $50,000 to cushion it against unexpected expenses or to allow it to take advantage of unanticipated opportunities.

The beginning cash in each month is the ending cash from the prior month.

The final two lines of the forecast represent the forecasted surplus or deficit cash position in each month. With this information, the firm can better manage its borrowing and investing activity.

B. Distribution Method

The distribution method is used in many short-term cash forecasting situations.

1. The distribution forecast is the total estimated cash flow to be allocated to the days of the forecast horizon. The total is spread over the days in the forecast horizon by multiplying the total by estimates of the proportions that will occur on each day.

2. These proportions can be estimated by taking a simple average of the amount of the cash flow that occurs on a given day.

Exhibit 10-1

Receipts and Disbursements Forecast

	January (000)	February (000)	March (000)
Cash Receipts	$1,000	$1,100	$ 950
Cash Disbursements	(870)	(1,450)	(1,000)
Net Cash Flow	130	(350)	(50)
Beginning Cash	100	230	(120)
Ending Cash	230	(120)	(170)
Minimum Cash Required	(50)	(50)	(50)
Financing Needed (deficit)		$ (170)	$(220)
Investable Funds	$ 180		

3. Regression analysis can be used if the amount of the cash flow that occurs on a particular day is influenced by more than one factor. For example, the amount of cash flow may depend on the day of the month and the day of the week in question.

4. For example, to apply this technique to determine the funding of monthly payroll, the total cash flow would be the total dollar amount of the payroll. The distribution method would estimate the percentage of the total that would clear on various business days after the payroll date.

5. The distribution method is accurate, allows seasonality and trends to be incorporated, and is easily and inexpensively prepared. However, a large amount of data is usually required to estimate the proportions used to spread the total, and proportions may need to be revised if conditions change.

6. Exhibit 10-2 is an example of forecasting using the distribution method.

Exhibit 10-2

Forecasting Using the Distribution Method

A company has used regression analysis to estimate the proportion of dollars that will clear on a given business day. It has determined that this proportion depends on the day of the week and the number of business days since the checks were distributed. The estimated proportions are given below.

Business Days Since Distribution	% of $ Expected To Clear	Day of the Week	Percentage (%) Effect
1	13	Monday	-2
2	38	Tuesday	0
3	28	Wednesday	2
4	13	Thursday	1
5	8	Friday	-1

Therefore, if $100,000 in payroll checks was distributed on Wednesday, May 1, the checks are estimated to clear according to the following schedule:

Date	Business Days After Distribution	Day of the Week	% Clearing	$ Forecast
May 2	1	Thursday	13%+1%=14%	$14,000
May 3	2	Friday	38%-1%=37%	$37,000
May 6	3	Monday	28%-2%=26%	$26,000
May 7	4	Tuesday	13%+0%=13%	$13,000
May 8	5	Wednesday	8%+2%=10%	$10,000

V. Long-Term Forecasting

Long-term forecasts project earnings, cash flow and cash requirements on an annual basis. The major techniques include:

A. Pro-Forma Statements

Projected income statements and balance sheets can form the basis of predicted cash flows over a longer forecast horizon. They are based on the percentage-of-sales method, as illustrated in Exhibit 10-3.

Percentage-of-Sales - With the percentage-of-sales method, financial statements are projected based upon future sales and the historical relationship between sales and balance sheet items such as cash, accounts receivable, inventory, and accounts payable.

The percentage of sales method can be developed in the following way:

1. Generate the sales forecast, working closely with sales managers, product managers and the top management of the company.

2. Determine the items on the balance sheet and income statement that can be assumed to be a constant percentage of sales. The percentage can be estimated from the most recent year's financial statements by using regression analysis.

3. Assume that the other balance sheet and income statement items are either constant or updated, based on available information. For example, the level of long-term debt is projected on the basis of the current amount outstanding plus scheduled changes.

4. After these projections are generated, total required assets usually do not equal total liabilities and equity. If the assets are smaller, the firm has a cash surplus; if the assets are larger, the firm has a cash shortage that will have to be financed through debt or equity.

B. Adjusted Net Income

Another approach to long-term forecasting is the adjusted net income method.

The projected sources and uses of funds are calculated from the firm's financial statements in order to derive projected cash flows. Non-cash charges and changes in balance sheet accounts are added back to the forecast of net income to forecast the net cash flow.

1. **Sources**

    *   Cash flows from operations (net profit plus non-cash charges) represent a source of cash.

    *   Decreases in assets

    *   Increases in liabilities

Exhibit 10-3

Forecasting with Pro-Forma Financial Statements

Assume the following income statement and balance sheet (in thousands) represent the firm's actual position as of December 31, 199X.

Income Statement

Sales	$2,000
Cost of Goods Sold	(1,500)
Selling & Administrative Expense	(200)
Depreciation	(100)
Interest Expense	(38)
Income Before Taxes	162
Taxes (34% x 162)	(55)
Net Income	$ 107

Balance Sheet

Cash	$ 100	Payables	$ 50
Receivables	300	Notes (12%)	150
Inventory	200	Bonds (10%)	200
Net Fixed Assets	400	Common Equity	600
Total Assets	$1,000	Total Liabilities & Equity	$1,000

To generate the percentage of sales forecast, the following assumptions are made (all numbers in thousands):
Cost of goods sold, selling & administrative expenses, payables and all current assets are a constant percentage of sales.
Depreciation will be $50.
Notes will be reduced to $100 at the beginning of the year.
Dividends will be $24.

Projected Income Statement (in thousands) December 31, 199X

Sales	$2,200	
Cost of Goods Sold	(1,650)	(75% of sales)
Selling & Administrative Expense	(220)	(10% of sales)
Depreciation	(50)	
Interest Expense	(32)	(.12 x 100 + .10 x 200)
Income Before Taxes	248	
Taxes (34% x 248)	(84)	
Net Income	$164	

Exhibit 10-3 (Continued)

Forecasting with Pro-Forma Financial Statements

Projected Balance Statement (in thousands) December 31, 199X

Cash	$ 110 (5% of sales)	Payables	$ 55 (2.5% of sales)
Receivable	330 (15% of sales)	Notes	100
Inventory	220 (10% of sales)	Bonds	200
Net Fixed Assets	350	Common Equity	740
($400 - depreciation)		(600 + retained earnings (164 - 24))	
Total Assets	$1,010	Total Liabilities and Equity	$1,095

Note that the difference, $85 represents the difference between total liabilities plus equity and total assets. This difference is usually plugged back into cash to balance the balance sheet. The same answer can be generated using the adjusted net income approach. Here, net cash flow is projected liabilities and net worth minus projected assets.

Adjusted Net Income

Sources of Cash		**Uses of Cash**	
Cash Flow from Operations	$214 (164+50)	Increases in Assets	$60 (10+20+30)
Decreases in Assets	0	Decreases in Liabilities	50 (150-100)
Increases in Liabilities	5 (55-50)	Dividends	24
Total Sources	$219	Total Uses	$134

Net Cash Flow $85

2. **Uses**

   • Increases in assets

   • Decreases in liabilities

   • Capital expenditures

   • Dividend payments

Net cash flow is equal to the sources minus the uses. This method is also illustrated in Exhibit 10-3.

VI. Medium-Term Forecasting

Medium-term forecasts range from one month to one year. The forecasting methods used by companies vary. All of the previously defined short- and long-term methods can be used.

VII. Statistical Forecasting

Statistical forecasting is based upon models using one or more equations to describe the relationship between the cash flow to be predicted and one or more input variables. Statistical forecasting can be useful when there is a large population to be sampled and when trend analysis can be applied.

A. Time Series Forecasting

A time series model seeks to forecast a variable based only on past observations of that variable.

1. **Simple Moving Average** - Simple moving averages are extrapolative methods that base a forecast on a simple average of past values of the variable to be predicted.

   A one-step ahead forecast is prepared by calculating the average of some number, (N), of the most recent actual values for the cash flow in question. Because each observation used in the estimation has the same weight, (1/N), the speed with which the forecast adjusts to trends or seasonal variations depends on N. When N is large (e.g., over 50), then the most recent cash flow has very little influence on the forecast.

   A forecast prepared using a simple moving average will always lag any trend in the actual cash flow.

2. **Exponential Smoothing** - Exponential smoothing is a variation on a simple moving average that may be more accurate. Different weights are assigned to each observation in the sample. The most recent observation is assigned the largest weight and earlier observations are assigned successively smaller weights.

   • A simple exponential smoothing forecast is given by the following expression:

   $$F_{t+1} = F_t + \alpha(X_t - F_t)$$

   Where: F_{t+1} = Cash Flow forecast for period (t+1)

   F_t = Cash flow forecast for period t

   α = Smooting constant ($0 < \alpha < 1$)

   X_t = Actual cash flow for period t

The equation shows that the exponential smooting forecast for the next period is equal to last period's forecast plus a correction α times the residual $(X_t - F_t)$ for the most recent forecast error.

- A large smoothing constant has the same effect as a small (N) in a simple moving average; a smoothing constant of 1.0 causes the forecast for the next period to be the same as for the current period actual. Regardless of smoothing constant size, the most recent observation exerts more influence on the direction of the forecast than do earlier observations.

  As in simple moving average forecasts, a simple exponential smoothing forecast will lag any trend in the data. To correct for this, and to allow seasonality in the forecast, there are extensions of exponential smoothing that allow the user to incorporate trend and seasonality.

Exhibit 10-4 *(page 196)* shows a forecast using both the moving average and exponential smoothing techniques.

B.   Regression Analysis

Regression analysis is a statistical technique that establishes the best linear relationship between the variable to be predicted, the independent variable, and one or more input, or explanatory variables. It is often used in conjunction with the distribution method for forecasting cash flows. A computer is necessary to develop regression models of any practical size.

Day	Cash Flow	Moving Average Forecast		Exponential Smoothing Forecast	
		Forecast (N = 5)	Error	Forecast (α = .4)	Error
1	110				
2	120				
3	115				
4	122				
5	126				
6	124	118.6	5.4	118.6*	5.4
7	129	121.4	7.6	120.76	8.24
8	133	123.2	9.8	124.06	8.94
9	132	126.8	5.2	127.64	4.36

For example, the moving average forecast for day 6 is:

(110 + 120 + 115 + 122 + 126)/5 = 118.6

which results is a forecast error of 124 - 118.6 = 5.4

The exponential smoothing forecast for day 7 is:

118.6 + (.4 x 5.4) = 120.76

which results in a residual of 129 - 120.76 = 8.24

* The exponential smoothing forecast for day 6 is assumed to be the average of the previous five observations. This is a rather arbitrary choice, but initialization of some type is always required for exponential smoothing.

Questions

The chapter questions are to test the information in the text and are not examples of CCM examination questions nor are they in the examination format.

Answers can be found at the back of the book on p. 328.

1. What are the major objectives of cash forecasting?

2. What is a cash forecasting horizon?

3. What are the major steps in the forecasting process?

4. What are the two major short-term forecasting methods?

5. One long-term forecasting method is the use of pro-forma statements. What is the technique that is used to prepare a pro-forma statement?

6. In the adjusted net income method, what are the major sources and uses of cash?

7. What is time series forecasting?

8. The following cash flow information is provided:

Day	Cash Flow
1	100
2	150
3	250
4	210

What is the moving average forecast for day 5?

9. How does exponential smoothing differ from the simple moving average forecast?

Investments ████

Chapter 11

Overview

This chapter compares the long- and short-term investment functions of the company. It describes why a short-term investment program is important and how investment policies and procedures are determined. The chapter includes a description of investment risks, frequently used short-term investment instruments, and examples of short-term investment strategies and guidelines.

Learning Objectives

Upon completion of this chapter and the related study questions, the reader should be able to do the following:

1. Discuss how authority and responsibility for short-term investments are usually assigned in the company.

2. Describe typical company investment guidelines.

3. Discuss factors that influence short-term investment yields.

4. Explain how prices are quoted for short-term investment instruments and how yields are calculated according to money market, bond-equivalent, and effective annual yield quoting conventions.

5. Explain the term structure of interest rates and how yield curves change under various market environments.

6. Describe the most frequently used short-term government, agency, municipal, bank, and corporate short-term investment instruments.

7. Discuss the difference between active and passive short-term investment strategies, and other more specific strategies such as matching, riding the yield curve, and dividend capture.

Outline

I. **Long- and Short-Term Investments**

    A. Liquidity Reserve

    B. Temporary Excess Funds

    C. Income Generation

II. **Investment Policies and Guidelines**

    A. Investment Objectives

    B. Responsibility

    C. Factors that Influence Investment Policies

    D. Investment Guidelines

III. **Factors that Influence Yields**

    A. Maturity and Yield Curves

    B. Marketability

    C. Default Risk

    D. Tax Status

IV. **Investment Instruments**

    A. Financial Markets

    B. U.S. Treasury Securities

    C. Federal Agency Securities

    D. Municipal Securities

    E. Bank Instruments

    F. Repurchase Agreements (Repos)

    G. Corporate Obligations

V. **Yield Computations**

    A. Yield Characteristics

    B. Yield Quoting Conventions

    C. Yield Calculations

Outline (Continued)

VI. Investment Strategies

    A.   Passive Strategies

    B.   Active Strategies

I. Long- and Short-Term Investments

Companies have both long- and short-term investments. Long-term investment decision making is oriented toward projects as described in Chapter 2, The Corporate Financial Function. After determining the businesses in which it wants to compete, the company carries out its strategy by investing in projects that may include capital equipment, marketing programs and by investing in, or divesting business units. The chief financial officer (CFO) is usually responsible for investment decision-making through the process of capital budgeting and monitoring the success of investments through internal and external financial reporting.

Short-term investments are generally the responsibility of the treasury function. Companies have short-term investment portfolios for the following reasons.

A. Liquidity Reserve

A company generally needs a liquidity reserve either in the form of excess funds, unused borrowing capacity or both. A reserve is needed to manage temporary cash shortages resulting from business seasonality or delayed collection of accounts receivable.

B. Temporary Excess Funds

A company may have temporary excess funds for any of the following reasons:

1. **Timing of Long-Term Financing -** Equity or bond offerings must be large enough to be economical, and their timing is determined primarily by market conditions. A company may raise funds that will not be needed for some time in the future.

2. **Sale of Assets -** A substantial asset may be sold to produce liquid funds that have not yet been redeployed.

3. **Positive Cash Flow -** A company may gradually accumulate excess cash through positive operating cash flow.

4. **Seasonality -** A business may generate a large portion of its cash in one season, and invest some of that cash for operating expenses in other seasons.

C. Income Generation

The company seeks to generate investment income within the constraints imposed by the need for liquidity and safety.

II Investment Policies and Guidelines

A company can incur opportunity costs and lose principal through poor investment judgment, assumption of imprudent risks, assignment of investment responsibilities to unqualified personnel and fraud. Because of these risks, a company should have clearly defined and published investment guidelines, including not only the criteria for acceptable investments but also specific personnel responsibilities for defining policy, carrying out day-to-day investing, reviewing performance, and auditing.

A. Investment Objectives

A company's basic investment objectives include:

1. **Liquidity** - A short-term investment portfolio is one of several ways to preserve corporate liquidity, in addition to maintaining steady cash flow from operations as well as the ability to borrow.

2. **Minimize Risk** - All investments have some degree of risk. Investment alternatives with higher returns usually have higher risks. Controlling risk involves identifying what the risks are and determining the relationship between additional risk and additional return. How companies define investment risk parameters is covered later in this chapter.

3. **Return** - Investments should generate acceptable returns. The level of returns considered acceptable may vary by company depending on factors such as risk tolerance and resources available for selecting and monitoring investments.

B. Responsibility

1. **Policy** - In most companies, investment policy is determined and monitored by the board of directors or the executive committee.

2. **Implementation** - Implementing and influencing the investment policy may be the responsibility of the treasurer, the cash manager, a specialized investment manager or an investment staff.

C. Factors that Influence Investment Policies

A company's investment policies and decisions are influenced by factors such as the following:

1. **Purpose** - Companies have different objectives for short-term investment, ranging from providing a source of liquidity, to generating income for the company.

2. **Timing** - A portion of a company's funds may be required at all times as a liquidity reserve, while other funds may be designated for future uses. Therefore, different types of investments may be appropriate for various segments of the portfolio.

3. **Tax Status** - A company's effective tax rate determines the after-tax return from taxable investments and the desirability of tax-advantaged investments. Investment funds that are tax-exempt, such as pension assets, are managed differently than taxable funds. The tax impact must be considered in decisions on the timing of investment gains and losses.

4. **Staffing** - Carrying out an active short-term investment program requires qualified people or an outside investment management firm.

5. **Investment Restrictions** - There may be legal restrictions, industry guidelines, or internal policies that restrict the types of instruments in a short-term investment portfolio.

6. **Financial Reporting** - A company may have to show a certain type of short-term investment on its balance sheet because of the requirements of stockholders, creditors, or industry regulators.

D. Investment Guidelines

1. **Acceptable Instruments** - A company generally has a list of acceptable short-term investment instruments based on the following factors:

   - *Maturity* - For fixed-income securities, this is often considered the most important investment guideline. The prices of long-term, fixed-income securities are volatile. Prices of fixed-income securities move inversely with interest rates, and the longer the maturity, the greater the effect of rate movements on price.

   - *Quality* - The credit quality of many instruments can be determined by ratings assigned by credit rating agencies. There are rating systems for corporate bonds, bank issues, municipal obligations, commercial paper, preferred stock, and money market funds.

     * In some cases such as buying unrated commercial paper or loan participation, the investor must analyze and evaluate the credit quality of the borrower.

     * In other cases, a financial intermediary will provide credit support or **credit enhancement** by issuing an instrument such as a standby letter of credit to guarantee the obligations of the borrower. The obligation is then given the credit rating of the institution providing the credit enhancement.

   - *Marketability* - Holding marketable securities provides liquidity for a company. A security is marketable if it can be sold in large volumes quickly without making a substantial price concession. A large, active secondary market for a security ensures its marketability. However, securities for which there is a limited secondary market are often included in portfolios because of their higher yields.

2. **Diversification** - An important risk-reduction technique is diversification in terms of issuer, instrument, maturity, or other investment characteristics. For example, there may be a limitation in the percentage of the portfolio, dollar amount, or both for securities of a single issuer or instrument.

3. **Dealer, Bank and Issuer Guidelines** - Companies have quality guidelines or specific names of acceptable dealers and banks.

4. **Authority of the Investment Manager** - What instruments the investment manager can buy and sell must be specifically defined in terms of dollar amount and maturity, as well as the type of instrument.

5. **Crisis Management** - When it is suspected that an issuer may default or it is determined that a broker/dealer has encountered problems, the guidelines may require the following steps:

   - Determine the specific amount of investment, type, maturity, location, and market value.

- Notify the Treasurer, Assistant Treasurer, and Investment Officer.
- Move quickly to limit loss by instructing the custodian to deliver the securities after arranging for sale.
- Do not sell to an entity at risk.

Exhibit 11-1 shows an example of investment guidelines.

III. Factors that Influence Yields

Yield is what an investor earns (income) divided by what the investor paid (principal), adjusted to be expressed as an annual percentage rate of return. Given the purpose of a short-term investment portfolio, yield is often of secondary importance to

Exhibit 11-1

**Example of
Investment
Guidelines**

Investment Objectives

To invest in high-quality, short-term debt obligations in order to achieve the maximum yield consistent with safety of principal and maintenance of liquidity. Liquidity and preservation of capital are the paramount considerations. Yield is important but secondary to these objectives.

Responsibilities

The treasurer shall have the responsibility to select and manage the short-term investments, maintain a reasonable relationship between short-term borrowings and short-term investments and maintain a level of liquidity adequate to meet the firm's financial obligations.

Approved Investments

The following are approved investment vehicles with attached limitations:

1. U.S. Government and Agency Securities - no limits
2. Money Market Funds - no more than $1 million may be invested in any one fund.
3. Banker's Acceptances - may be up to 40% of the portfolio.
4. Repurchase Agreements - may be up to 20% of the portfolio.
5. Commercial Paper - the maximum per issuer is $2 million. Holdings of commercial paper may not make up more than 60% of the portfolio.
6. Certificates of Deposit - may represent up to 50% of the portfolio.

Exhibit 11-1 (Continued)

*Example of
Investment
Guidelines*

Constraints

Diversification

Foreign denominated securities may not exceed 10 percent of the portfolio.

Options and futures contracts may only be used in hedging positions.

Credit Quality

All domestic commercial paper purchased must be rated the equivalent of A-1 or A-1+.

All domestic CDs must be rated the equivalent of AA or higher.

Maturity

The portfolio should be mixed with 65 percent up to 2 months' maturity. The remainder may not exceed one year.

Safekeeping

Securities purchased by the company should be delivered against payment and held in a custodian account by one of the company's principal banks.

---

liquidity and safety of principal. However, there are wide variations in before- and after-tax yields even within the constraints imposed by the need for safety and liquidity. The four factors that explain the major differences in yield among potential investments are maturity, marketability, default risk, and tax status.

A. Maturity and Yield Curves

The relationship between market yields and maturity is described by a yield curve, as illustrated in Exhibit 11-2. A yield curve is a graphic representation of the differences in yield on securities that are identical except for their dates of maturity.

1. **Normal Yield Curve** - The relationship between interest rates and the prices of debt instruments is inverse. As rates rise on current issues, the prices of existing issues fall. The longer the maturity, the greater the risk of a price decline. Consequently, the most common shape of the yield curve is upward sloping, reflecting the increased risk and return associated with the increased maturity.

Exhibit 11-2

Sample Yield Curves

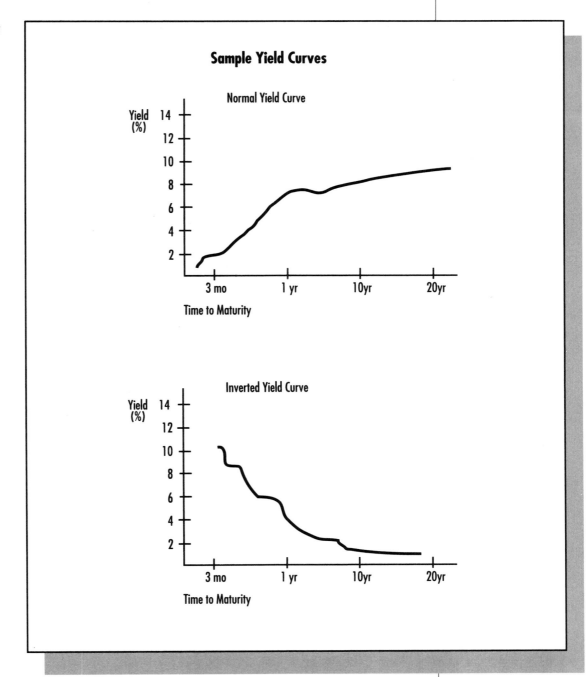

Sample Yield Curves

2. **Inverted Yield Curve -** Long-term rates may be lower than short-term rates when short-term interest rates are expected to fall. Investors buy long term securities to lock in good long-term yields. Their demand drives long-term rates down. At the same time, borrowers, awaiting lower long-term rates in the future, continue to push short-term rates up through short-term borrowing. A downward sloping yield curve is less common than an upward sloping yield curve.

B. Marketability

The marketability of securities affects the yield, because investors require a higher yield as compensation for holding securities that are more difficult to sell.

C. Default Risk

Investors require higher yield to compensate for the risk that the principal will not be repaid under the original terms. The greater the likelihood of default, the higher the risk premium, and the higher the expected yield. A risk premium is the extra yield above the yield of a risk-free security that investors require as compensation for assuming the additional risk. U.S. Government securities are considered to have no default risk, and other short-term securities are evaluated in comparison to them. Default risk is evidenced by the credit rating that is given the issue.

D. Tax Status

1. States are constitutionally forbidden to tax obligations of the U.S. Government. The income from obligations of state and local governments is exempt from federal income taxes. Securities issued by a given state are often exempt from taxes in that state, but may not be exempt from taxes in other states. Tax-exempt securities provide a lower pre-tax yield than taxable securities of similar maturity and default risk.

2. When comparing investment alternatives of taxable and tax-exempt instruments, the tax-advantaged yield is usually converted to a taxable equivalent yield as follows:

$$Y = 100 \times \frac{r}{1.0 - T}$$

Where: Y = taxable equivalent yield
T = marginal tax rate
r = taxable yield

Given a marginal tax rate of T percent on ordinary income and a taxable yield of r percent, a taxable security must yield Y percent for it to return the same after-tax yield as the tax-exempt security. For example, given a corporate tax rate of 34 percent, a tax-exempt yield of 6 percent is equivalent to a taxable yield of 9.09 percent.

$$100 \times \frac{.06}{1.0 - .34} = 9.09\%$$

IV. Investment Instruments

A company has a wide variety of short-term investment options with differing credit quality, yields, maturities and marketability.

A. Financial Markets

The financial markets can be divided into two categories. These are:

1. **Capital Market -** The capital market consists of both equity and debt instruments that mature in more than one year.

2. **Money Market -** The money market consists of debt instruments that mature in one year or less. The money market is actually a group of markets for common instruments such as Treasury bills, Federal Agency securities, municipal notes, commercial paper, bankers' acceptances, negotiable certificates of deposit, loans to security dealers, repurchase agreements (repos), and Federal funds. At the center of the market are money center banks, about 40 U.S. and foreign government securities dealers, some of which are large financial institutions, about a dozen commercial paper dealers, bankers' acceptance dealers, and money brokers specializing in short-term instruments.

B. U.S. Treasury Securities

The U.S. Government securities market consists of U.S. Treasury securities and Federal Agency securities. It is an actively traded, liquid market that appeals to a broad spectrum of investor groups.

1. **Background -** The U.S. Treasury securities market is the world's largest credit market. U.S. Treasury securities are sold to finance gaps between the Government's receipts and expenditures.

   • Yields on Treasury securities are generally the benchmark against which rates and prices in the other fixed income securities markets are compared.

   • Treasury securities are issued in both registered and bearer form. A **registered security** is registered in the name of the investor, and only that party can collect interest and principal or sell the security. There is no registration for **bearer securities**, also known as bearer paper. The holder can collect interest or principal at maturity as well as sell the security.

   • All Treasury Bills and a large fraction of all other marketable securities are now in **"book entry"** form. The physical securities do not move when they are traded. They stay in a vault at the Federal Reserve Bank of New York, and book entries are made when ownership changes.

   • Since 1971, virtually all Treasury offerings have been sold at auction. When Treasury bills are to be offered, the Treasury issues a notice of the new offering, inviting bids. Banks and broker/dealers, and other private and governmental entities tender bids for specific amounts of securities at specific yields. The securities go to those bidders offering the highest price, or lowest yield/interest cost to the Treasury.

2. **Securities** - In its financing operations, the Treasury issues the following:

- *Treasury Bills (T-Bills)* - T-Bills are the most liquid securities in the money market because of their credit quality, short maturities and volume. They are issued each week on a discount basis in maturities of 13, 26, and 52 weeks. T-Bills are available in denominations of $10,000, $15,000, $50,000, $100,000, $500,000 and $1,000,000. They are usually traded in round lots of $1,000,000. The discount rate on T-Bills is quoted in terms of the actual number of elapsed days divided by 360.

- *Treasury Notes (T-Notes)* - T-Notes are issued with original maturities of 2, 3, 4, 5, 7, and 10 years. They are available in $1,000, $5,000, $10,000, $100,000 and $1,000,000 denominations. A round lot is $1,000,000. T-Notes are interest bearing securities on which interest is paid semi-annually. Interest is calculated on the actual number of elapsed days and a 365-day year.

- *Treasury Bonds (T-Bonds)* - T-Bonds are similar to T-Notes, but with maturities ranging from 10 to 30 years.

3. **Advantages** - Treasuries offer investors several advantages such as:

- *Liquidity* - Treasury securities are actively traded in the secondary market in large volume and at narrow spreads between the bid and asked prices.

- *Credit Risk* - Treasuries are considered to be free from credit risk.

- *Taxation* - Interest income on Treasuries is exempt from state taxation. Other investment alternatives generally trade at yields above those of the government.

C. Federal Agency Securities

1. **Background**

- Federal credit agencies act as financial intermediaries. They borrow funds and use them to make various types of loans to specific classes of borrowers.

- The major federal agencies that issue debt to the market include the Federal Farm Credit Bank (FFCB), the Federal National Mortgage Association (FNMA or Fannie Mae), the Student Loan Marketing Association (SLMA or Sallie Mae), the Federal Home Loan Mortgage Corporation (FHLMC or Freddie Mac), and the Government National Mortgage Association (GNMA or Ginnie Mae). A brief overview of each agency follows.

2. **Advantages**

- *Liquidity* - Although Agency issues are smaller than Treasury issues, the liquidity of most Agencies compares favorably with other money market instruments. Agencies trade at higher yields than Treasuries of the same maturity.

- *Credit Risk* - While credit risk exists, Agency securities represent reasonable risk. Most Agency securities are not direct or indirect obligations of the government, but they are obligations of entities dealing largely with federally regulated institutions and often involve federal sponsorship and, in some cases, guarantees.

- *Taxation* - Income earned on many Agency issues is exempt from state and local taxation.

3. **Federal Farm Credit Bank (FFCB)** - The Federal Farm Credit System is a cooperatively-owned nationwide system of banks and associations that provides mortgage loans, short-and intermediate-term credit, and related services to farmers and ranchers. The Federal Farm Credit System banks issue securities on a consolidated basis under the name of the FFCB. FFCB securities are not guaranteed either directly or indirectly by the U.S. Government. Interest derived from these securities is subject to federal taxation but exempt from state and local taxation.

4. **Federal National Mortgage Association (FNMA or Fannie Mae)** - FNMA is a privately owned corporation whose function is to buy government-insured or guaranteed and conventional mortgages. To finance its mortgage purchases, FNMA relies primarily on the sale of debentures and short-term discount notes. FNMA securities are not backed by the federal government.

5. **Government National Mortgage Association (GNMA or Ginnie Mae)** - GNMA is a wholly government-owned corporation within the Department of Housing and Urban Development that makes real estate investment more attractive to institutional investors by administering mortgage-backed securities programs. Those programs provide a vehicle for channeling funds from the securities and bond markets into the mortgage market, thus increasing the overall supply of mortgage credit available for housing. GNMA guarantees timely payment of principal and interest on private issues backed by pools of mortgages which carry the full faith and credit of the U.S. Government.

6. **Student Loan Marketing Association (SLMA or Sallie Mae)** - SLMA is a stockholder-owned corporation which was established to provide liquidity to banks, S&Ls, educational institutions, state agencies and other lenders to increase the amount of funds available for lending, and to support the credit needs of students.

7. **Federal Home Loan Mortgage Corporation (FHLMC or Freddie Mac)** - The FHLMC was created to promote the development of a nationwide secondary market in conventional residential mortgages. FHLMC may purchase mortgages only from financial institutions that have their deposits or accounts insured by agencies of the federal government. FHLMC sells its interest in the mortgages it purchases through mortgage-backed securities.

D. Municipal Securities

Municipal securities are debt securities issued by state and local governments and their agencies.   Agencies of state and local governments include school districts, housing authorities, sewer districts, municipally-owned utilities, and authorities running toll roads, bridges and other transportation facilities.

1. **Bonds and Notes -** Municipalities generally issue bonds or notes.

   - *Bonds -* Most municipals are long-term bonds. State and local governments generally sell long term bonds to finance the construction of schools, housing, pollution-control facilities, roads, bridges, and other capital projects. There is an ongoing secondary market for municipal bonds which is not as active as the market for newly issued bonds.

   - *Variable-Rate Demand Bonds (VRDBs) -* VRDBs are tax-exempt obligations which may have an original maturity of five or more years and which allows the investor upon proper advance notice to tender the obligation back to the remarketing agent once a week on a predetermined day. The interest rate on VRDBs is reset weekly and paid usually on the tender date monthly or quarterly.

   - *Notes -* Municipal notes are typically sold in anticipation of the receipt of other funds.

2. **Revenue and General Obligation Securities -** Municipal securities fall into two broad categories. These are:

   - *General Obligation Securities -* General obligation securities have the full faith, credit, and taxing power of the issuing entity securing the payment of principal and interest. This usually means that the securities are backed by all of the issuer's resources and its pledge to levy taxes.

   - *Revenue Securities -* Payments of interest and principal on revenue securities are made from revenues derived from tolls, user charges, or rents paid by those who use the facilities financed by the proceeds of the security issue. Sometimes they are credit enhanced.

E. Bank Instruments

Domestic and foreign banks issue short-term certificates of deposit, time deposits and acceptances that offer higher yields than Treasuries.

1. **Certificates of Deposit (CDs)**

   - *Domestic CDs -* Domestic certificates of deposit are coupon instruments with original maturities ranging from 14 days to 5 years. Most CDs have maturities of less than one year. The minimum investment is $100,000 but CDs are usually traded in $1,000,000 units.

     * *Fixed-Rate CDs -* The interest rate is established at the time of issue. Interest is paid at maturity for CDs that mature in less than one year and semi-annually for those maturing in more than one year.

* *Floating (Variable) Rate CDs* - Interest is adjusted periodically to reflect prevailing interest rates. On 6- month CDs, interest is paid and the rate is reset every 30 days. For CDs with maturities of one year or longer, interest is paid and the rate is reset every three months. The rate is a spread over a widely-used index rate such as the 90-day T-Bill or a composite of LIBOR from several banks.

* *Yankee CDs* - U.S. dollar-denominated CDs issued by foreign banks through their branches in the U.S. market.

* *Eurodollar CDs* - U.S. dollar denominated CDs issued by banks, including branches of U.S. banks, outside the U.S. Original maturities vary from 14 days to several years, though most have maturities of six months or less. There is a large secondary market for Eurodollar CDs. Eurodollar CDs offer marginally higher yields than domestic CDs because they are slightly less liquid and expose the investor to sovereign risk. Sovereign risk is the risk that a foreign country will not allow an obligation to be paid. It is further discussed in Chapter 15, International Cash Management.

2. **Eurodollar Time Deposits (Euro-TDs)** - Non-negotiable, fixed-rate time deposits with maturities ranging from overnight to several years issued by banks outside the United States. Most have maturities in six months or less. Eurodollar time deposits offer higher yields than similar domestic time deposits because of sovereign risk.

3. **Banker's Acceptance (BA)** - A banker's acceptance is a short-term obligation of a bank arising from an international trade transaction, generally the shipment or storage of goods.

   A BA is created when the obligor, under a letter of credit, draws a draft on a bank, receiving funds and agreeing to repay in a specified number of days. The bank stamps the draft "accepted" and sells it in the money market. A BA is the obligation of both the bank and the underlying borrower. It is a discount instrument. The discount includes both the bank's underlying interest rate and commission. Bankers acceptances are discussed in detail in Chapter 15, International Cash Management.

F. Repurchase Agreements (Repos)

1. A repurchase agreement (repo) is a transaction between a securities dealer and an investor in which the dealer sells the security to the investor with an agreement to buy the security back from the investor at a specific time and at a price that will result in a predetermined yield to the investor. The investor is lending the dealer money and the dealer is lending the investor securities. Repo transactions are done overnight, for a specified number of days, or as a continuing open contract.

2. In a reverse repurchase agreement (reverse repo), the corporate borrower (the investor) sells securities to the dealer with an agreement to buy them back for a specific price at a specific time. The corporate borrower is lend-

ing the dealer securities and the dealer is lending money to the corporate borrower.

3. The repo mechanism helps the liquidity of the government securities market overall. A repo helps dealers finance their inventory of government securities, and a reverse repo helps dealers borrow the inventory to make deliveries. The repo market itself is highly liquid, and repos offer returns slightly above treasuries for investors.

4. In a repo transaction the investor takes collateral, but is still exposed to the creditworthiness and business practice of the dealer. If a dealer fails the investor in a repo could lose the amount invested. Also, the investor must continually monitor the value of the collateral to make sure it does not drop below the value of the repo.

Investors may take collateral in the following ways, in decreasing order of effectiveness:

- Having securities physically delivered to a custodian.

- Having a custodian acknowledge that it is holding securities for the corporation's account.

- Having the dealer write a letter to the investor stating that collateral is being held for the investor's account.

G. Corporate Obligations

1. **Commercial Paper (CP)** - Commercial paper is an unsecured promissory note issued for a specific amount to mature in 270 days or less. It is issued by domestic and industrial corporations, finance companies and bank holding companies. Bank holding companies are parent companies of commercial banks.

   - Commercial paper may be interest-bearing or discounted; it is usually discounted.

   - Issuers sell commercial paper directly to investors or through dealers. Dealers include securities firms and commercial banks.

   - The issuer's obligation may be backed by a standby letter of credit, which is similar to a guarantee from a major bank or insurance company with a high credit rating.

   - Commercial paper is rated by major credit rating agencies based on factors such as liquidity, cash flow potential, earning trends, position in the industry, quality of management, and backup credit facilities.

   - Unrated commercial paper is also sold by some dealers. It is issued by companies that lack either the size or the credit quality required for a rating. Substantially higher yields are available on unrated CP, but the investor incurs greater credit risk and must analyze and follow the issuer's creditworthiness.

2. **Preferred Stock** - Preferred stock is a type of equity instrument that has preference over common stock in its share of earnings and assets. Preferred dividends are paid before common stock dividends. Preferred as well as common stock offers a tax advantage to corporate investors. Currently, a corporate investor can exclude 70 percent of dividends received from a stock from current income if they hold the stock for at least 46 days.

3. **Adjustable-Rate Preferred (ARP)** - Adjustable-rate preferred stock (ARP) is a form of preferred stock where the dividend rate is adjusted quarterly,based on current treasury yields.

4. **Money Market Preferred (MMP)** - Money market preferred stock, also known as auction-rate preferred, adjusts the dividend rate every 49 days, which is beyond the minimum holding period for the corporate dividend exclusion. The dividend rate adjustment is based on current treasury yields. Securities dealers are invited by the issuer to bid in a Dutch Auction every seven weeks. The rate that the issuer accepts at a Dutch Auction is the lowest rate at which all of the securities can be sold. Existing holders may retain their shares and receive dividends at the new rate.

V. Yield Computations

A. Yield Characteristics

Not all yields quoted in the markets are comparable. Investors and borrowers have a problem in comparing all of their financing and investment alternatives because yields for various financial instruments are quoted and priced differently, and interest payments are timed differently.

1. **Interest Bearing Instruments** - Some instruments, for example, certificates of deposit (CDs), and Eurodollar deposits, pay interest in arrears, or at the end of the financing period. They are called interest bearing instruments. Eurodollar deposits are U.S dollar-denominated deposits in banks or bank branches located outside the United States, but not necessarily in Europe.

2. **Discount Instruments** - Other instruments, such as Treasury bills and bankers' acceptances are discounted; the investor pays the face value of the instrument minus the interest (the discount) and receives the face value at maturity. The discount is the face value multiplied by the discount rate, times the number of days divided by 360.

   • A discount rate understates yield because it is calculated from the face value, whereas yields are computed as a percentage of purchase price.

   • The investor's yield for the investment period is the discount divided by the price paid (the face value minus the discount.)

3. **Days in the Year** - Most short term instruments, commercial paper and Treasury bills, for example, pay interest calculated on a 360 day basis. Treasury bonds and treasury notes pay interest on a 365 day basis.

4. **Nominal Yield** - The quoted yield on an annual basis for most instruments is a simple annual rate, called a nominal yield, and does not reflect compounding.

5. **Effective Annual Yield** - The most reliable way to compare all of these instruments is to calculate their effective annual yields. Effective annual yields assume compounding and are calculated on a 365 day basis. Because of compounding, effective annual yields are higher than simple annualized yields. By assuming compounding, an effective annual yield assumes that the investor always has the opportunity to reinvest funds at the same rate.

6. **Bond Equivalent Yield** - Bond equivalent yield is the nominal yield quoted on a 365-day basis.

B. Yield Quoting Conventions

To compare the yields on two different investment instruments it is often necessary to convert from one yield quoting convention to the other. A simpler way may be to convert both to an effective annual yield.

An easy way to remember the different conventions and how they relate to each other is to remember the logic of the sequence above, starting with the discount rate, converting to the simple annualized but not compounded money market yield on a 360-day year basis, moving to the still non-compounded bond-equivalent yield calculated on a 365-day basis, and finally moving to the effective annual yield, both compounded and calculated on a 365-day basis.

Summary of Yield-Quoting Conventions

Yield-Quoting Convention	Characteristics
Money Market Yield	Annualized Not Compounded 360-Day Year
Bond Equivalent Yield	Annualized Not Compounded 365-Day Year
Effective Annual Yield	Annualized Compounded 365-Day Year

C. Yield Calculations

The following formulas and sample calculations show the relationships among the dollar discount, the discount rate, the purchase price, and the discount rate for a T-bill.

Where   D =   Dollar discount
        DR = Discount rate
        PP = Purchase price
        FV = Face value (redemption value)
        DM = Days to maturity

1.   **Purchase Price for a Discounted Instrument** - The Discount is equal to the Discount Rate multiplied by the Face Value. This is multiplied by the number of days to maturity divided by 360.

$$D = (DR \times FV) \times \frac{DM}{360}$$

The Discount Rate on a period basis is equal to the discount divided by the face value. To annualize that rate, divide by the number of days in the period and multiply by 360.

$$DR = \frac{D}{FV} \times \frac{360}{DM}$$

The Purchase Price is equal to the Face Value minus the Dollar Discount

$$PP = FV - D$$

Example:

What is the purchase price of a 91-day $100,000 T-bill sold at a 7.91% discount rate?

$$D = (DR \times FV) \times \frac{DM}{360}$$

$$D = (.0791 \times \$100,000) \times \frac{91}{360}$$

$$D = \$1,999.47$$

$$PP = FV - D$$

$$PP = \$100,000 - \$1,999.47$$

$$PP = \$98,000.53$$

$$DR = \frac{D}{FV} \times \frac{360}{DM}$$

$$DR = \frac{\$1,999.47}{\$100,000.00} \times \frac{360}{91} = .0791 \text{ or } 7.91\%$$

2. **Money Market Yield for a Discounted Instrument** - The money market yield (MMY) states the annual yield of a discounted security on a short-term interest-bearing basis with a 360-day year.

$$MMY = \frac{D}{PP} \times \frac{360}{DM}$$

The above represents a two-step process. D / PP is the formula for period yield, which is then annualized. A period yield is the effective yield for a particular period such as a week, a month or a year. A 30-day instrument with a simple annual yield of 12% has a period yield of 1%.

Example:

What is the money market yield of the previous 91-day $100,000 T-bill with a discount rate of 7.91 %?

$$MMY = \frac{D}{PP} \times \frac{360}{DM}$$

$$MMY = \frac{\$1,999.47}{\$98,000.53} \times \frac{360}{91}$$

$$= 8.07\%$$

3. **Converting to Bond Equivalent Yield from a Discount Rate or Money Market Yield** - The following formula and calculation shows how the yield on a discounted security can be converted to the bond equivalent yield (365 days). Remember, this is still a nominal yield with no compounding.

$$BEY = \frac{D}{PP} \times \frac{365}{DM} \text{ or } MMY \times \frac{365}{360}$$

Example:

What is the bond-equivalent yield of the previous 91-day $100,000 T-bill with a 7.91% discount rate?

$$BEY = \frac{D}{PP} \times \frac{365}{DM}$$

$$BEY = \frac{\$1,999.47}{\$98,000.53} \times \frac{365}{91}$$

$$= 8.18\%$$

VI. Investment Strategies

A short-term investment strategy may be either passive or active, depending on the company's objectives.

A. Passive Strategies

1. With a passive strategy the investor does minimum decision making, incurs minimum credit risk, and keeps funds liquid at all times. Passive investment strategies are appropriate for companies that want to be assured that their principal is safe, and do not have the resources and risk tolerance to warrant a more active strategy and the increased yield that it may bring.

2. Overnight investment is the most basic passive investment strategy. Funds available, e.g. the amount that exceeds the target bank balance, are invested daily in a money market instrument or a fund that a bank manages for overnight investments. Many banks provide this service in the form of a sweep account that automatically transfers excess balances into an interest-earning account.

3. Firms can carry out their own overnight investment programs by investing in instruments such as repos, Eurodollar time deposits, or commercial paper. Overnight investment programs produce the lowest available rates, but they also entail minimum risk and time commitment.

B. Active Strategies

1. **Matching** - Matching is the purchase of a security with a maturity on the date that funds are required to make a payment.

   - The investor has an incentive to invest for longer periods because in a normal, upward-sloping yield curve environment investing for longer maturities produces higher yields.

   - An accurate forecast of future requirements is required to ensure that the security can be held to maturity. If cash is required sooner than expected, the security may have to be sold at a loss because of marketability problems or interest rate changes.

   - Because of these risks, companies normally match fund a portion but not all of their short-term investment reserves.

2. **Riding the Yield Curve** - In contrast to matching, the investor may choose to ride the yield curve, buying highly liquid and marketable securities such as T-bills that mature on a day different from the day a payment must be made. With such a strategy, the investor aims to take advantage of the current yield curve. There are two ways that this can be done.

   - **Normal Yield Curve/Long Maturity** - With a normal yield curve, longer-term securities offer higher yields. To take advantage of this, the firm purchases a security that matures at a time beyond a known cash need. At the time of sale, the security has a shorter maturity than it did when it was purchased. Unless interest rates have risen considerably,

Exhibit 11-3

Riding the Yield Curve

Assume a firm has a cash need in 30 days. The discount rate is 8.0 percent on T-Bills with 30 days to maturity and 8.5 percent on T-Bills with 60 days to maturity. The bond equivalent yield on matching strategy is:

$$r = \frac{365 \times .08}{360 - (.08 \times 30)} = .082 = 8.2\%$$

The bond equivalent yield from riding the yield curve (buying the 60-day bill and selling it after 30 days) is:

Price paid: $\quad P = 100 \left[\frac{1 - (.085 \times 60)}{360} \right] = 98.58$

Sale price: $\quad S = 100 \left[\frac{1 - (.08 \times 30)}{360} \right] = 99.33$

Yield: $\quad r = \frac{(99.33 - 98.58) \times 365}{98.58 \times 30} = 9.3\%$

Note that here the yield has improved by 110 basis points. While no additional *default* risk has been incurred, *reinvestment* or *interest rate risk* has. If the yield curve does not shift over the investment horizon, the firm realizes a higher yield than that afforded by other strategies. On the other hand, riding the yield curve can provide lower yields than matching if market interest rates change during the investment horizon. For example, if interest rates rose during the 30-day investment period, so that when the 60-day bill was sold the 30-day T-Bill discount was 9.5 percent, the yield would be below the yield on the matching strategy. The new sales price is:

$$S = 100 \left[\frac{1 - (.095 \times 30)}{360} \right] = 99.2$$

and the yield is:

$$S = 100 \left[\frac{1 - (.095 \times 30)}{360} \right] = 99.2$$

the price of the security will be higher when it is sold than when it was purchased. The investor's yield is higher than it would have been with a security maturing on the date cash was needed. A sample of this strategy is illustrated in Exhibit 11-3.

- **Inverted Yield Curve/Short Maturity** - With an inverted yield curve, shorter-term securities offer higher yields. The investor buys a security that matures before the known cash need, and reinvests the proceeds when it matures. As long as the yield curve does not shift, the investor earns higher rates by rolling over shorter-term investments than on an investment whose maturity matched the time cash was required.

3. **Dividend Capture** - Companies may increase the yield on their short-term investment portfolios through a dividend capture or dividend rollover program. Under this type of tax-motivated trading program, a corporation buys a stock just before the ex dividend date, the first date on which a new holder of the stock does not receive the last dividend. The stock is held for a period long enough to receive the dividend and at least 46 days to qualify for the 70 percent exclusion from taxable income.

4. **Swaps** - Swaps are exchanges of securities for other securities of similar credit quality to improve yields. In understanding swaps, it is useful to envision an investment portfolio with specific guidelines on the amount of securities in each credit quality category and a carefully managed maturity structure.

   For example, the investor analyzes the yield curve to determine the increase in yield that would result from extending a maturity, i.e., selling a security and buying one with similar credit quality but longer maturity. The investor must then determine whether the increased yield justifies assuming the additional market exposure.

   The type of swap explained here is different from interest rate and currency swaps, which are described in Chapter 13, Foreign Exchange and Interest Rate Risk Management.

Questions

The chapter questions are to test the information in the text and are not examples of CCM examination questions nor are they in the examination format.

Answers can be found at the back of the book on p. 329.

1. What are the major purposes of having a short-term investment portfolio?

2. What are some of the factors that influence a company's investment policy?

3. What are the three major areas that influence the acceptability of a financial instrument for inclusion in the portfolio?

4. What is meant by "crisis management" in conjunction with investing?

5. What are the four factors that influence yield?

6. What is an inverted yield curve?

7. What are the two major categories of financial markets?

8. What is meant by "book entry"?

9. What are the three major U.S. Treasury securities?

10. What are Federal agency securities?

11. What are the two broad categories of municipal securities?

Questions (Continued)

12. What makes municipal securities an attractive investment?

13. What are Eurodollar CDs?

14. When are banker's acceptances used?

15. What is a repo?

16. What is the maximum time-to-maturity for commercial paper?

17. What is money market preferred stock?

18. What is the purchase price of a 182-day, $100,000 T-Bill sold at a 4.53% discount rate?

19. What is the bond equivalent yield of the T-Bill in Question 18?

20. What bank product is frequently used in an overnight investment strategy?

21. What are the two major active investment strategies?

22. A firm needs cash to pay taxes in 90 days. It plans to do so by using a $10,000 T-Bill. The following maturities and rates are available:

> 90 days-4.75%
>
> 180 days-5.00%

Compare the gain from riding the yield curve with that of following a matching strategy.

Borrowing

Chapter 12

Overview

This chapter covers borrowing objectives, strategies and responsibilities. It discusses the principal types of debt instruments used by companies and how they are priced. It also covers the legal considerations and mechanics of borrowing.

Learning Objectives

Upon completion of this chapter and the related study questions, the reader should be able to do the following:

1. Describe company borrowing objectives, strategies and responsibilities.

2. Describe the principal features of borrowing instruments such as bonds, term loans, short-term bank loans, commercial paper and bankers' acceptances.

3. Discuss the most common provisions of loan agreements.

4. Describe the usefulness of credit enhancement and securitization.

5. Calculate the all-in cost for lines of credit, commercial paper and bankers' acceptances.

Outline

I. **Corporate Borrowing Strategy and Objectives**

    A. Strategy

    B. Objectives

II. **Cost of Borrowing and Credit Ratings**

    A. Rate Definitions

    B. Credit Ratings

    C. Credit Enhancement

III. **Short-Term Debt Instruments**

    A. Lines of Credit

    B. Banker's Acceptances (BAs)

    C. Commercial Paper (CP)

    D. Loan Sales and Participations

    E. Master Notes

    F. Grid Notes

    G. Trade Credit

    H. Asset-Based Borrowing

    I. Export Financing Programs.

    J. Securitization

IV. **Medium- and Long-Term Borrowing Instruments**

    A. Bonds

    B. Special Types of Bonds

    C. Debt-Equity Hybrids

    D. Industrial Revenue Bonds (IRBs)

    E. Term Loans

    F. Private Placements

    G. Medium-Term Notes

Outline (Continued)

V. Repayment of Principal

    A. Amortization

    B. Sinking Fund

VI. Legal Aspects of Borrowing

    A. Loan Agreements

    B. Promissory Notes

I.   Corporate Borrowing Strategy and Objectives

A.   Strategy

A company's borrowing strategy is part of its overall financing strategy as discussed in Chapter 2, The Corporate Financial Function. Developing and implementing a financing strategy are some of the most important ways the corporate finance function serves to maximize shareholder value. The financing strategy must be coordinated with capital budgeting, the process in which a company decides on the projects in which to invest. The process of formulating a financing strategy is based on several decisions, including the following:

* the mix between debt and equity

* the mix between fixed- and floating-rate debt

* the mix between long- and short-term debt

* the use of hedging instruments such as swaps, options and futures, described in Chapter 13, Foreign Exchange and Interest Rate Risk Management

B.   Objectives

The objectives of a company's borrowing program include the following:

1.   **Availability -** Ensure the continued availability of borrowed funds.

2.   **Cost -** Minimize the cost of borrowing.

3.   **Risk -** Minimize and balance the risks of unfavorable interest rate movements and unavailability of debt financing.

4.   **Flexibility -** Maintain as much flexibility as possible among sources of borrowed funds.

II.   Cost of Borrowing and Credit Ratings

A.   Rate Definitions

A company may borrow at either fixed or floating rates. Most long-term bonds are at fixed rates. Pricing varies with the company's credit rating. The following base rates are used to determine pricing:

1.   **London Interbank Offered Rate (LIBOR) -** The London Interbank Offered Rate is the rate offered by banks in the Eurodollar market for short-term placement of funds by other banks. LIBOR is quoted for a full range of short-term maturities including 30, 60, 90 and 180 days. It is the most commonly used base rate for international lending and is used as a base rate for domestic U.S. lending as well.

2.   **Prime Rate -** Until the mid-1970s, the prime rate was defined as the interest rate that banks charged their most creditworthy customers. It is used primarily for middle-market companies today. Large companies with top

credit ratings can usually negotiate rates at spreads over LIBOR or U.S. Treasuries, which amount to an effective cost below prime.

3. **Other Base Rate -** Other base rates that may be used include the bankers' acceptance rate, the certificate of deposit rate, and the Treasury Bill rate.

B. Credit Ratings

Credit rating agencies rate corporate bonds and commercial paper based on factors such as current earnings, leverage, future prospects of the company, and the amount of collateral assigned to the debt issue in question.

1. Credit ratings are services that issuers pay for to broaden the marketability of their debt.

2. A rating applies to a specific issue, not to the company.

3. The most widely used credit rating services include Moody's, Standard & Poor's, Fitch, and Duff & Phelps.

C. Credit Enhancement

Credit enhancement is a process in which a bank or insurance company guarantees the debt obligations of a borrower using an indemnity bond or letter of credit and the borrower's debt is issued and traded with the credit rating of the guarantor.

III. Short-Term Debt Instruments

Short-term debt instruments mature in less than one year. They are generally used to finance current assets such as accounts receivable and inventory.

A. Lines of Credit

A line of credit is an agreement between the bank and a customer in which the customer can borrow up to a specified amount during a year.

1. The major purpose of a credit line is to provide temporary or short-term funding, to back commercial paper or to provide a liquidity cushion. Some firms with very seasonal borrowing requirements have loan agreements in which the maximum amount available varies over the year.

2. Lines of credit are typically unsecured.

3. Lines of credit are either uncommitted or committed.

   • Uncommitted lines are usually made available for a one year period and can be canceled at any time by the bank. This line of credit may also be referred to as a money market line.

   • When a committed line is used, there is usually a formal loan agreement with the bank that requires compensation in the form of balances or fees. Under a committed facility the bank is obligated to provide funding up to the credit limit stipulated in the agreement.

4. In an advised line of credit, the company is formally notified of the line, its amount, availability, rates and other compensation.

    Other credit may be made available to a company once a credit relationship is established. These are referred to as internal guidance lines and do not carry terms, require compensation or attract an interest charge. They are not formal or committed facilities and usually relate to such things as foreign exchange trading activity and other services provided by the bank.

5. Bank revolving credit agreements are credit multi-year facilities in which the borrower can borrow, repay and reborrow up to a defined amount. Revolving credits are contractual commitments with loan agreements, including covenants. Usually there is a commitment fee on the unused portion, as well as a facility fee.

6. Pricing is negotiated. Some banks are willing to make a trade-off between compensating balances and the interest rate charged on advances under a line, though a formal requirement for compensating balances has become less common in recent years. The bank may take into account other aspects of the overall bank-corporate relationship in pricing the line.

7. Borrowing against the line is commonly in the form of notes drawn for varying maturities, such as overnight, 7 days or 60 days.

8. Sometimes the bank requires a clean-up period (frequently 30 to 60 days) during which there are no borrowings on the line, though this has become less common in recent years. This is to assure the bank that the line is not being used as a permanent source of funds.

9. Pricing for bank lines has three basic components:

    - *Interest Rate.* This is normally variable and tied to either the prime rate or to a money market rate, such as the Fed funds rate, or a bank rate such as LIBOR.

    - *Commitment Fee.* For committed lines, the bank charges a percentage fee, either on the total amount of the commitment or on the unused portion of the commitment. Payment is usually made quarterly. Fees vary, depending on the creditworthiness of the firm, the stated purpose of the line, and the term of the line.

    - *Compensating Balances.* Compensating balances reduce the usable amount of the loan. The balance requirement can be specified as a percentage of the total commitment, the unused amount of the commitment or the amount used. If a firm already maintains transaction balances at the credit bank, it may not need to borrow to meet the compensating balance requirement. A formal requirement for compensating balances has become less common in recent years.

10. To compute the effective borrowing rate for a line of credit, the following formula is used:

$$i = \frac{I + F}{L} \times \frac{365}{t}$$

where

i = the effective annual borrowing rate

I = the total dollars of interest paid

F = the dollar amount of fees if any, for example commitment fees, placement fees and issue costs.

L = the average usable loan (i.e., after deducting compensating balances)

t = the number of days the loan is outstanding

Example:

- A firm has an average loan outstanding of $1,000,000.
- The line of credit is a commitment for $3,000,000
- It requires no compensating balances
- The commitment fee is .25% on the unused portion of the line.
- The interest rate charged is 10%. The effective annual interest rate is:

$$i = \frac{.10(1,000,000) + .0025(2,000,000)}{1,000,000} \times \frac{365}{365} = 10.5\%$$

The commitment fee adds 50 basis points to the nominal interest rate of 10%. Had there been compensating balance requirements, the amount of compensating balances, calculated as a percentage of the total facility, would have been subtracted from the amount of usable funds in the denominator.

B. Banker's Acceptance (BA)

1. A banker's acceptance is a time draft drawn on a bank. In accepting the draft, the bank promises to pay the person holding the draft the amount stated on the maturity date. By substituting its own credit for that of the borrower, the bank creates an instrument that is negotiable, and discounts that instrument in the money market. BAs are a widely used short-term investment instrument for corporate and institutional investors.

2. Acceptances are discounted short-term instruments used primarily to finance the import, export or domestic shipment of goods or the storage of readily marketable staples. Acceptance financing is often provided to a buyer or seller in connection with a letter of credit, but acceptances can be created to finance open account transactions as well.

3. The all-in rate for acceptance financing includes the acceptance discount rate plus the bank's acceptance commission. This often compares favorably with bank short-term borrowing.

4. Acceptance financing, including the criteria for eligibility, and examples, are discussed in further detail in Chapter 15, International Cash Management.

C. Commercial Paper (CP)

Commercial paper is an unsecured promissory note issued for a specific amount, with maturities ranging from overnight to 270 days. SEC registration is required on debt instruments with a maturity of more than 270 days.

1. **Cost -** Large companies with the highest credit rating can generally borrow through issuing commercial paper at a lower rate than through bank debt. In effect, the borrower is going directly to the investor. The underwriter or agent takes a fee. In contrast, a bank that makes a loan and keeps that loan on its balance sheet must charge a higher rate because it has both administrative costs and capital requirements.

2. **Distribution -** Commercial paper is usually sold through a dealer, either an investment banking firm or a commercial bank. Some companies sell commercial paper directly to investors.

3. **Back-Up Lines of Credit -** Commercial paper borrowers arrange back-up lines of credit that may be used if market conditions are not conducive to issuing commercial paper.

4. **Credit Rating -** Commercial paper is credit rated by the major rating agencies.

5. **Unrated Commercial Paper -** Unrated commercial paper at relatively high interest rates is sold by some dealers to sophisticated investors who are willing to analyze and follow the borrower's credit. This provides an additional source of funds to some borrowers that are below investment grade.

6. **All-In Cost for Commercial Paper -** Assume that a company is issuing $20,000,000 of commercial paper with a 30-day maturity at a discount rate of 8%. The paper is sold through a dealer at an annual charge of 1/8 of 1%. The company has a backup line of credit in the amount of $20,000,000 and pays an annual commitment fee of .25% on the line.

- Since the commercial paper is sold at a discount, the firm will receive only $20,000,000 less 30 days' worth of interest at 8%. The amount of usable funds is:

Face value x (1 - discount x $\frac{\text{maturity}}{360}$)

= $20,000,000 x (1 - .08 x $\frac{30}{360}$)

= $19,866,667

(Note that the maturity is divided by 360, following the U.S. convention.)

- The interest cost is the difference between the face value of $20,000,000 and the funds received, $19,866,667, which equals $133,333.

- The dealer cost is:

(0.00125 x $20,000,000) x (30/360) = $2,083.

- The back-up line of credit has a total annual cost of:

(.0025 x $20,000,000) = $50,000.

However, if the intention is to use commercial paper on a fairly continuous basis, only one-twelfth of this cost, $4,167, is attached to this issue. The total issuing costs are:

$133,333 + $2,083 + $4,167 = $139,583.

- The effective annual interest cost is determined by dividing the total costs by the amount of usable funds and annualizing this rate. The effective annual cost is:

$$\frac{\$139,583}{19,866,667} \times \frac{365}{30} = 8.55\%$$

- The yield to the investor is:

$$\frac{\$133,333}{19,866,667} \times \frac{365}{30} = 8.17\%$$

D. Loan Sales and Participations

In a **loan sale** program, a bank makes a loan and sells all or a part of that loan to investors. In a **participation,** a bank signs an agreement to share part of an existing loan with another lender. Loan sales and participations are generally done only with the borrower's concurrence. Investors include the full range of institutional investors, including foreign and regional banks. The bank may sell the loan at a spread below the rate paid by the borrower. For example, the borrower may pay the bank 8% and the bank may sell the loan to the investor at a 7-7/8% yield. When banks make loans with the intention of reselling them they can sometimes charge lower rates than if they planned to keep those loans on their balance sheets. A loan sale program can be a useful funding source for a company not large enough, or with financing needs not large enough to justify a commercial paper program.

E. Master Notes

This type of borrowing is between highly rated companies and the trust departments of major banks. The borrowing company creates a note with a maturity of two or three years. It specifies a maximum and a minimum amount that the trust department will lend to the company. The amount loaned can fluctuate on a daily basis. The pricing is often set at a small spread above the company's commercial paper rate. This rate is set and confirmed by telephone daily.

F. Grid Notes

This arrangement under a line of credit is intended to simplify the paperwork connected with the loans. The company signs one comprehensive promissory note under which borrowing takes place. Any loans under the terms of the note are simply recorded on the note.

G. Trade Credit

Trade credit consists of terms provided by vendors, for example with **open account**, the buyer can generally pay for merchandise up to thirty days after invoice date with no financing charge. Taking full but not excessive advantage of trade credit is normally part of a company's overall financing plan. This is covered in Chapter 5, Accounts Receivable and Credit Management.

H. Asset-Based Borrowing

Financial institutions specialize in lending based on the pledging of accounts receivable and inventory as collateral for the loan.

1. **Accounts Receivable**

    - In the case of accounts receivable financing, lenders get to know the type of customers who buy from the borrower and the delinquency and losses the borrower has experienced.

    - Lenders monitor the borrower's accounts receivable aging schedule.

    - An advance rate governs the maximum amount that can be borrowed; it is a percentage of accounts receivable.

- Customers of the borrower may be required to send payment directly to the lender

2. **Inventory**

   - The lender becomes familiar with the industry and how to value inventory.

   - Generally, lenders are more willing to advance against finished goods than work in process.

   - As with accounts receivable financing, borrowing is limited by the advance rate. In determining the advance rate, the lender has to consider the risk that the borrower will not be able to sell the inventory for reasons such as spoilage or obsolescence.

3. **Factoring -** Factoring is the sale or transfer of title of the accounts receivable to a third party (factor). A factor is a financing institution that discounts acceptable accounts receivable with or without recourse to the company discounting the receivables in the event of a loss.

   - The borrower's customers are notified to remit directly to the factor. For this service, the factor charges a percentage commission on the amount of receivables discounted.

   - The borrower may collect funds from the factor on the average due date, or pay additional financing charges for earlier funding.

4. **Floor Planning -** This type of financing is used frequently to support the inventory of high value items such as automobiles, trucks and farm equipment dealers. The lender advances funds to the manufacturer as each unit is sold and retains legal title to the automobile until it is sold.

I.   Export Financing Programs

Export financing is available from commercial banks and from the Export Import Bank of the United States. It is discussed in detail in Chapter 15, International Cash Management.

J.   Securitization

Securitization is a financing technique in which a company issues securities backed by selected financial assets. Debt service for the securities is supported by the cash flow from these assets.

1. Securitization is a type of off-balance sheet financing. Neither the financing nor the assets financed appear on the company's balance sheet. Off-balance sheet financing can be advantageous for two reasons. These are:

   - Removing debt financing from the balance sheet improves leverage ratios and protects borrowing capacity.

   - Securitized financing with a specific source of repayment such as accounts receivable may command a better borrowing rate than financing based on the company's balance sheet.

2. Assets suitable for securitization have the following characteristics:

   - A determinable, steady cash flow to service the debt

   - A low level of historical loss experience that can reasonably be predicted to remain steady in the future.

3. The most widely issued securitized debt instruments have financed credit card and automobile loan portfolios. Equipment leases and aircraft leases have been securitized as well.

4. Securitized issues achieve a high credit rating through one or more of the following types of credit enhancement:

   - Over-collateralization—selling assets that have a higher present value than that of the securities.

   - Letter of credit from a bank with a high credit rating.

   - Spread account—a reserve built from an excess of cash flow from underlying assets over cash flow required for debt service.

   - Recourse to the originator.

IV. Medium- and Long-Term Borrowing Instruments

Medium-term debt is generally considered to mature between one and five years from the date of issuance. Long-term debt has a maturity of more than five years.

A. Bonds

A bond is an interest-bearing certificate of debt by which the issuer becomes obligated to repay the principal on a specified maturity date, usually five years or more from the date of issue, and to pay periodic interest.

1. In the U.S., interest is usually paid semi-annually.

2. Bonds are usually traded publicly through securities dealers and securities exchanges, but may also be sold directly to institutional investors.

3. An investor may collect interest by presenting coupons that are detachable from the bond. Alternatively, in the case of registered bonds, which are payable only to the registered owner, the issuer mails checks to the owner.

4. A bond indenture is an agreement among all the parties to a bond issue. It defines details of the issue such as property to be pledged, if any, and the duties of the trustee.

5. Corporate bonds are administered through a trustee which is usually a bank. The trustee is responsible for ensuring that the bonds are authentic, ensuring that sinking fund and interest payments are properly paid and applied, and administering redemption. In the event of default, the trustee represents the bondholders in legal proceedings.

6. Bonds are either senior or subordinated. Holders of senior bonds have first claim on the assets of a company in the event of liquidation. All other debt

is subordinated. Subordinated debt will typically have a higher yield, because it is riskier than the senior debt. The more junior the debt, the higher the yield.

7. Bonds may be either secured or unsecured. Secured bonds are collateralized by a specific asset. Unsecured bonds, called debentures, offer no collateral. Debenture holders have a general claim against a company but not against a specific asset.

   • Secured debt gives the investor a lien against a corporate asset. Bonds may be secured by various assets including inventories, real estate or fixed (capital) assets.

   • A subordinated debenture is an unsecured bond on which payment to the holder will take place only after the senior debt has been fully paid, in the event of corporate liquidation.

   • In the event of liquidation, holders of secured debt, whether senior or junior, will be paid off before holders of unsecured debt. Then senior unsecured debt holders will be paid out before the subordinated debenture holders.

8. Corporate bonds are rated by a number of services such as Moody's and Standard & Poor's according to factors such as the financial strength and future prospects of the company and the amount of security assigned to the bond. The ratings apply to the bonds themselves, not the company.

9. A call feature on a bond allows the issuer to retire the security before maturity. Bondholders must sell the security back to the company at a predetermined premium over face value. A call provision is often useful for the issuer if there is a good possibility that interest rates will fall during the life of the bond. The firm can call the bond and refinance with less expensive debt.

B. Special Types of Bonds

1. **Junk Bonds -** Junk bonds are high-yield, below-investment grade securities. Generally a junk bond has a rating below BBB.

2. **Eurobonds -** Eurobonds are bonds issued outside the country where the currency of those bonds is domiciled. For example, dollar-denominated Eurobonds are bonds issued in U.S. dollars outside the U. S.

3. **Foreign Bonds -** Foreign bonds are issued in the country of their currency by non-residents of that country. Foreign bonds, which are issued in other than the issuer's principal operating or functional currency, appeal primarily to companies with international operations.

C. Debt-Equity Hybrids

Debt-Equity Hybrids have both debt and equity qualities.

1. **Convertible Bond -** A convertible bond is a type of bond convertible into shares of the company's common stock at a defined price. Convertible bonds allow investors to benefit from possible appreciation in the common

stock price. They provide the borrower with a lower interest rate than non-convertible bonds and the opportunity to convert debt to equity on the balance sheet.

2. **Equity Warrant -** An equity warrant is a long-term option to buy a stated number of shares of stock at a specified price (exercise price). Warrants usually have an exercise price greater than the market price of the stock when the warrants were issued. They may be purchased separately in the open market, but are generally part of a debt or preferred stock issue and are included to make the security issue more attractive. The value of a warrant moves with the value of the underlying stock.

D. Industrial Revenue Bonds (IRBs)

IRBs are a special classification of municipal bonds issued by a municipality to provide funds for a facility such as a plant that the municipality is trying to attract to the area. The 1986 Tax Reform Act limited IRBs to mostly public projects.

E. Term Loans

Term loans are made for a fixed period of time, usually several years, often with a fixed repayment schedule.

F. Private Placements

A private placement is an unregistered direct sale of securities by a company to institutional investors such as insurance companies or pension funds.

1. Terms and conditions are spelled out in an agreement called a note-purchase agreement.

2. A private placement can be arranged by an investment banking firm, a commercial bank or the borrower itself.

3. Private placements are usually less costly to arrange than publicly issued debt, and may offer longer and more flexible terms than commercial bank term loans.

G. Medium-Term Notes

Medium-term notes are notes similar to commercial paper and are usually sold in 2 to 10 year maturities. They have been useful instruments for automobile finance companies.

V. Repayment of Principal

Corporate debt can be structured to allow for any schedule of principal and interest payments. Two important considerations in debt structuring are:

A. Amortization

Amortization is the liquidation of a debt on an installment basis i.e., the repayment of the loan principal in installments over the life of the loan. Amortization schedules vary depending on the type and maturity of the loan. Many loans are amortized over their life to require the borrower to pay off the principal gradually, rather than at one point in the future. This reduces the lender's or investor's risk by shortening the amount of time the principal and interest are at risk. Some schedules provide for equal installments over the life of the loan, and others such as mortgages have equal payments incorporating both principal and interest over the life of the loan. An amortization schedule may be matched to the cash flows expected from the project or equipment being financed. Options that may be incorporated into an amortization schedule are:

- Grace periods before any principal payments are due

- Balloons, which are payments concentrated toward the final periods

- Bullet maturities in which the entire principal amount is due on the final maturity date

- Zero coupon bonds could be considered "the ultimate bullets" because no principal or interest is due until the final maturity date.

B. Sinking Fund

A sinking fund is used to retire a bond in an orderly way over its life. A company sets aside a sum of money equal to a percentage of the bond issue either annually or semi-annually. These funds are held in either cash or marketable securities or, more frequently, are used by a trustee to purchase the bonds in the open market and retire them. The investor is protected as the company will not have to retire the entire issue at maturity.

VI. Legal Aspects of Borrowing

A. Loan Agreements

1. **Covenants** - Covenants are provisions in loan agreements that restrict the borrower's activities in ways that protect the lender during the term of the agreement. Examples of covenants in loan agreements include the following:

   - *Financial Ratios:*

     Maximum debt to equity ratio

     Minimum interest coverage ratio

     Minimum net worth

     Minimum current ratio or working capital

- *Borrower Limitations:*

  Limitations on capital expenditures

  Limitations on new leases

  Limitations on incurring other debt

  Limitations on payment of dividends

  Limitations on mergers and acquisitions

  Limitations on sale or pledge of assets

  Limitations on stock or debt repurchase

- *Borrower Obligations:*

  Requirement to maintain properties

  Requirement to maintain insurance

2. **Events of Default -** Events of default include violation of covenants, not paying interest or principal when due and material adverse changes in the condition of the borrower. An event of default allows the lender to demand payment of the outstanding debt prior to its maturity, terminate the agreement or both. Covenants are often designed so that the borrower will discuss material adverse changes with the lender before they take place, and so that a waiver may be negotiated and granted at the lender's discretion.

3. **Representations and Warranties -** Representations and warranties refer to the conditions before and at the time the loan agreement is executed. They include the valid legal existence of the borrowing corporation, a resolution by the borrowers' board of directors authorizing the borrowing and the authority of the corporate officers signing the loan agreement. They may include a representation that the company is in compliance with Employee Retirement Income and Security Act (ERISA) and an indemnity protecting the lender from environmental liabilities. Some clauses may appear either as covenants or representations and warranties.

B. Promissory Notes

Promissory notes are often used for borrowings under lines of credit. A promissory note is an unconditional promise to pay a specified amount plus interest at a specified rate either on demand or on a certain date.

Questions

The chapter questions are to test the information in the text and are not examples of CCM examination questions nor are they in the examination format.

Answers can be found at the back of the book on p. 333.

1. What are the major objectives of a company's borrowing program?

2. What is LIBOR?

3. What is credit enhancement?

4. What is a committed line of credit?

5. A firm has an average loan outstanding of $200,000 on a $500,000 line of credit. There is a commitment fee of .25% on the unused portion of the line, and the interest rate on the borrowed funds is 7%. If there is no compensating balances requirement, what is the effective annual interest cost of the loan?

6. How are lines of credit used in conjunction with commercial paper?

7. A company issues $1,000,000 of commercial paper with a 60-day maturity at a discount rate of 6%. The paper is sold through a dealer for a charge of 1/4 of 1%. There is no backup line of credit. What is the effective annual percentage cost of issuing the commercial paper?

8. What is a loan participation?

9. What is floor planning?

Questions (Continued)

10. What are the two characteristics which show that an asset is suitable for securitization?

11. What is a bond indenture?

12. What are covenants?

13. Why will a company issue convertible bonds?

14. What may the lender do if a default occurs?

Foreign Exchange and Interest Rate Risk Management

Chapter 13

Overview

In recent years, there have been periods of substantial interest rate and currency volatility and methods have been developed for companies to protect themselves against these movements. This chapter describes how companies hedge themselves against interest rate and currency movements.

Learning Objectives

Upon completion of this chapter and the related study questions, the reader should be able to do the following:

1. Understand why foreign currency rates fluctuate.

2. Understand how foreign exchange rates are quoted.

3. Describe discounts, premiums, and the cash, spot and forward foreign exchange markets.

4. Understand why foreign exchange and interest rate risk are managed.

5. Understand how foreign currency and interest rate exposures may be hedged.

Outline

I. **Foreign Exchange and Interest Rate Volatility**

   A. Company Exposure

   B. Historical Background

II. **Foreign Exchange**

   A. Foreign Exchange Rates

   B. Bid-Offer Spreads

   C. Spot Market

   D. Forward Market

   E. Discounts, Premiums and Par

   F. Foreign Exchange Exposure

   G. Foreign Exchange Hedging

III. **Interest Rate Exposure Management**

   A. Interest Rate Futures

   B. Interest Rate Options

   C. Interest Rate Swaps

   D. Caps, Collars and Floors

I. Foreign Exchange and Interest Rate Volatility

A. Company Exposure

Many companies are exposed either directly or indirectly to some type of foreign exchange or interest rate risk. Here are a few of these risks:

1. An importer who agrees to pay in foreign currency in the future is exposed to an increase in the price of that currency in U.S. dollar terms.

2. An exporter who agrees to receive foreign currency in the future is exposed to a decrease in the value of the foreign currency received in relation to the U.S. dollar.

3. In both of the cases previously discussed, the importer and the exporter are equally exposed to a gain or loss. In other words, the exporter's gain is equal to the importer's loss and vice versa.

4. Exporters, importers and even companies that neither export nor import are exposed to the effect of fluctuating foreign exchange rates on foreign competitors' costs and prices. For example, inexpensive foreign imports can undermine a domestic manufacturer in its home market.

5. A company with a loan at a floating rate based on an index such as LIBOR is exposed to interest rate risk.

6. A company that borrows at fixed rates, for example in the bond market, is exposed to a possible opportunity cost if rates decline after it has borrowed a large amount. Investors may also be adversely affected.

B. Historical Background

1. **Prior to World War II -** In the late nineteenth century, there were no explicit international agreements on exchange rates, but most major trading nations established values of their currencies in terms of gold as the amount of cross-border trade grew in the late nineteenth century. This was called the Gold Standard. The Gold Standard worked reasonably well until World War I disrupted international trade. Between World War I and World War II, exchange rates were allowed to fluctuate. They were distorted by speculative pressures, competitive devaluations, and tended not to settle at a reasonable equilibrium based on supply and demand.

   In the late 1930s, the U.S. dollar was the only truly convertible currency. A convertible currency is one into which other principal currencies can be readily converted. The dollar in this period served as the principal reference against which the value of other currencies was quoted.

2. **Bretton Woods -** The Bretton Woods conference in 1944 established the International Monetary Fund, the International Bank for Reconstruction and Development (the World Bank) and the Gold Exchange Standard.

   - The International Monetary Fund provided temporary assistance to countries having difficulty maintaining their exchange rates or having structural trade problems.

- The World Bank provided loans to public agencies in developing countries for infrastructure projects and to private companies as well.

- Under the Gold Exchange Standard, each country fixed an exchange rate in relation to gold, though only the U.S. dollar would be actually convertible into gold. Countries agreed to try to keep the value of their currencies within one percent of the par values they had established. A devaluation of more than ten percent required International Monetary Fund approval.

- The Bretton Woods agreement collapsed in the 1970s when the U.S., desiring to devalue the dollar, withdrew.

3. **Cooperation Among the Top Industrial Nations -** The finance and foreign ministers of the seven leading industrial nations, the G-7 Group (U.S., Japan, England, France, Germany, Canada, and Italy), meet periodically to discuss measures to reduce foreign exchange volatility. Central banks intervene in the currency markets through buying and selling currencies in order to influence exchange rates. Sometimes the possibility of central bank intervention proves to be enough to influence the market in a particular direction.

4. **Interest Rate Volatility of the Early 1980s -** Corporate treasurers became increasingly sensitive to interest-rate exposure in the early 1980s when the Federal Reserve Board adopted a monetarist policy in fighting inflation and was willing to let short-term rates exceed 20 percent.

5. **New Hedging Products -** Increasing concern with both foreign exchange and interest rate volatility led to the development of new financial products. Interest rate and currency swaps, options, and futures and other derivative products were introduced.

II. Foreign Exchange

This section describes how foreign exchange rates are quoted, how foreign exchange transactions are implemented, and how a company quantifies its foreign exchange exposure.

A. Foreign Exchange Rates

A foreign exchange rate is the equivalent number of units of one currency per unit of a different currency. There are two ways to quote foreign exchange rates: the U.S. dollar equivalent of a unit of the foreign currency, or the amount of the foreign currency per U.S. dollar. Financial newspapers such as The Wall Street Journal quote rates for major currencies in both ways on a daily basis.

The following example shows how the rates of selected foreign currencies are sold are quoted every business day in The Wall Street Journal:

	U.S. $ Equivalent	Currency per U.S. $
British Pound (GBP)	1.68	.59
German Deutschemark (DEM)	.57	1.75
Japanese Yen (JPY)	.0073	136.99

In this example, a British Pound would cost $1.68 or a U.S. dollar would cost £.59.

B. Bid-Offer Spreads

Banks and other dealers quote both bid and offer rates for foreign currency. The bid rate is the rate at which a bank is willing to pay to purchase currency. The offer rate is the rate at which a bank is willing to sell currency. The spread between the bid rate and the offer rate provides income for the bank. For example, if the bank provided a quote of DEM 2.89 -.95 = $1, it would purchase a dollar for 2.89 DEM (bid) and would sell a dollar for 2.95 DEM (offer).

C. Spot Market

A rate quoted in the spot market for currency is called a **spot foreign exchange rate (spot rate).** These rates are generally quoted for delivery two business days from the date of the transaction. Exceptions may be made, but usually at the expense of a rate higher than the quoted spot rate. In the North American market, the Canadian currency spot value is quoted for delivery the next business day.

D. Forward Market

The forward foreign exchange market is a market in which an exchange rate for a future exchange of currencies can be fixed today.

1. A forward foreign exchange rate (forward rate) is an exchange rate established today for a currency transaction that settles more than two days in the future.

2. A forward foreign exchange contract is a commitment to buy or sell a specified quantity of foreign currency at an exchange rate set today for delivery on a specific date more than two business days in the future for major currencies, and more than one business day for Canadian dollars.

3. Forward foreign exchange rates are based on the spot exchange rate and the borrowing and lending interest rates in the two currencies. This phenomenon is known as interest rate parity.

E. Discounts, Premiums and Par

The terms discount, premium and par, describe the relationship between spot and forward exchange rates. In the forward market, every currency can be said to trade at a discount, a premium or par with respect to the spot rate for that currency.

1. A currency is at a discount if it is worth less in the forward market than in the spot market.

2. A currency is at a premium if it is worth more in the forward market than it is in the spot market.

3. If the spot and forward values are the same, then the forward rate is at par to the spot rate.

F. Foreign Exchange Exposure

There are three different types of foreign exchange exposure: transaction, translation and economic exposure.

1. **Transaction Exposure** - Transaction exposure is the exposure of balance sheet accounts such as accounts receivable, accounts payable or loans to a change in foreign exchange rates between the time a transaction is booked and the time it is paid.

   For example, a U.S. exporter sells merchandise to a French buyer, agreeing to accept payment in French francs three months from now. The exporter books the account receivable now. The exporter is exposed to a possible loss if the value of the French franc declines in dollar terms. For example, the exchange rate for the French franc may change from two francs to the dollar to four francs to the dollar between now and when the payment is received.

2. **Translation Exposure** - An exposure is created when a foreign subsidiary's financial statements are translated into U.S. dollars in order to be consolidated into the parent's financial statement. Translation exposure is the net total of the exposed assets less the exposed liabilities. The Financial Accounting Standards Board (FASB 52) requires a company to include in its income statements gains and losses on import and export transactions and to report gains and losses on the value of its non-domestic subsidiaries as an adjustment to equity except when the subsidiary is in a high inflation country, as defined by the FASB. These adjustments do not have any impact on either the parent's or the subsidiary's cash flow. There is also no effect on earnings per share.

3. **Economic Exposure** - Economic exposure is the long-term effect of transaction exposure on the present value of cash flows to the firm. For multinational firms, this arises primarily because the firm is doing business in many different currencies and, in the long term, will always be subject to additional fluctuations in its cash flows because of exchange rate changes. Economic exposure even exists for firms dealing in domestic sales denominated solely in U.S. dollars. It arises because changes in foreign exchange rates can alter the competitive relationship with other firms, which may be non-U.S. firms or U.S. firms with foreign manufacturing capabilities.

G. Foreign Exchange Hedging

Once a company has identified and quantified its foreign exchange exposure it can decide whether to hedge it fully, partially or not at all.

The tax consequences of the various strategies should be assessed before implementation.

1. **Forwards** - The most common form of foreign currency hedging is arranging a forward contract at a specific date in the future to either buy or sell a specific amount of foreign currency. An importer arranges to buy the amount of currency needed when the payment is due. An exporter arranges to sell the amount of currency received when the payment is expected. Forward contracts are typically for six months or less but may be arranged for periods of up to three years.

2. **Futures** - Foreign exchange futures are similar in concept to forwards but are highly standardized contracts offered for only a few major currencies like the British pound and the Japanese yen. Futures contract involve large amounts of the currency and mature at fixed dates. They are traded on the International Monetary Market of the Chicago Mercantile Exchange and on the New York Futures Exchange. Because the contracts trade on their own they do not require an underlying commercial transaction. Futures contracts are available on a variety of other financial instruments and commodities.

3. **Options** - An option is a right, but not an obligation, to buy or sell foreign currency at a specific price within a fixed period of time. Options are available on a variety of other financial instruments and on the futures contracts for those instruments.

   - A call option gives the holder the right to buy foreign currency.

   - A put option gives the holder the right to sell foreign currency.

   - The price at which the option can be exercised in the current market is called the strike price.

   - The buyer of the option pays a premium to the seller of the option. If the buyer exercises the option, the option is binding on the seller.

   - An American option can be exercised at any time up to and including the expiration date. A European option can be exercised only on the expiration date. Either type can be bought or sold any time prior to expiration.

   - The buyer of a call option and the seller of a put option will benefit from an increase in the price of the underlying currency. Conversely, the buyer of a put and the seller of a call will benefit from a decrease in the price of the underlying currency. The roles of buyers and sellers in option transactions are illustrated in Exhibit 13-1.

   - A call option in which the market price of the underlying currency has risen above the strike price is said to be in-the-money. The option holder could "call" (buy) the currency at the strike price then sell it in the

Exhibit 13-1

Option Buy-Sell Grid

	Call	Put
Option Buyer	Has Right To Buy	Has right to sell
Option Seller	May have to sell	May have to buy

market at a profit. If the strike price equals the market price the option is in-the-money. Otherwise the option is out-of-the-money.

- A put option in which the market price of the underlying currency has fallen below the strike price is said to be in-the-money. The option holder can purchase the currency at the market price and sell it for the strike price, realizing a profit. If the strike price is equal to the market price the option is at-the-money. Otherwise the option is out-of-the-money

- Option pricing varies with the price of the underlying currency, the price volatility of the underlying currency, and tends to decrease as the expiration date draws closer.

4. **Currency Swaps -** A foreign currency swap is a transaction in which two counterparts exchange specific amounts of two different currencies at the outset, and repay these amounts over time with interest. The payment flows incorporate repayment of principal and the interest rates in each currency, which can be fixed or floating.

Foreign currency swaps may allow a company to do the following:

- Reduce overall borrowing costs by enabling the company to borrow in those capital markets that provide the best comparative advantage.

- Take advantage of preferential interest rates without exchange risk. A company that borrows unhedged in a foreign currency runs the risk that the value of that currency will rise, reducing or even reversing the interest rate saving.

III. Interest Rate Exposure Management

Interest rate futures and options can be used as a hedge against interest rate risk.

A.   Interest Rate Futures

Interest rate futures are legally binding commitments to sell financial instruments at a specified future date at a specified price. They are not generally used for buying and selling financial instruments, but for generating gains and losses on the value of specific financial instruments through the purchase and sale of futures contracts.

1.   The short-term financial instruments most actively traded in the futures market are 90-day Eurodollar time deposits, 90-day Treasury Bills and 90-day bank certificates of deposit. The most actively traded long-term instruments are 30-year U.S. Treasury bonds, 10-year U.S. Treasury notes, and 5-year U.S. Treasury Notes.

2.   For both the 90-day Eurodollar and the 90-day T-Bill contracts, the face amount per contract is $1,000,000. Pricing for the Eurodollar contract is based on the London Interbank Offer Rate (LIBOR) and pricing for the T-Bill is based on the three-month T-Bill discount rate.

B.   Interest Rate Options

Interest rate options are options on financial instrument futures. If interest rates rise, the price of a financial future will fall, and if interest rates fall, the price of the future will rise.

1.   A borrower can protect interest expense for a three-month period by purchasing a three-month put option, which is an option to sell a financial future at the end of the three-month period. If interest rates rise above the strike price, the price of the financial future will fall, and the borrower can exercise the put option. That allows the sale of the financial future at a price above the prevailing market. The profit will offset the increase in borrowing cost.

2.   An investor can buy a call option to protect against a decline in interest rates for a three-month period. If rates go down, the price of the underlying financial future will go up. An investor can exercise the call, buying the financial future below market, and profiting sufficiently to offset the loss of investment income.

C.   Interest Rate Swaps

A interest rate swap occurs when two parties agree to exchange interest obligations for a specified period of time or when the sale of a security is coupled with a simultaneous purchase of a similar security with a different coupon rate.

1.   **Purpose of an Interest Rate Swap** - The purpose of an interest rate swap between two parties is usually for one party to convert a fixed-interest rate payment into a variable-rate payment while the other party takes the opposite position.

2.   **Use of Swaps** - Interest rate swaps exist because of differences in financial markets, such as different risk premiums between markets.

D.   Caps, Collars and Floors

Caps and collars allow companies to benefit from the low cost of adjustable-rate financing while protecting themselves against interest rate movements.

1.   **Interest Rate Caps** are arrangements by lenders guaranteeing that interest rates on floating-rate loans or variable-rate securities will not exceed specified levels. If a defined floating-rate index such as LIBOR exceeds the cap, then the lender pays the difference to the borrower. When rates are lower than the level defined, the borrower enjoys the full benefit, minus the cost of the cap. Pricing is either a fee or an adjustment to the interest rate on the loan.

2.   **Interest Rate Floors** are minimum interest rates for a loan or variable-rate security. They guarantee that the borrower will pay no less than an agreed-upon interest rate. For the borrower, a floor is the equivalent of writing a call option. The borrower receives the equivalent of a premium for bearing the risk that rates will decline below a certain level i.e., the strike price. If rates go below that level, the borrower must make up the difference to the lender.

3.   **Interest Rate Collars** are combinations of caps and floors, giving the holders ranges of minimum and maximum interest rates. Because the buyer of a collar is being paid for selling the floor in addition to buying the cap, a collar is less expensive than a cap.

Questions

The chapter questions are to test the information in the text and are not examples of CCM examination questions nor are they in the examination format.

Answers can be found at the back of the book on p. 336.

1. What was the purpose of the Bretton Woods Conference?

2. A bank provides a quote of SF 1.59 - .64 = $1. How much will it pay for one U.S. dollar?

3. A company purchases Japanese yen in the spot market on Thursday. When will delivery be?

4. How are forward exchange rates determined?

5. What creates translation exposure?

6. What are the four major hedging vehicles used to manage foreign exchange exposure?

7. Can foreign currency futures be used to hedge all types of foreign exchange exposures?

8. If a call option is in-the-money, what is the relationship between the market price and the strike price of the underlying currency?

9. How may an investor use an interest rate call option to protect against falling interest rates?

10. What is the purpose of an interest rate swap?

11. What are interest rate collars?

Bank Relationship Management

Chapter 14

Overview

This chapter describes how companies select banks, how bank relationships are managed, how bank services are priced, and how companies analyze bank creditworthiness.

Learning Objectives

Upon completion of this chapter and the related study questions, the reader should be able to do the following:

1. Describe how companies select banks.

2. Describe how bank relationships are managed.

3. Explain how banks are compensated.

4. Develop an understanding of account analysis.

5. Explain the methods used to evaluate bank creditworthiness.

Outline

I.   **Objectives of Bank Relationship Management**

II. **Bank Selection**
     A. Criteria for Selecting Banks
     B. Optimizing the Number of Banks

III. **Managing the Relationship**
     A. Relationship Documentation
     B. Bank Performance Measurement and Evaluation
     C. Audit and Control

IV. **Bank Compensation and Account Analysis**
     A. Bank Service Charges
     B. Fee versus Balance Compensation
     C. Account Analysis
     D. Comparing Bank Service Charges

V.   **Bank Creditworthiness**
     A. Rating Agencies
     B. Bank Credit Analysis

I. Objectives of Bank Relationship Management

A company may work with one or more banks in many ways including borrowing, investing excess funds and using a wide variety of services. Therefore, the corporate/bank relationship has many facets and involves a number of people on both sides. The treasurer tends to orchestrate the relationship on the corporate side, but the cash manager usually has the most contact with banks on a daily basis. The objectives of bank relationship management include:

- *Credit Facilities* - Ensure the company has adequate credit facilities. This has traditionally been the company's most important reason for a banking relationship.

- *Services* - Equip the company with necessary banking services, including cash management, investment, trust and interest rate and currency risk management.

- *Cost* - Manage total banking costs. This involves selecting cost-effective service providers and optimizing the number of banking relationships.

- *Compensation* - Ensure that bank compensation is fair and reasonable. While not overcompensating the bank, the company generally wants to be considered a desirable relationship.

- *Bank Exposure* - Control exposure to banks. The failure of a bank could cost a company the loss of uninsured deposits, the loss of credit facilities, and the need to replace operating service providers.

II. Bank Selection

Selecting appropriate banks for each service and optimizing the number of banks for the company's needs have become more critical. Banks have different strengths and specialties. Some have found it necessary to discontinue or sell businesses that are not profitable and concentrate their resources on services in which they have the most competitive advantage.

A. Criteria for Selecting Banks

The following are important criteria for selecting and maintaining banking relationships:

- Willingness to be a reliable provider of credit at competitive rates

- Ability to structure flexible loan terms and conditions and provide financial advice

- Knowledge of company and/or specific industry

- Responsiveness to questions and understanding of needs. Quality customer service

- Bank strategy and future direction. Commitment to a company, industry or service

- Quality and expertise of bank management, relationship managers, and technical specialists

- Financial strength of the bank

- Offering of a specific service. Ability to customize services. Innovativeness in developing new products or finding improvements for the company

- Long-term relationship orientation

- Geographic considerations and convenience

- Pricing of banking services

- Political considerations

B. Optimizing the Number of Banks

1. There are internal and external costs for each banking relationship, resulting in an incentive not to have more banking relationships than necessary.

2. Many companies seek multiple banking relationships to ensure that they have adequate credit facilities.

3. Each bank should serve a purpose in the company's banking network. Because of the increasing specialization of banks, a company may want to add a bank or justify keeping a bank because it stands out in a particular service.

4. When a company has multiple banking relationships, often one is designated a lead bank. There may be different lead banks for credit and other banking services.

5. There has been a trend toward fewer banking relationships.

III. Managing the Relationship

A. Relationship Documentation

There are important documents associated with the establishment of a banking relationship. These are:

1. **Account Resolution** - This document is the basic account authorization and is usually a board of directors' resolution.

   - It describes what banking functions can be performed by specific individuals or job titles, lists signers on the account and covers a variety of liability issues.

   - The resolution may be rather broad in scope or it may address very specific transactions and limit actions that can be taken on the part of the company.

- Many banks have standard resolutions; however, companies may have their own resolutions.

2. **Signature Cards -** Most banks require companies to furnish signatures of authorized signers or specimens of facsimile or computerized signatures.

3. **Service Agreements -** Service agreements are required for most services. Over the years, these agreements have become more formalized. The following are elements that may be included in a service agreement:

   - Operational procedures include the detailed processing requirements for the service, information needs, and identifying people who are authorized to make changes.

   - Performance standards define agreed-upon service quality.

   - Compensation includes pricing, method of payment, payment frequency, handling of residual balances, excess/deficit arrangements, contract length and adjustments.

   - Liability defines how risks will be shared.

B. Bank Performance Measurement and Evaluation

Service quality is a very important criterion in evaluating the on-going banking relationship. One of the most difficult tasks is to determine exactly what operating quality means and what is reasonable error rates for the various services. More formal methods for measuring and evaluating bank performance are being developed. The Bank Administration Institute (BAI) has undertaken a project in this area.

1. **Bank Report Cards.** - Once standards have been established with the bank, it is important to give the banks periodic feedback. Report cards can be effective tools in resolving issues and obtaining better service. They contain:

   - Number of errors by service

   - Reporting times for information services

   - Responsiveness to questions

   - Timeliness of error resolution

   - Effectiveness of certain bank personnel

   Bank report cards can be done monthly, quarterly, or annually. Some companies rank banks by specific service.

2. **Relationship Review -** Bank reviews can be done in the normal course of conversation between a company and its bank or in a more formal setting. In the latter situation, a variety of people from both the company and the bank may be involved. A formal agenda is usually prepared.

   Often the relationship review includes both senior officers and day-to-day contacts for both sides. Topics to be covered include financial performance of both parties, problems and their resolution, meeting performance standards, plans for the upcoming year, and a review of current services in use, as well as new products being introduced by the bank.

C.   Audit and Control

Audit and control of bank relationships typically involve the following:

- Institute procedures for opening bank accounts including, but not limited to, approval policies for opening of accounts, use of banks' corporate resolution or in-house developed resolution, individuals authorized to open accounts or contract for bank services, and authorized signatories.

- Establish policies and procedures for reconciliation of bank accounts. These policies and procedures should provide for timely reconciliation and segregate reconciliation duties and transaction initiation duties.

- Maintain records of bank account documentation including corporate resolutions, contracts for special services and signatories on accounts. Records must be updated for changes in services and signatories on a timely basis.

IV. Bank Compensation and Account Analysis

A.   Bank Service Charges

Banks allow companies to pay for services in fees, balances or a combination of both.

1.   **Bank Compensation Terms** - In determining the balances required for bank compensation, several terms are used.

- Collected balances required are the collected balances needed to cover the cost of services.

- Service charges are the charges, fees or costs of services provided by the bank.

- Earnings credits are used by banks to offset service charges, because banks, by law, cannot pay interest on demand deposits (Reg. Q).

- An earnings credit rate is the rate used to calculate earnings credits. It is determined by each bank and is usually tied to the T-bill rate or another measure of the bank's cost of funds.

- Reserve requirements are the balances that must be maintained by banks at the Federal Reserve. In computing bank compensation, a bank may use a percentage other than that set by the Federal Reserve.

2. **Collected Balance Calculation -** Many banks request compensation for service charges in the form of collected balances. The following formula is useful in converting service charges to collected balances required for services and vice versa:

$$CB = \frac{SC}{\left(ECR \times \frac{D}{365}\right) \times (1 - RR)}$$

Where:

CB = collected balances required for services

SC = service charges, fees or costs

ECR = earnings credit rate

RR = reserve requirement

D = number of days in the month; instead of D/365, some banks divide the ECR by 12

Example:

A company uses services with charges that total $10,000 per month. The bank's earnings credit rate is 5 percent. The reserve requirement is 10 percent. Using the formula above, the average collected balances required to compensate the bank for the services used is:

$$CB = \frac{10,000}{\left(.05 \times \frac{30}{365}\right) \times (1 - .10)}$$

$$= \frac{10,000}{(.0041 \times .90)}$$

$$= \frac{10,000}{.0037}$$

$$= \$2,702,702$$

When $1.00 is used as the service charge in the above formula, the balance multiplier is calculated. This number, multiplied by the charge for a specific service, gives the collected balances required to pay for this service. It is very useful in comparing bank prices when they are paid for in balances.

3. **Earnings Credits Calculations** - Earnings credits may only be used at a particular bank for compensation purposes.

A sample earnings credit calculation is:

Assumptions:

Average ledger balance	$250,000
Deposit float	30,000
Reserve requirement	10%
Earnings credit rate	5%
Service charges for the month	1,000

Calculations:

Average ledger balance	$250,000
Less: deposit float	(30,000)
Equals: average collected balance	$220,000

$$EC = CB \times (1 - RR) \times \left(ECR \times \frac{D}{365} \right)$$

Where:

EC = earnings credit

CB = collected balances required for services

SC = service charges, fees or costs

ECR = earnings credit rate

RR = reserve requirement

D = number of days in the month; instead of D/365; some banks divide the ECR by 12.

$$EC = 220,000 \times (1 - .10) \times \left(.05 \times \left(\frac{30}{365} \right) \right)$$

$$= 220,000 \times (.90) \times (.0041)$$

$$= \$811.80$$

$$SC = (\$1,000)$$

$$\text{Excess (Deficiency)} = (\$188.20)$$

4. **Bank Compensation Policies** - If a company has an excess balance, it cannot be paid to the firm in cash according to current regulations. Some banks allow carryovers only for limited periods, such as a quarter. Excess credits are eliminated at the end of the quarter while deficiencies must be paid to the bank in fees at that time. Other banks allow the excess (or deficiency) to be carried over into subsequent months. The period of carryover may be for one year or sometimes more. Some banks absorb the excess and start the month with no credits. Such banks usually require fee payments for deficiencies monthly.

   Most banks calculate the earnings credit on collected balances net of reserve requirements (net collected balances). Traditionally it has been applied to the monthly average net collected balance. A number of banks are applying this rate to daily positive net collected balances. With this scenario, net collected balances are not allowed to be averaged over the course of a month. A borrowing rate is applied on days when there is a negative net collected balance.

   For compensation purposes, accounts may be considered individually or on a combined basis where all the accounts for a company are added together. The latter approach is useful for a company that has excess balances in one account but a deficit in another. By combining the balances, banking costs can be reduced. With the increase in banks that have multistate banking facilities, some of them will aggregate balances throughout the entire network rather than at each individual bank.

B. Fee versus Balance Compensation

From the perspective of both the company and the bank there are advantages and disadvantages to both fee and balance compensation. In selecting the most appropriate compensation method, a company should consider the following factors:

1. **Corporate Perspective**

   - *Factors Favoring Fee Compensation:*

     * *Reserve Requirement* - Companies can generally earn higher rates on the balances than the bank can pay in earnings credits. The primary reason for this is the reserve requirement percentage and the fact that banks typically pay a very conservative earnings credit rate (ECR).

     * *Explicit Control of Bank Costs* - Many firms have changed to fee compensation for purposes of tighter cost control. Fees can be budgeted and compared with other costs, while balances are not as directly comparable.

     * *Fees Prevent Overcompensation* - Excess balances are a form of overpayment.

   - *Factors Favoring Compensation by Balances:*

     * *Transaction Balances* - In deposit systems, information and clearing delays may cause several days to elapse between the time of deposit

and the removal of funds from the deposit bank. The concentration system may be unsuccessful in removing all of these transaction balances. These balances can be used for compensation. This means payment by fees could result in overcompensating the bank.

* *Banking Relations* - Banks may view the relationship more favorably if balances are used for compensation.

* *Differential Charges for Fee Compensation* - A few banks prefer balances strongly enough to levy higher charges if services are to be paid for with fees.

* *Soft Dollar Budgeting* - Balances can be used to hide certain costs because they are not clearly identifiable for budget purposes.

- **Factors Favoring a Combination of Fees and Balances:**

* Balances can be used as the compensation base with any deficiencies being paid for with fees. In this way, the maximum amount can be invested, and the likelihood of overcompensation reduced.

2. **Bank Perspective**

- *Factors Favoring Fee Compensation*

* Bank analysts tend to regard fee income as an important element of recurring, low-risk earnings.

* For some large banks increased deposits may be considered costly because they inflate the balance sheet and contribute directly to capital requirements.

- *Factors Favoring Balance Compensation:*

* Some banks may have funding strategies which require attracting additional demand deposits.

* Because of the spread between the ECR and the actual bank investment rates, services may be more profitable when paid for in balances.

* Some banks have such strong preferences for balances that they levy higher service charges or surcharges for payment in fees, rather than balances. This cost differential must be taken into account when comparing alternatives.

3. **Target Balances** - A target balance is the desired average collected balance a company may maintain to compensate a bank for services provided. A company compensating with only fees may set a target as low as zero.

C.   Account Analysis

An account analysis is a statement, usually prepared monthly for a company by each bank, summarizing a company's transaction activity, average balances and service charges.

1. **TMA Account Analysis Standard** - In 1987, to address the problem of comparability among account analyses, the Treasury Management Association (TMA) (formerly NCCMA) with active member participation developed a standard account analysis format and a glossary of terms.

   It consists of sections with the following information:

   - Customer information

   - Current and historic balance and compensation information

   - Adjustment detail

   - Management summary of accounts

   - Service description and cost information

2. To address the problem of comparing services and service options among banks, the TMA (formerly the NCCMA) developed product family service codes descriptions. Below are some examples of these TMA service code product families:

   - *Depository services (020)* - Included here are services related to the depositing of checks or cash for credit to an account. The checks may be encoded and sorted or unencoded and mixed. Checks and drafts presented for collection, as well as the handling of all unpaid return items and all coin and currency transactions, are also a part of this product family.

   - *Lockbox services (030)* - The two fundamental aspects of these services, whether wholesale or retail, are check processing and remittance information capture and distribution. Check clearing, invoice data entry, payee verification, photocopies, reports, document scanning and the maintenance of the lockbox are the elements of this product family.

   - *Disbursement Services (040)* - All products related to the issuing, control and posting of paper-based payments are part of this product family. The handling of stop payments and other exceptions are all included services.

   - *Reconciliation Services (060)* - These products focus on the reconciliation of check payments, providing the matching of checks issued and checks paid information. Reports and document handling are among the main services. However, the reconciliation of all transactions or any subset (wire transfers, deposits, ACH transactions, etc.) are also within this product family. Matching of expected transactions to actual debit/credit postings is the essential element. TMA service codes are being revised with publication planned for mid-1993.

3. The American National Standards Institute (ANSI) has developed a standardized format, (ANSI 822 Customer Account Analysis), for banks to use in sending account analyses to companies electronically. Not all banks are currently sending account analyses in this fashion. The ANSI 822 transaction set can accommodate the TMA (formerly NCCMA) Standardized Account Analysis Format. TMA published an "Implementation Guide for Customer Account Analysis Transaction Set 822" in mid-1991.

D. Comparing Bank Service Charges

Companies compare bank service charges when selecting bank service providers as well as when reviewing on-going banking relationships.Service charges can vary widely among banks for the following reasons:

1. Banks have different cost structures and pricing strategies.

2. Prices may vary depending on the amount of work the company is willing to do. For example, check deposit charges vary depending on the degree of sorting, encoding, and machine readability.

3. Service charges may be bundled or unbundled. Bundling is charging for a group of several related services and service options whether or not the customer uses all of them. Unbundling is charging individually for each service used.

4. It is often difficult for a company to compare services from one bank to another because of bundling. It is necessary to know all the service charge components that make up a service. A number of companies are taking a bank's unbundled prices and rebundling them in order to compare total prices. For example, with controlled disbursement, one bank might have all of its charges combined in a single per-item price. Another bank might have a charge for each check paid, one for account reconcilement services, another for reporting the amount of checks clearing each day, another for funding the account, etc.

V. Bank Creditworthiness

Bank creditworthiness has been a growing concern for the corporate treasurer and cash manager because of the increasing number of bank failures and the weakened condition of many financial institutions.

A. Rating Agencies

Bank rating and analysis have become increasingly important. A number of firms compete in this market. Some offer only ratings, while others support their ratings with detailed reports. These reports may be based on interviews with bank management and conclusions based on financial analyses.

B. Bank Credit Analysis

A bank credit analysis may be divided into five components. These are:

1. **Liquidity -** A bank should have sufficient liquid reserves to meet its obligations. For example, if a bank relies heavily on large, uninsured deposits, it is relatively vulnerable to sudden withdrawal by depositors in the event of bad news or rumors.

2. **Asset Quality -** Declining asset quality has been associated with many bank failures and credit downgrades. Bank credit analysis examines factors such

as the amount of non-performing loans, the amount of charge-offs, the loan loss reserve and the provision for loan losses.

3. **Earnings -** The level and stability of a bank's earnings are also important indicators of its financial health. Bank credit analysis examines factors such as net interest margin (the difference between the cost of funds and the yield on loans and investments on a percentage basis), the ratio of operating expenses to income, and pre-tax operating profit.

4. **Capital -** Regulatory standards are a minimum, and banks normally try to have capital levels in line with other banks of similar size. Some of the bank rating services compare a bank to its peer group in all of the ratios.

   Capital should be sufficient to act as a cushion against risk. A bank with asset quality problems needs to have a higher level of capital to be considered creditworthy.

5. **Holding Company -** Some rating services view the holding company and its banks only on a consolidated basis. Others look at holding companies on both a consolidated and a parent-only basis. By analyzing the parent separately, one can focus on double leverage and dividends paid by banks to the parent.

   • Double leverage is the degree to which the holding company has borrowed and invested in the stock of bank subsidiaries. A highly leveraged bank holding company is very dependent on continued bank earnings to service its term debt.

   High bank dividends to the parent are often for the purpose of servicing the parent's term debt. An otherwise healthy bank can be deprived of its ability to build capital by a highly leveraged parent. The parent may also draw dividends from a healthy bank to fund a weaker bank subsidiary.

Questions

The chapter questions are to test the information in the text and are not examples of CCM examination questions nor are they in the examination format.

Answers can be found at the back of the book on p. 337.

1. What are the major objectives of bank relationship management?

2. What are some of the criteria for selecting banks?

3. What are the major documents associated with the establishment of a banking relationship?

4. What types of performance should be graded on a bank report card?

5. What are the major audit and control issues regarding bank relationship?

6. How may banks be compensated?

7. A company uses services with charges that total $4,000 per month. The bank's earnings credit rate is 6% and the reserve requirement is 10%. What is the average collected balance required to compensate the bank for services used?

8. The following information is provided:

Average ledger balance	$100,000
Deposit float	19,000
Reserve requirement	10%
Earnings credit rate	6%
Service charges for the month	$650.

Are the earnings credits sufficient to cover the service charges?

Questions (Continued)

9. What are the major factors favoring fee compensation from the corporate perspective?

10. What are target balances?

11. What is an account analysis?

12. What is bundling of service charges?

13. What are the five components of bank credit analysis?

14. Why does a company seek to optimize the number of banks with whom it has a relationship?

International Cash Management

Chapter 15

Overview

This chapter describes the principal methods of international cash management including the application of cash management principles to the business environment of other countries and techniques specific to cross-border cash management. It describes the principal international trade payment methods, letters of credit, documentary collections and open accounts, and introduces export financing and insurance.

Learning Objectives

Upon completion of this chapter and the related study questions, the reader should be able to do the following:

1. Describe the organization of international cash management responsibilities.

2. Discuss the principal reasons for financing overseas.

3. Understand how payment methods and banking systems vary among countries.

4. Describe how cross-border check payments and wire transfers are made.

5. Discuss the basic functions and reasons for using netting, reinvoicing, and internal factoring.

6. Understand the principles behind foreign tax credits and international tax planning.

7. Discuss how an exporter selects and uses letters of credit and documentary collections, and how to open accounts for international trade payments.

8. Describe the principal methods of export insurance and financing.

Outline

I. **Objectives of International Cash Management**

II. **Organization for International Cash Management**
   A. Control
   B. Structure

III. **Offshore Financing**
   A. Reasons for Offshore Financing
   B. Offshore Finance Companies

IV. **Variations in Cash Management**
   A. Payment Practices
   B. Banking Systems

V. **Cross-Border Cash Management**
   A. Check Clearing - Inter-country
   B. Balance Reporting Services
   C. Intercept Accounts
   D. Netting
   E. Leading and Lagging
   F. Reinvoicing
   G. Internal Factoring

VI. **Tax Considerations**
   A. Foreign Tax Credits
   B. Foreign Tax Planning
   C. Tax-Advantaged Business Centers

Outline (Continued)

VII. **International Trade Payment Methods**

    A.   Letters of Credit

    B.   Documentary Collections

    C.   Open Accounts

    D.   Other Trade Payment Methods

    E.   Banker's Acceptances (BAs)

VIII.   **Export Financing and Credit Management**

    A.   Foreign Credit Evaluation

    B.   Foreign Credit Insurance

    C.   Financing Foreign Buyers

I. Objectives of International Cash Management

The objectives of international cash management are similar to those for U.S. cash management. International cash management is the application of basic functions such as collection, concentration, disbursement, investment, borrowing and information management to the international environment. International Cash Management is also concerned with cross-border funds movement, foreign exchange, and cash management practices within countries outside the U.S.

II. Organization for International Cash Management

The organization of the international cash management function may be centralized, decentralized or a combination of the two, based on a number of factors. These factors are:

A. Control

1. Some companies maintain centralized control over international cash management giving relatively little autonomy to non-domestic treasury personnel. Reasons for this approach include the following:

   - A centralized function may provide economies of scale for services, resulting in lower costs to the company.

   - Non-domestic personnel may have relatively little experience in international cash management.

   - The company may not be able to justify hiring highly qualified treasury professionals in its international offices.

2. Other companies with decentralized international treasury operations often exercise control by requiring non-domestic treasury personnel to send in weekly and monthly reports summarizing bank balances, borrowing, investments and other indicators of performance. Headquarters personnel may make periodic visits to international offices to audit and train treasury personnel.

B. Structure

1. A company with relatively autonomous international subsidiaries capable of operating as independent companies is more likely to be decentralized.

2. A company with sales subsidiaries that interact primarily with the U.S. parent is more likely to be centralized.

III. Offshore Financing

A. Reasons for Offshore Financing

Offshore financing involves raising funds outside a company's home country. Companies may finance outside their country for the following reasons:

1. A company may want to diversify its funding sources rather than depend on one market.

    - Too much debt in a particular market may saturate investors' desire for a company's debt, and as a result, raise the cost of borrowing.

    - In times of tight credit, it is helpful to have relationships with a number of different lenders.

2. Long-term debt in a foreign currency can hedge a long-term investment in the same currency. Similarly, short-term debt can hedge current assets such as accounts receivable in the same currency. For example, if a U.S. company had accounts receivable denominated in pound sterling, it may consider short-term debt denominated in sterling. In both long- and short-term cases, if foreign currency-denominated assets depreciate, liabilities denominated in the same foreign currency depreciate as well.

3. As described in Chapter 13, Foreign Exchange and Interest Rate Risk Management, a company may be able to borrow in a foreign currency at a lower borrowing rate than its U.S. borrowing rate, even after hedging.

4. An international subsidiary may be able to borrow in its local market from one of its local banks at lower rates than it can from its parent company.

5. There may be tax advantages available in the subsidiary's home country.

B. Offshore Finance Companies

Companies may establish offshore financing subsidiaries to obtain funding and benefit from favorable tax regulations. A company may fund the needs of a number of subsidiaries in different countries through its offshore finance company, thus taking advantage of lower rates by borrowing in large amounts.

IV. Variations in Cash Management

A company with international subsidiaries must coordinate and supervise cash management operations in countries where payments systems and bank services vary considerably. In analyzing cash management in each country, a summary of corporate payment and collection practices, banking services, bank compensation and other cash management functions should be prepared. This section contains examples of how cash management may differ among countries.

A. Payment Practices

1. **Electronic Payment** - Electronic payment of company obligations is more common in some areas of the world than it is in the U.S..

2. **Giros -** Most European countries have giro systems which generally operate through their postal systems. Giro systems allow payments from one giro account to another using direct debits and credits.

3. **Collection -** The banking system is utilized to collect payments in various ways in different countries. For example, in Spain and France, a payor may accept a draft drawn by the payee as evidence of the payor's payment obligation. The payee holds the draft and collects it through its bank and the payor's bank when due. The payee may discount the draft through its bank.

   In Japan and Korea, buyers sign promissory notes that sellers collect through the banking system. Prompt payment is customary and expected. As a result, bank account balances are predictable, and some companies do not require balance reporting.

B. Banking Systems

Each country's banking system has different regulations, capabilities and products.

1. **Branches -** A number of countries, including the U.K. and Canada, have countrywide banking.

2. **Pooling -** In some countries, the U.K. for example, a special procedure is offered by banks in which excess funds in the accounts of some subsidiaries may be used to offset deficits in the accounts of other subsidiaries.

   • Positive and negative balances may be aggregated each day for the calculation of interest earned or due. Normally, no funds are actually transferred; only the interest calculation is made.

   • Divisions or subsidiaries may have zero balance accounts.

3. **Interest -** Unlike the U.S., many countries allow the payment of interest on demand deposits.

4. **Overdraft Banking -** In most European countries, a company may have either a positive balance in a bank account and earn interest or a negative balance and pay interest.

5. **Value Dating -** In most other countries, banks use the technique of value dating to compensate themselves for providing services to their customers. Under a value dating system, the bank sets the dates upon which it grants credit for deposits or debits the account for checks written. Value dates may have no relationship at all to actual clearing dates for checks.

   • The forward value date is the date upon which the firm will be granted credit for deposited items. In some countries, this date is based on the date of the check rather than on the date of deposit in order to adjust for delayed presentment of the check.

- The back value date is the date upon which checks written on an account are debited from that account. The value date is also usually based on the date of the check.

- Value dating may be negotiable, depending upon the bank and the country.

6. **Check Clearing - Intra-country -** Some countries have countrywide check clearing systems; others do not.

- Germany has separate clearing systems for different types of banks including commercial banks, cooperative banks, savings banks and the postal girobank.

- Italy does not have a countrywide clearing system. Clearing is done either through networks of large countrywide banks or through correspondent arrangements.

V. Cross-Border Cash Management

A. Check Clearing - Inter-country

A check clears in the home country of its currency. For example, a check payable in French francs must ultimately be paid by a bank in France even though the drawee and payee may be outside France.

When the payee receives a check payable in a different country, for example, when a U.S. exporter receives a check denominated in Deutschemarks, it cannot clear the check through normal check clearing channels but must submit it for collection.

- The payee submits the check to a U.S. bank for collection. The check is sent by the collecting bank to the drawee bank in Germany for payment.

- The drawee bank in turn sends a check in U.S. dollars drawn on a bank in the U.S. or wire transfer funds from a correspondent bank in the U.S. to the collecting bank. The amount of the check is reduced by the drawee bank's collection fee. The rate used by the drawee bank for conversion from Deutschemarks to dollars provides the bank a profit.

- After receiving funds from the drawee bank, the collecting bank credits the payee's account. The process may take from two weeks to more than two months. During that period, the party that submitted the check incurs the risk of a change in the exchange rate that may reduce the value of the check.

B. Balance Reporting Services

Major banks in Europe and Asia have been reporting balances and transactions electronically since the mid-1980s. Such reporting services allow both local and international access.

For example, the balances and debit and credit details for a Dutch subsidiary of a U.S. company can be reported to local management in the Netherlands as well as to the parent. Major international banks and third-party service providers can consolidate reporting by a company's banking network and produce a report each day.

C. Intercept Accounts

Some U.S. companies have intercept accounts for countries in which they do a significant amount of business. An intercept account is a deposit account in another country that is used to accept payment from customers in that country, making cross-border payments unnecessary. The seller has the flexibility to use the funds for local operating expenses or remit funds to headquarters. Reducing the frequency of cross-border payments reduces fees and improves control.

Some banks in international centers such as London or Luxembourg offer multicurrency accounts. A **multicurrency account** is an account that allows for the transfer of payments in any readily convertible currency to and from one designated account. The currency denomination of the account is at the discretion of the account holder. Such accounts are useful for companies that do not have sufficient sales volume to justify intercept accounts in several countries.

D. Netting

Netting is a system designed to reduce the number of cross-border payments among units of a company through elimination or consolidation of individual funds flows.

1. **Bilateral Netting -** In a bilateral netting system, purchases between two subsidiaries of the same company are netted against each other so that over time, typically one month, only the difference is transferred.

   For example, subsidiaries of a multinational, one located in France and another in Germany, hold payments until one or two regularly scheduled times during the month. Prior to the settlement date, the payments in both directions are totalled, the net due one of the subsidiaries determined, and a single transfer is scheduled.

2. **Multilateral Netting -** The system is similar to bilateral netting, but with more than two units. Each unit informs a central treasury management center of all planned cross-border payments. Payments are totalled and each unit is informed prior to the settlement date of the net amount to pay or to be received in its own currency. The netting center makes the necessary foreign exchange conversions. Although multilateral netting is used primarily for intra-company transactions, some companies include third-party payables in their systems.

   The mechanics of multilateral netting are illustrated in Exhibit 15-1.

3. **Advantages.**

   - The number of foreign exchange transactions as well as cross-border wire transfer transactions is reduced.

Exhibit 15-1

Illustration of Multilateral Netting

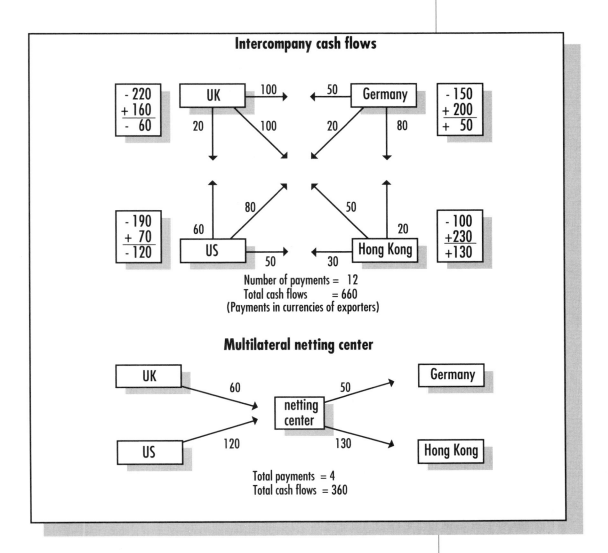

Intercompany cash flows

Number of payments = 12
Total cash flows = 660
(Payments in currencies of exporters)

Multilateral netting center

Total payments = 4
Total cash flows = 360

- Pricing is favorable for larger foreign exchange transactions.

- Pre-planning cross-border payments improves cash forecasting for both the subsidiary and the parent.

- Float can be eliminated and value dating can be assured and tracked more effectively.

4. **Disadvantages.**

- Netting may be illegal in some countries.

- There may be significant costs to set up a netting system as well as service fees for its operation.

- Local formal approval may be required to set up a netting system.

E. Leading and Lagging

Netting systems may be used to implement leading and lagging. This involves making cross-border payments between subsidiaries either ahead of schedule (leading) or behind schedule (lagging). Liquidity is moved from one subsidiary to the other. Leading can be helpful when a currency is expected to depreciate while lagging will be used when the currency is expected to appreciate relative to the parent's home currency.

F. Reinvoicing

Reinvoicing is a method of centralizing the responsibility for tracking and collecting international accounts receivable and for managing the related foreign exchange exposure. The reinvoicing center, a company-owned subsidiary, buys the goods from the exporter and sells the goods to the importer. The exporting unit receives funds from the reinvoicing subsidiary in its own currency, and the importing unit pays funds to the reinvoicing subsidiary in its own currency.

1. **Advantages.** Advantages of a reinvoicing center include:

   - Centralizing foreign exchange exposure, removing all such risks from foreign subsidiaries. This allows the company to control its cash flow better and can simplify the monitoring of intracompany receivables and payables.

   - It can also improve worldwide short-term liquidity management by providing flexibility in inter-subsidiary payments. For instance, this enables leading and lagging arrangements to be implemented easily, improving export trade financing and collections, reducing bank costs and improving foreign exchange rates by trading in larger amounts.

2. **Disadvantages.** Disadvantages of a reinvoicing center include:

   - Establishing a reinvoicing center requires local approval and negotiation on how the subsidiary will be taxed.

   - Tax authorities in each country may monitor transactions to ensure that taxable income is not being shifted from the seller's country to the country of the reinvoicing center.

   - As with netting, the use of a reinvoicing center may reduce local autonomy.

   - Reinvoicing center expenses include physical location costs as well as costs associated with netting centers.

   - Reinvoicing centers are almost always handled in-house by multinational companies.

   Reinvoicing is illustrated in Exhibit 15-2.

G. Internal Factoring

The purpose of an internal factoring center is similar to that of reinvoicing. Rather than taking actual title to the goods as with reinvoicing, the internal factoring unit buys accounts receivable from the exporting unit and bills and collects from the importing unit.

Exhibit 15-2

Illustration of Reinvoicing

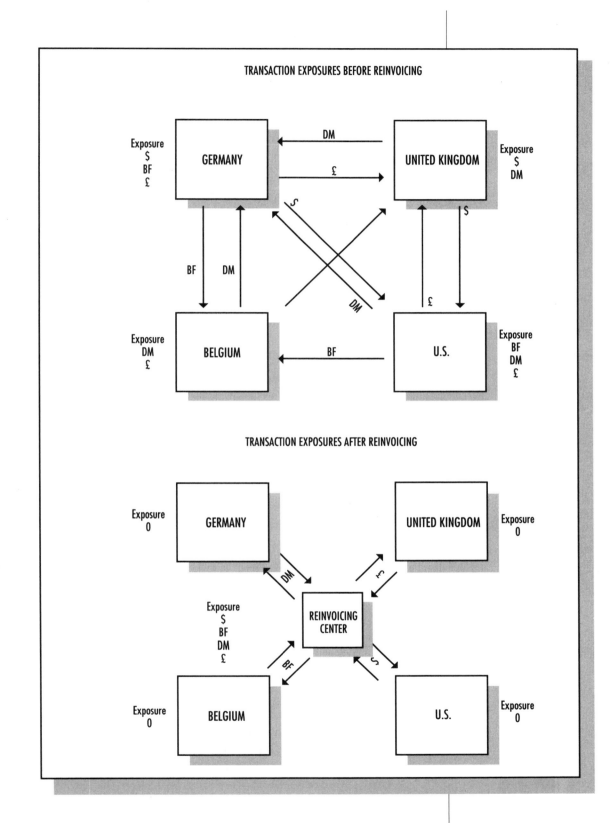

VI. Tax Considerations

A. Foreign Tax Credits

A U.S. company's income derived from its foreign operations may have to be included in its U.S. income tax return. This may occur when a dividend is paid from a foreign subsidiary to the U.S. parent. That same income may also have been included in an income tax return of the country in which the subsidiary is located. The result is that the foreign income is double taxed.

To relieve the effect of this double taxation, the U.S. tax law allows a U.S. company a dollar-for-dollar tax credit against its total U.S. income tax liability for those foreign income taxes paid by the parent and its subsidiaries. This credit is called the foreign tax credit (FTC). The FTC is allowed only for those foreign taxes paid which are income taxes.

A separate FTC calculation must be computed for each type of income. For example, incomes from manufacturing in one country can only be combined with manufacturing-derived incomes from other countries. U.S. tax law allows FTC to be carried back two years, and forward five years.

B. Foreign Tax Planning

The complexity of the law regarding the taxation of non-domestic income makes it important for treasury personnel to work with tax experts.

C. Tax-Advantaged Business Centers

To attract multinational businesses and related employment opportunities, a number of countries, such as Belgium and Ireland, offer tax incentives for subsidiaries that perform certain administrative and financial functions.

1. Permissible activities include support services such as research, financial coordination, advertising, promotion, and data processing.

2. A relatively low tax base is calculated, based on the costs allocated to the center. Withholding tax exemptions, real estate tax exemptions, and employee tax concessions are provided.

VII. International Trade Payment Methods

In the U.S., it is customary for a seller to check the credit standing of a buyer prior to selling on open account. Invoices are often sent with each shipment and included in a statement of amounts due at the end of the month. When a seller is exporting goods to a non-domestic buyer, more credit protection is frequently needed, particularly for a new business relationship. The most frequently used international trade payment mechanisms, letters of credit, collections and open account, can be explained as a hierarchy. Letters of credit offer the most protection, but they are also the most expensive, while open account offers the least protection but are also the least costly.

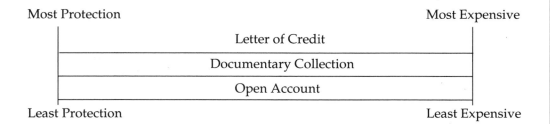

A. Letters of Credit

1. A letter of credit (LC) is a document issued by a bank, guaranteeing the payment of a customer's draft up to a stated amount for a specified period if certain conditions are met. An LC substitutes a bank's name and credit for that of the buyer, and eliminates the seller's risk.

2. The banks may have the following roles:

   - *Issuing Bank* - The issuing bank is the buyer's bank that issues the LC in favor of the beneficiary (seller).

   - *Advising Bank* - The advising bank advises the beneficiary of an LC in its favor.

   - *Negotiating Bank* - The negotiating bank examines the documents presented by the beneficiary, charges the account of the issuing bank and pays the beneficiary. The advising and negotiating bank may be the same.

   - *Confirming Bank* - A confirming bank guarantees to the beneficiary that payment will be made if documents meet the terms and conditions of the LC, regardless of the issuing bank's ability to pay. Confirmation is done at the issuing bank's request and a fee is imposed. The confirming bank assumes the credit risk of the issuing bank.

3. The LC provides for immediate or deferred payment to the beneficiary.

   - When the beneficiary presents a sight draft, which is a draft payable on demand, the negotiating bank pays the seller immediately, and is reimbursed by the issuing bank.

   - The seller may also present a time draft which provides for payment at a future date. The seller may in turn discount the draft with the local bank for immediate funds. This process is a way for the seller to provide credit terms to the buyer.

   - A deferred payment LC provides for presentation of one or more sight drafts at specified dates in the future, and this sometimes extends over several years. When medium-term financing is provided for the export of capital goods, a deferred payment LC may be used in conjunction with a term loan agreement.

4. Letters of credit are generally irrevocable. This means that if all required documentation is presented, the issuing bank must honor all drafts pre-

sented by the seller (generally to its bank). Also, changes must be agreed to by all parties to the transactions.

Once ongoing business relationships have been established, however, the seller may require only revocable letters of credit. These are cheaper but do not carry the issuing bank's guarantee to honor all drafts presented. They are used, for example, when joint venture partners trade with each other. Letters of credit may specify payment in either the importer's or the exporter's currency. Therefore, only one of the parties bears the exchange rate risk.

5.   The bank's role in an LC transaction is the examination of documents, not merchandise. It is the responsibility of the importer opening the credit to specify the documents that the exporter must present after shipment as a condition for payment. Naturally the use of documents has its limitation as a protective mechanism to ensure that the importer gets exactly what it wants.

6.   With an export letter of credit, a U.S. bank assumes the credit risk of the non-domestic bank issuing the Letter of Credit (LC) in favor of the U.S. beneficiary. With an import letter of credit, the U.S. bank issuing the credit assumes the credit risk of the U.S. importer that is opening the credit in favor of the non-domestic exporter.

7.   Banks or external consultants may be helpful in counseling exporters on whether or not to require a letter of credit and how to prepare documents for shipment and presentation to the bank. Exporters are concerned with the amount of time a bank takes to examine and pay against documents as well as the negotiating bank's punctuality in contacting the overseas bank to request a waiver for discrepancies such as late shipment.

8.   A **commercial letter of credit** is issued by a bank to another bank on behalf of a commercial customer stating that payment will be made if documents are presented as provided in the credit.

9.   A **standby letter of credit** is an LC used as a guarantee issued on behalf of a bank's customer in favor of a beneficiary stating that the bank will pay the latter upon presentation of a statement signed by the beneficiary stating that the bank's customer has not fulfilled the terms of the contract.

Exhibit 15-3 illustrates a commercial letter of credit:

B.   Documentary Collections

Documentary collections are credits tied to a set of documents specifying the conditions of the sale. They are a simpler and less expensive alternative to letters of credit for the exporter in collecting payments from non-domestic buyers.

1.   The exporter's bank forwards documents to the importer's bank with its collection letter, which also contains instructions such as whether to wire transfer or airmail the proceeds, whether charges are for account of the exporter or the importer, and whether or not to issue a formal protest if the draft is not paid. A protest of a commercial draft is treated seriously in the

Exhibit 15-3

**Illustration of a
Letter of Credit
Transaction**

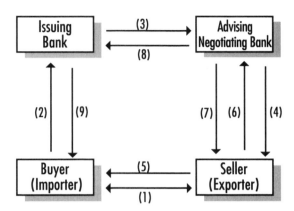

1. The buyer and the seller agree to a sales contract in which the buyer is required to open an LC in favor of the seller.

2. The buyer chooses a bank in its country and opens an LC in favor of the seller.

3. The issuing (buyer's) bank sends the LC to a bank in the seller's country. The latter bank becomes the advising bank.

4. The advising bank sends details of the credit to the seller, who is the beneficiary of the credit.

5. The seller ships the merchandise to the buyer.

6. The seller presents the draft and documents to the advising/negotiating bank.

7. The advising/negotiating bank examines the documents and pays the seller if the documents meet the terms of the LC.

8. The advising/negotiating bank sends the documents to the issuing bank and charges the issuing bank's account.

9. The issuing bank examines the documents, charges the buyer's account, and releases the documents to the buyer. With the documents, the buyer is able to claim the merchandise.

legal codes of many countries and is therefore used with discretion. The availability of protest is one of the advantages of a documentary collection over open account, which is described in the next section.

2. When the importer pays the amount due to the foreign collecting bank, the bank releases the documents, and the importer is able to take possession of the documents and delivery of the merchandise.

3. The banks in the countries of the buyer and seller do not assume any credit risk but act solely as agents in the collection process.

4. A disadvantage of documentary collections is that the exporter must wait for payment until the merchandise arrives in the importer's country. There is no assurance of payment as provided with the letter of credit.

5. The exporter is protected by the collecting bank's practice of not releasing documents until payment is made or a time draft is signed. Some banks overseas are stricter than others in adhering to this procedure, and payments may be made as long as 30 or 40 days after presentation of a sight draft.

Exhibit 15-4 illustrates a documentary collection.

C. Open Accounts

Under the open account method, the seller ships the merchandise and sends an invoice.

1. The open account method is the least secure, but also the least costly.

2. The open account is the most frequently used method of payment for well established relationships. For example, a company may switch from using letters of credit to using open accounts for large shipments after having sufficient credit experience with the customer.

3. The currency of billing is a marketing and financial decision for the seller. A seller of high-technology products with little competition may be sufficiently confident of its market position to require payment in U.S. dollars. Other sellers may bill in local currency and bear the foreign exchange risk. An exporter who bills in U.S. dollars avoids transaction exposure but still has economic exposure. If the dollar rises in value against the currencies of competitors, then the competitors' products become cheaper in the local market. This is further explained in Chapter 13, Foreign Exchange and Interest Rate Risk Management.

D. Other Trade Payment Methods

Other less frequently used international trade payment mechanisms include cash before delivery, consignment, barter, countertrade and forfeiting.

1. **Cash Before Delivery (CBD) -** Cash before delivery is used when the seller requires the total protection of receiving payment before shipment of goods. The opportunity cost can be substantial if competitors do not require such terms.

Exhibit 15-4

Illustration of a Documentary Collection

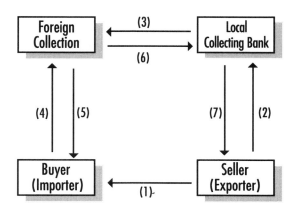

1. The seller ships merchandise to the buyer.

2. The seller delivers the draft and documents to the local collecting bank.

3. The local/collecting bank forwards the documents to the buyer's bank, the foreign collecting bank.

4. The buyer makes payment to the foreign collecting bank in the case of a sight draft, or accepts a time draft.

5. The foreign collecting bank releases the documents so that the buyer may take delivery of the merchandise.

6. The foreign collecting bank remits funds to the local/collecting bank.

7. The local/collecting bank pays the seller.

2. **Consignment -** The seller consigns goods to a foreign agent, but retains title to the goods. The agent pays the exporter when the goods are sold. Title remains with the seller until payment date. Regaining possession of the goods if they are not sold may be difficult and costly.

3. **Barter -** Barter is the direct exchange of goods or services without using money.

4. **Countertrade -** Countertrade is a method of payment used by countries that do not have sufficient hard currency (internationally traded currencies such as the U.S. dollar or the Japanese yen) to pay for imports from other countries. A seller in a country such as the U.S. ships merchandise to the countertrading country, and takes in exchange merchandise that can be sold in the U.S.

5. **Forfaiting** - Forfaiting is a specialized form of export financing which provides both short- and medium-term financing. The seller accepts a note from the buyer which may have a maturity of up to three years. The note can be discounted in a specialized market in London. It may be available in some situations in which confirmed letters of credit are not.

6. **Trading Companies** - An exporter (seller) can also sell its products, at a discount, to an export trading company that does business with developing countries.

E. Banker's Acceptance (BA)

Acceptance financing is most often used to finance the import, export or domestic shipment of goods but can also be used to finance domestic or overseas storage of those goods. Acceptances are commonly, but not necessarily, used in conjunction with letters of credit.

An acceptance is a time draft, on the face of which the drawee has written the word "accepted" over its signature. The date and place payable are also indicated. The party accepting or agreeing unconditionally to pay the draft at a particular time and place is known as the acceptor.

A banker's acceptance is a time draft drawn on, and accepted by a bank. By accepting the draft, the bank creates a banker's acceptance and indicates its commitment to pay the face amount at maturity to anyone who presents it for payment at that time. In this way, the bank backs the instrument with its name and credit and assumes the credit risk of the obligor, but at the same time creates a short-term investment instrument that is negotiable in the money market. The bank can either hold the acceptance in its own portfolio or sell it through a broker to an investor.

1. **Cost -** The cost of acceptance financing to the customer has two components: the discount rate (the rate earned by the investor) and the bank's acceptance commission.

2. **Eligibility -** Most acceptance financing is done with eligible acceptances. An eligible banker's acceptance is an acceptance that may be discounted at the Federal Reserve. To be eligible for discount, the acceptance may not have a maturity of more than 180 days. Eligible underlying transactions include the following:

   - Import or export of goods
   - Domestic storage transactions with shipping documents conveying title attached
   - Storage of readily marketable staples secured by warehouse receipts
   - Certain transactions that create U.S. dollar exchange with a maximum maturity of three months

3. **Example** - The mechanics and potential uses of bankers' acceptances can be illustrated by the following example:

   - A U.S. exporter agrees on the terms of sale with a foreign buyer, which include a requirement for the buyer to open an LC. An LC is opened at a foreign bank and advised through a U.S. bank.

   - The seller has offered terms on the sale of goods, so the draft drawn by the seller (usually on the advising bank) when documents are presented calls for payment a specified number of days after shipment or after sight, or on a specific future date. The advising bank forwards the documentation to the drawee bank.

   - The drawee bank accepts the draft, and the beneficiary becomes the owner of a banker's acceptance.

   - The seller may hold the draft until maturity, or may discount the draft with a bank. In the latter case, the bank advances the discounted proceeds to the beneficiary and most likely sells the acceptance in the open market.

VIII. Export Financing and Credit Management

Providing financing to a non-domestic buyer can be a crucial competitive factor for an exporter, particularly in the case of large-ticket sales such as airplane sales or construction contracts.

A. Foreign Credit Evaluation

It may be difficult for a U.S. company or bank to evaluate the credit of a non-U.S. buyer because of the scarcity of credit information and differing accounting practices. Collecting delinquent accounts in other countries is both difficult and expensive for a U.S. exporter.

B. Foreign Credit Insurance

Another way of ensuring payment is export insurance. This insurance is provided by the Export Import Bank of the United States (Eximbank) through an independent contractor, FCIA Management Co. Inc., and by certain private insurers.

Insurance coverage is available for shipment to almost every country with which the U.S. has diplomatic relations. Eximbank offers insurance, through its agent, which covers political and commercial risks on export receivables. The insurance is not backed by the U.S. government but rather by a private insurer through Eximbank.

Private insurance can be obtained for some countries for which FCIA insurance is not available, although it is often more expensive.

From a buyer's viewpoint, insurance can be preferable to letters of credit. As an example, when a buyer opens an LC, it may reduce the available line of credit the buyer has established with its bank.

C. Financing Foreign Buyers

1. **Commercial Banks** - Some commercial banks in the U.S. specialize in providing direct financing to the foreign buyers of U.S. exports.

2. **Export-Import Bank of the U.S. (Eximbank)** - The Eximbank is an independent agency of the U.S. Government established to finance and guarantee U.S. export loans. The Bank is directed by its corporate charter:

   - to make export financing competitive with foreign credit agencies

   - to ensure that loans are to borrowers with a reasonable capacity to repay

   - to supplement but not compete with financing offered by private commercial banks.

   The Eximbank's programs include a working capital program aimed at small businesses, a loan guarantee program to encourage private-sector loans and a direct loan program used in a situation in which the competition receives subsidized financing.

Questions

The chapter questions are to test the information in the text and are not examples of CCM examination questions nor are they in the examination format.

Answers can be found at the back of the book on p. 340.

1. What are the two major factors that determine whether the international cash management function should be centralized or decentralized?

2. What are some of the reasons a company may wish to get part of its financing off shore?

3. How do payment practices vary outside the U.S.?

4. What is pooling, as applied in non-U.S. banking systems?

5. What is value dating?

6. What must a payee do if it receives a check drawn in a different country?

7. What is a multi-currency account?

8. What are the major advantages of using a netting system?

9. What is a reinvoicing center?

10. What risk is eliminated by the use of a letter of credit?

11. What is an irrevocable letter of credit?

Questions (Continued)

12. What is a stand-by letter of credit?

13. What is the major difference in the role of the banks under a documentary collection as opposed to a letter of credit?

14. What is countertrade?

15. What is the maximum maturity for a banker's acceptance to remain eligible for discount at the Federal Reserve?

16. What is the Eximbank?

Acronyms

ACH-Automated Clearing House

ANSI-American National Standards Institute

ARP-adjustable-rate preferred stock

ATM-automated teller machines

BA-Banker's acceptance

BAI-Bank Administration Institute

BIF-Bank Insurance Fund

CBD-cash before delivery

CCD-cash concentration and disbursement

CCD+-cash concentration and disbursement plus addendum

CD-certificate of deposit

CHIPS-Clearing House Interbank Payments System

COD-cash on delivery

CP-commercial paper

CTP-corporate trade payment

CTX-corporate trade exchange

DDA-demand deposit account

DIDMCA-Depository Institutions Deregulation and Monetary Control Act (1980)

DSO-days' sales outstanding

DTC-depository transfer check

EDI-electronic data interchange

EDT-electronic depository transfer

EFAA-Expedited Funds Availability Act (1988)

EFT- electronic funds transfer

EFTA-Electronic Funds Transfer Act (1978)

ERISA-Employee Retirement Income and Security Act

FAS-Financial Accounting Standards

FASB-Financial Accounting Standards Board

FDIC-Federal Deposit Insurance Corporation

FED-Federal Reserve System

FFCB-Federal Farm Credit Bank

FHLMC-Federal Home Loan Mortgage Corporation (Freddie Mac)

FIRREA-Financial Institutions Reform, Recovery and Enforcement Act (1989)

FNMA-Federal National Mortgage Association (Fannie Mae)

FOMC-Federal Open Market Committee

FSLIC-Federal Savings and Loan Insurance Corporation

FTC-foreign tax credit

FTD-federal tax deposit

GAAP-Generally Accepted Accounting Principles

GIC-guaranteed income contract

GNMA-Government National Mortgage Association (Ginnie Mae)

HDGS-high dollar group sort

IRB-industrial revenue bond

IRR-internal rate of return

LC-letter of credit

LIBOR-London Interbank Offered Rate

MICR-Magnetic Ink Character Recognition

MIS-management information system

MMP-money market preferred stock

NACHA-National Automated Clearing House Association

NCUA-National Credit Union Administration

NOW-negotiable order of withdrawal

OCC-Office of the Comptroller of the Currency

OTS-Office of Thrift Supervision

PAC-preauthorized check

PC-personal computer

PID-payable if desired

PIN-personal identification number

POD-proof of deposit

POS-point of sale

PPD-prearranged payment and deposit

PTD-payable through draft

RCPC-Regional Check Processing Center

RTC-Resolution Trust Corporation

S&L-savings and loan association

SAIF-Savings Association Insurance Fund

SEC-Securities and Exchange Commission

SLMA-Student Loan Market Association (Sallie Mae)

SWIFT-Society for Worldwide Interbank Financial Telecommunications

TMA-Treasury Management Association

TMIS-treasury management information system

TXP-tax payment format

UCC-Uniform Commercial Code

VAN-value-added network

VRDB-variable-rate demand bond

WACC-weighted average cost of capital

ZBA-zero balance account

Glossary

Account analysis—Statement, usually prepared monthly for a company by each bank, summarizing a company's transaction activity, average balances, and service charges.

Adjusted net income—Long-term cash forecasting method which uses a company's projected sources and uses of funds to derive projected cash flows.

Adjustable rate preferred (ARP)—A form of preferred stock whose dividend rate is adjusted quarterly, based on current treasury yields.

Agency—A role in which a bank or trust institution manages assets in which the title remains with the owner.

Aging schedule—A list of the percentages and/or amounts of outstanding accounts receivable classified as current or past due in 30-day increments.

ANSI—American National Standards Institute, the recognized coordinator and clearing house for information on national and international standards including those for electronic transaction formats that are used in electronic data interchange (EDI).

Anticipation—The initiation of a transfer before cash becomes available at the deposit bank.

Asset-based borrowing—Lending based on the pledging of accounts receivable and inventory as loan collateral.

Auction rate preferred—A form of preferred stock whose dividend rate is set every 49 days through an auction process which is beyond the minimum holding period for the corporate dividend exclusion. The dividend rate adjustment is based on current treasury yields. Also called money market preferred (MMP).

Automated clearing house (ACH)—A domestic payment system providing an electronic parallel to the Federal Reserve check clearing system. An ACH transfer can contain more information than a check and is generally more reliable and cost efficient.

Availability float—The delay between the time a check is deposited and the time the firm's account is credited with collected funds.

Availability schedule—A schedule that specifies when a bank or the Federal Reserve grants credit for deposited checks in the form of an increase in the depositor's available or collected balance.

Bank Insurance Fund (BIF)—A fund administered by the Federal Deposit Insurance Corporation (FDIC), which insures the deposits of commercial banks and mutual saving banks.

Banker's acceptance (BA)—A short-term obligation of a bank arising from an international trade transaction, generally the shipment or storage of goods.

Basis point—The minimum price change in interest rates is one basis point (.01%).

Bearer security—A treasury security where the holder can collect interest or principal at maturity as well as sell the security.

Bilateral netting—System in which purchases between two subsidiaries of the same company are netted against each other, so that over time, typically one month, only the difference is transferred.

Bond—An interest-bearing certificate of debt by which the issuer becomes obligated to repay the principal on a specified maturity date and to pay periodic interest.

Bond equivalent yield—Nominal yield on a long-term instrument quoted on a 365-day basis.

Book entry—Securities do not move when traded; they are stored at the Federal Reserve Bank of New York, and entries are made when ownership changes.

Call back—A return call to a company to ensure a transaction has been authorized; a call is placed after the transaction has been entered, but before it is executed.

Call option—The holder of a security has the right, but not the obligation, to purchase the foreign currency at a given price.

Cap—A ceiling on the maximum interest rate for a loan or variable-rate security.

Capital market—A financial market that consists of both equity and debt instruments that mature in more than one year.

Captive finance company—Typically, a wholly owned subsidiary whose major purpose is to perform credit operations and obtain receivables financing.

Cash before delivery (CBD)—Credit terms requiring payment, often in the form of a check; a cashier's or certified check may be required before the order is shipped.

Cash concentration and disbursement (CCD) (format)—Electronic payment format used for concentration and disbursement of funds within or between companies.

Cash concentration and disbursement plus addendum (CCD+) format—Electronic payment format identical to the CCD format, but containing one additional addendum record.

Cash forecasting—The process of predicting cash flow for the purposes of liquidity management and financial control.

Cash letter—A bundle of one or more checks accompanied by a list of individual items and dollar amounts together with deposit tickets and other control documents.

Cash on delivery (COD)—Credit terms in which goods are shipped and the buyer must pay upon delivery.

Cash terms—Credit terms under which the buyer generally has a week to 10 days to make the payment.

Cash transfer scheduling—The decision on when and how much cash to transfer.

Certificates of deposit (CDs)—Negotiable or non-negotiable obligations of a bank, that may have a fixed or a variable interest rate.

Check—A demand instrument to transfer funds from the payor to the payee.

Check float—The delay between the receipt of an invoice and the clearing of the check. It has two components: collection float and disbursement float.

Check truncation—The process by which essential information contained on a conventional paper check is captured electronically and the electronic information, not the paper check, is sent through the clearing system.

City items—Checks drawn on banks located in Federal Reserve cities.

Clearing float—The delay between the time the check is deposited and the time it is presented to the payor's bank for payment. It has two components: availability float and clearing slippage float.

Clearing House Automated Payment Service (CHAPS)—A London-based payment system for high-value, same-day settlement of transactions.

Clearing House Interbank Payment System (CHIPS)—An independent message-switching system that permits international financial transactions to be settled among New York banks. It is operated by the New York Clearing House Association.

Clearing slippage float—The delay between the time the payee receives collected funds and the time the payor's account is debited. Also called Fed float.

Collar—An agreement between a borrower and a bank that includes both a cap defining the maximum level of interest that the borrower will pay and a floor defining the borrower's minimum rate.

Collected balances—Balances in a customer's account required to cover the cost of services provided by the bank. It is the difference between ledger balances and deposit float.

Collection float—The delay between the time the payor mails a check and the time the payee receives available funds. It has three components: mail float, processing float and availability float.

Commercial letter of credit—Letter of credit issued by a bank to another bank on behalf of a commercial customer stating that payment will be made if documents are presented as provided in the credit agreement.

Commercial paper—An unsecured promissory note issued for a specific amount with a maturity of 270 days or less.

Company processing center—A collection system in which the company does its own processing and depositing of payments.

Compensating balances—Balances held by a company in the form of collected balances to pay for bank services.

Concentration—The movement of funds from outlying depository locations to a central bank account, where it can be utilized and managed most effectively.

Controlled disbursement—A bank service that provides same-day notification, usually by early or mid-morning, of the dollar amount of checks that will clear against the controlled disbursement account that day.

Covenants—Provisions in loan agreements that restrict a borrower's activities in ways that protect the lender during the term of the agreement.

Convertible bond—A type of bond convertible into shares of the company's common stock at a defined price.

Corporate trade exchange (CTX) format—Electronic payment format for corporate-to-corporate payments that contains additional addenda records in the ANSI X12 format.

Corporate trade payment (CTP) format—Electronic payment format for corporate-to-corporate payments. It contains additional addenda records for remittance information.

Corporate trustee—As a trustee for a corporate bond or preferred stock issue, a bank monitors compliance with the indenture agreements between issuers and investors.

Correspondent balances—Demand deposits held by one bank at another bank to facilitate check clearing, securities, letters of credit and other transactions.

Country items—Checks drawn on banks located outside the area served by a Federal Reserve city or RCPC.

Credit enhancement—Use of an indemnity bond or letter of credit to back a debt issue, thereby substituting the creditworthiness of the guarantor for the borrower's creditworthiness.

Credit scoring—A type of statistical analysis that uses multiple discriminant analysis (MDA) to classify credit applicants as good or bad credit risks.

Currency swaps—Agreements between borrowers with debt in different currencies to exchange payments in different currencies. They are normally arranged through bank intermediaries.

Daylight overdraft—An intra-day exposure of a bank when an account is in an overdraft position at any time during the business day.

Days' sales outstanding (DSO)—A credit measurement ratio calculated by dividing accounts receivable outstanding at the end of a time period by the average daily credit sales for the period.

Demand deposit account (DDA)—Bank account from which funds can be transferred to a third party with a check, a wire transfer or an ACH transfer.

Deposit float—The sum of each check deposited multiplied by its availability in days.

Depository Institutions Deregulation and Monetary Control Act of 1980 (DIDMCA)—Federal law that required the Federal Reserve to eliminate or price Federal float and to charge for its services explicitly. Commonly referred to as the Monetary Control Act.

Depository Transfer Check (DTC)—A preprinted, unsigned, restricted-payee instrument used by a company to transfer funds from one of its outlying depository locations to its concentration account.

Direct send—cash letter that bypasses the local Federal Reserve clearing system and is sent via courier directly to a non-local Federal Reserve bank or to a correspondent bank.

Disbursement float—The delay between the time a payor issues the check and the time when the funds are debited from the payor's account. It has the following components: mail float, processing float and clearing float

Disbursement network—A system of check mailing locations and drawee banks based on disbursement studies and designed to maximize disbursement float.

Discount—The face value multiplied by the discount rate times the number of days divided by 360.

Discount rate—Interest rate charged by the Federal Reserve for loans to depository institutions.

Distribution method—A forecasting technique used in cash scheduling wherein the distribution of cash flow over a given time period is estimated.

Documentary collections—Credit tied to a set of documents specifying the conditions of the sale. Also called draft bill of lading.

Dollar-days—The usual measurement for float, calculated by multiplying the time lag in collections by the dollar amount being delayed.

Douglas Amendment—Federal law enacted in 1956 that allows banks to merge across state lines if each of the states involved permits it. It also prohibits bank holding companies from acquiring banks across state lines.

Drawdown wire—A company initiates instructions to debit its own or another party's account. The party being debited must authorize the transfer.

Dual balances—A situation in which available balances exist simultaneously in two banks. It occurs when availability is granted by the depositing bank before a check is cleared at the payor's bank.

Earnings credit—A bank credit used to offset service charges; by law, banks cannot pay interest on corporate demand deposits.

Earnings credit rate (ECR)—A bank-specific rate used to calculate earnings credit; it is usually tied to the T-bill rate or another measure of the bank's cost of funds.

Economic exposure—The exposure reflected by the potential decline in the value of a company that may result from changes in the exchange rate.

Edge Act—Federal act that permits banks to invest in corporations that engage in international banking and finance and allows banks to develop domestic networks of Edge Act corporations devoted to international transactions.

Effective annual yield—A compounded, annualized yield calculated on a 365 day basis.

Electronic data interchange (EDI)—The movement of business data electronically between or within firms (including their agents or intermediaries) in a structured computer-processable data format that permits data to be transferred without re-keying.

Electronic depository transfer (EDT)—An ACH transaction used for concentration of funds; also known as electronic depository transfer check (EDTC).

Electronic funds transfer (EFT)—The movement of funds by non-paper means (i.e., electronically), usually through a payment system such as the automated clearing house network.

Electronic Funds Transfer Act—Federal law enacted in 1978 that defines the rights and responsibilities of users and providers of consumer EFT services.

Electronic payable through draft—ACH debits to a company's account in which the company is notified in time to pay or reject each item.

Encryption—A process that scrambles a message so that it cannot be read by someone who may intercept it.

Eurobond—A bond issued outside the country where the currency of the bonds is domiciled.

Equity warrant—A long-term option to buy a stated number of shares of stock at a specified price.

Eurodollar CD—U.S. dollar-denominated CD issued by banks, including branches of U.S. banks, outside the U.S.

Eurodollar deposits—U.S. dollar-denominated deposits in banks or bank branches located outside the U.S., but not necessarily in Europe.

Eurodollar time deposits (Euro-TDs)—Non-negotiable, fixed-rate time deposits with maturities from overnight to several years, issued by non-U.S. banks and branches of U.S. banks outside the U.S.

Excess balances—Average collected balances in a company's bank account above the average required for bank compensation.

Expedited Funds Availability Act (EFAA)—Federal law that defines check availability time periods, payable-through draft and check return procedures.

Exponential smoothing—A time series forecasting technique that assigns declining weights to past values.

Factoring—The sale or transfer of title of the accounts receivable to a third party (factor).

Federal Deposit Insurance Corporation (FDIC)—Independent federal agency that insures deposits in member banks. It has its own reserves and can borrow from the U.S. Treasury.

Federal Reserve System (Fed)—An independent agency of the U.S. government which plays a central role in monetary policy, domestic payments system and the regulation of financial institutions.

Federal Reserve float (Fed float)—The difference between the availability granted to a clearing bank and the time required for the Fed to present the item to the drawee bank.

Fed funds—Funds deposited by commercial banks at Federal Reserve banks, including funds in excess of bank reserve requirements. Banks may lend federal funds to each other on an overnight basis at the federal funds rate to help the borrowing bank satisfy its reserve requirements.

Federal agency securities (Agencies)—Discount and coupon obligations of the federal agencies that were established by Congress to provide credit to specific sectors of the economy.

Fedwire—The real-time system operated by the Federal Reserve for funds transfer.

Fee compensation—Compensation for bank services by direct, explicit fee payment.

Fiduciary—An individual or institution to whom certain property is given to hold in trust according to a trust agreement.

Financial Accounting Standards Board (FASB)—An independent accounting organization responsible for publishing the "Generally Accepted Accounting Principles (GAAP)." FASB is the public accounting profession's self-regulatory organization.

Financial leverage—The use of debt to finance a company.

Floor—A minimum interest rate for a loan or variable-rate security.

Foreign bonds—Bonds issued in the country of their currency by non-residents of that country.

Foreign currency swap—A transaction in which specific amounts of two different currencies are exchanged, and the amounts are repaid over time.

Foreign exchange (FX) rate—The equivalent number of units of one currency per unit of a different currency.

Forward foreign exchange contract—A contract to purchase or sell a specified quantity of a foreign currency at an exchange rate established today for delivery on a specific date in the future.

Forward foreign exchange rate—An exchange rate established today for a currency transaction that settles more than two days in the future.

Freight payment services—Specialized payment services offered by banks and third parties that effect payment for the client directly to freight carriers and offer data bases that assist in determining cost-efficient freight distribution methods.

Futures contract—A standardized, exchange-traded contract for future delivery of a financial or real asset.

GAAP—Generally Accepted Accounting Principles. See Financial Accounting Standards Board.

Garn-St. Germain Act—Federal law enacted in 1982 that extends the legal lending limit of banks.

General obligation securities—A form of municipal security backed by the issuer's resources and its pledge to levy taxes.

Giro systems—Centralized payment systems, common in Europe, generally operated by the postal service using direct debits and credits.

Glass Steagall Act (Banking Act of 1933)—Federal law prohibiting commercial banks from securities underwriting. It requires the Federal Reserve to establish interest rate ceilings and established the FDIC.

Grid notes—A type of bank credit arrangement in which a company signs a comprehensive promissory note under which borrowing takes place and is recorded on the note.

High Dollar Group Sort (HDGS)—A program of the Federal Reserve to expedite the processing of high-dollar-checks through the system.

Imprest accounts—An account maintained at a prescribed level for a particular purpose or activity; it is periodically replenished to the prescribed level.

Indenture agreement—Formal agreement between an issuer of bonds and the bondholder.

Industrial revenue bonds (IRBs)—A special class of municipal bonds issued to provide funds for a facility the municipality is trying to attract for the area.

Intercept account—A deposit account in another country that is used to accept payment from customers in that country, making cross-border payments unnecessary.

Interest rate swaps—A swap between two parties usually for one party to convert a fixed-interest rate payment into a variable-rate payment while the other party takes the opposite position.

Internal rate of return (IRR)—The discount rate at which the net present value is equal to zero.

Invoicing float—The delay between the purchase of goods and services and the receipt of the invoice by the customer.

Leading and lagging—A technique for making cross-border payments from one subsidiary to another either ahead of schedule (leading) or behind schedule (lagging) as a means of moving liquidity from one unit to another.

Ledger balances—Bank balances that reflect all accounting entries that affect a bank account, regardless of any deposit float.

Letter of credit (LC)—A document issued by a bank, guaranteeing the payment of a customer's draft up to a stated amount for a specified period if certain conditions exist.

London Interbank Offered Rate (LIBOR)—Rate offered by banks in the Eurodollar market for short-term placement of funds by other banks.

Line of credit—An agreement between a bank and a customer in which the customer can borrow up to a specified amount during a year.

Liquidity—The ability to convert assets into cash or cash equivalents without significant loss.

Loan participation—A bank agreement to share part of an existing bank loan with another lender.

Loan sale—A bank program where the bank makes a loan and sells all or a part of the loan to investors.

Lockbox—A collection system in which a bank or a third party receives, processes and deposits a company's mail receipts. Also known as a lockbox processor.

Lockbox networks—Collection systems that offer multiple locations to receive customer remittances through one organization.

Magnetic Ink Character Recognition (MICR) Line—Lower part of a check that contains the special character information necessary to process checks by machine.

Mail float—The delay between the time a check is mailed and the date it is received by the payee or at a processing site.

Master account—Account used to fund zero balance accounts automatically.

Master notes—A form of borrowing between highly rated companies and the trust departments of major banks. The amount loaned can fluctuate daily.

McFadden Act—Federal law enacted in 1927 that established the state as the foremost party in determining geographic restrictions for commercial banks and prohibited banks from accepting deposits across state lines.

Message authentication—A digital signature used to protect the integrity of a message and ensure that it is unchanged.

Money market—Financial markets consisting of debt instruments that mature in one year or less.

Money market deposit accounts—Short-term deposit accounts created by Garn-St. Germain Act that pay an unregulated rate of interest determined by the bank and allow limited check-writing.

Money market preferred (MMP)—See auction-rate preferred.

Money market yields—Nominal yield quoted on a 360 day basis.

Multicurrency accounts—An account that allows for the transfer of payments in any readily convertible currency to and from one designated account.

Multilateral netting—System in which purchases among participating non-domestic subsidiaries of the same company are netted so that each participant pays or receives only the net amount of its intracompany sales and purchases.

Multiple drawee checks—Checks that can be presented for payment at a bank other than the drawee bank; both bank names appear on the check. Also called payable-if-desired (PID) checks.

Municipal securities—Debt securities issued by state and local governments and their agencies.

NACHA—National Automated Clearing House Association, the membership organization that provides marketing and education and established rules, standards and procedures that enable financial institutions to exchange ACH payments on a national basis.

Netting—A system to reduce the number of cross-border payments among units of a company either through the elimination or consolidation of individual funds flow. There are two types: bilateral and multi-lateral.

Negotiable order of withdrawal (NOW)—Bank accounts that offer unrestricted check-writing and pay unregulated rates of interest.

Nominal yield—The quoted yield on an annual basis for most instruments is a simple annual rate.

Normal yield curve—There is an inverse relationship between interest rates and the prices of debt instruments; as rates rise on current issues, the prices of existing services fall.

OCC—The Office of the Comptroller of the Currency (OCC) grants charters to and regulates, supervises and examines national banks. It monitors bank performance, issues supervisory agreements and determines loan credit quality ratings.

Open account (Open book credit)—Type of commercial trade credit in the U.S. in which the seller issues an invoice, which is formal evidence of an obligation, and records the sale as an account receivable.

Open market activities—The purchase and sale of securities from the Federal Reserve's portfolio, respectively increasing or decreasing the money supply.

Opportunity cost—The price or rate of return that the best alternative course of action would provide.

Options—The holder has the right, but not the obligation to sell (put option) or buy (call option) financial instruments at a specified price (strike price) within a fixed period of time.

Over-the-counter/field deposit—Collection system in which funds are received and deposited by local operating units in the field in the form of cash, checks, or credit card vouchers.

Payable-if-desired (PID)—See multiple drawee checks.

Payable through draft (PTD)—A payment instrument resembling a check that is drawn against the payor, not the bank, and on which the payor has a period of time in which to honor or refuse payment.

Paying agent—Agent, usually a bank, that receives funds from an issuer of bonds or stock and in turn pays principal and interest to bondholders and dividends to stockholders.

Payments finality—The Federal Reserve's guarantee of funds received. For example, on Fedwire, the Fed guarantees the transferred funds to the receiving bank if the sending bank fails to settle.

Payor Bank Services—An information service in which the Federal Reserve electronically notifies controlled disbursement banks early in the morning of all checks that will be presented that day.

Percentage of sales—A forecasting method in which financial statements are projected based on future sales and the historical relationship between sales and balance sheet items.

Personal identification number (PIN)—A unique number assigned to an individual that is used to determine that the person is authorized to execute the transaction.

Pooling—A special procedure offered by banks in a few countries outside the U.S. in which excess funds in the accounts of some subsidiaries may be used to offset deficits in the accounts of other subsidiaries.

Positive Pay Service—A bank service used for fraud control. A list of checks issued by a company is transmitted to a bank which matches the serial number and the dollar amount. Only those checks that match are paid.

Prearranged payment and deposit (PPD) format—The automated consumer payment application by which a consumer may authorize debits or credits to a personal account by a company or financial institution.

Preauthorized debit (PAD)—A payment method in which the payor approves in advance the transfer of funds from the payor's bank account to the payee's bank account.

Prenotifications (prenotes)—Zero-dollar entries that are sent through the ACH system at least ten days prior to live entries to provide a verification function at the receiving bank before entries for settlement are processed.

Prime rate—The interest rate banks charge to their most creditworthy customers; it applies primarily to middle-market companies.

Private placement—An unregistered direct sale of securities by a company to institutional investors.

Processing float—The delay between the time the payee or the processing center receives a check and the time the check is deposited.

Promissory note—An unconditional promise to pay a specified amount plus interest at a specified rate either on demand or on a certain date.

Proof of deposit (POD)—A bank procedure for verification of the dollar amount of a check being deposited. Also called item-by-item.

Put options—The holder has the right to sell foreign currency, or other financial instruments at a given price.

RCPC items—Checks drawn on banks served by a Federal Reserve regional check processing center (RCPC).

Receivables balance pattern—The percentage of credit sales in a time period (usually a month) that remains outstanding at the end of each subsequent time period.

Registered securities—A treasury security registered in the name of an investor, and only that party can collect interest and principal or sell the security

Registrar—Agencies responsible for monitoring the owners of bonds and the issuance of stock to ensure that no more than the authorized amount of stock is in circulation.

Regression analysis—A statistical technique that establishes the best linear relationship between the variable to be predicted, the independent variable and one or more input or explanatory variables.

Reinvoicing—A method for centralizing the responsibility for tracking and collecting international accounts receivable and for managing the related foreign exchange exposure.

Remote disbursement—A disbursement method designed to delay the collection and final settlement of checks by using bank locations with longer clearing times.

Repurchase agreement (Repo)—A transaction between a securities dealer and an investor in which the dealer sells the security to the investor with an agreement to buy the security back at a specific time and price that will result in a predetermined yield for the investor.

Reserve requirements—Federal Reserve balances that must be maintained by a bank.

Resolution Trust Corporation (RTC)—The organization that manages and resolves troubled savings institutions that have been turned over to the RTC; it manages and liquidates assets controlled by insolvent S&Ls.

Retail lockboxes—Lockboxes characterized by a large number of relatively small-dollar remittances, usually from consumers.

Reverse repurchase agreement (Reverse repo)—The borrower/investor sells the securities to a dealer with an agreement to buy them back for a specific price at a specific time.

Revolving credit agreement (revolver)—Multi-year bank credit facilities in which a borrower can borrow, repay and reborrow up to a defined amount.

Revolving credit terms—A form of trade and consumer credit in which credit is granted without requiring specific approval for each transaction as long as the account is current and below the maximum limit.

Riding the yield curve—The investor buys highly liquid and marketable securities that mature on a day different from the day a payment must be made.

Robinson Patman Act—Federal law that prohibits price discrimination among customers when a cost basis cannot be demonstrated as the reason for price differences.

Savings Association Insurance Fund (SAIF)—A fund administered by the Federal Deposit Insurance Corporation (FDIC). It insures the deposits of savings and loan associations.

Securitization—A financing technique in which a company issues securities backed by selected financial assets.

Sender net debit cap—Limits set by the Federal Reserve and based on a bank's self-evaluation. These limits set the maximum intraday overdraft that a bank can incur over all the large-dollar payment systems.

Settlement dates—Dates of ACH transactions that determine the availability of funds.

Sight draft—A draft that is payable when presented. Generally it must be accompanied by other documents showing that the terms of a transaction have been met.

Simple moving averages—Extrapolative methods that base a forecast on a simple average of past values of the variable to be predicted.

Society for Worldwide Interbank Financial Telecommunications (S.W.I.F.T.)—The major international financial telecommunications network that transmits international payment instructions as well as other financial messages.

Sovereign risk—The risk that a foreign country will not allow an obligation to be paid.

Spot foreign exchange rate—Currency rates generally quoted for delivery two business days from the date of the transaction.

Staggered funding (delayed funding)—A method of bank account funding that uses a forecast or formula based on historical clearing patterns for transferring funds into a disbursement account.

Standby letter of credit—A letter of credit used as a guarantee issued on behalf of a bank's customer in favor of a beneficiary stating that the bank will pay the latter upon presentation of a statement signed by the beneficiary stating that the bank's customer has not fulfilled the terms of the contract.

Swaps—Exchanges of securities for other securities of similar credit quality to improve yields.

Sweep account—A bank account that automatically transfers excess balances into an interest-earning account with the same bank.

S.W.I.F.T.—See Society for Worldwide Interbank Financial Telecommunications.

Target balance—Average collected balance that must be maintained to compensate a bank for all the services provided to the company. Targets are often set monthly and monitored daily.

Term loan—A loan for a fixed period of time, usually several years, often with a fixed repayment schedule.

Time deposits—Deposits that must be held at a bank for a specified time period.

Time draft—A draft similar to a sight draft payable to a third party on a specified future date.

Transaction balances—Bank balances held by firms for collection and disbursement activities.

Transaction exposure—The exposure of balance sheet accounts to a change in foreign exchange rates between the time a transaction is booked and the time it is paid.

Transaction sets—The electronic analog of a paper business document or form.

Transfer agent—Individual or company that keeps a record of the shareholders of a corporation by name, address and number of shares.

Translation exposure—The exposure of balance sheet accounts when a non-domestic subsidiary's financial statements must be translated into U.S. dollars to be incorporated into the parent company's financial statement.

Treasury Bills (T-Bills)—Discount instruments issued by the U.S. Treasury in original maturities of 13, 26 and 52 weeks.

Treasury Bonds (T-Bonds)—Coupon securities issued by the U.S. Treasury with interest paid semi-annually in original maturities of 10-30 years.

Treasury Notes (T-Notes)—Interest-bearing securities issued by the U.S. Treasury with original maturities of 2-10 years.

Treasury securities—"Full faith and credit" obligations of the U.S. Government issued by sale at periodic auctions, delivered and cleared electronically. There are two types: registered and bearer.

Treasury management information system (TMIS)—Configurations of hardware, software and information sources designed to assist in the collection and formatting of information and routine calculations.

Uniform Commercial Code (UCC)—A uniform set of laws governing commercial transactions enacted separately in each state. It defines the rights and duties of the parties in a commercial transaction and provides a statutory definition of commonly used business practices.

Value dating—A system used in some banks outside the U.S. in which the bank sets the dates at which it grants credit for deposits or debits the account for checks written. Value dates may not have any relationship to the actual clearing dates of checks.

Value-added networks (VANs)—Third-party communications providers that play a major role in EDI processing and serve as intermediaries between trading partners.

Variable-rate demand Bonds (VRDB)—A tax-exempt municipal obligation with an original maturity of 5 or more years. It allows an investor to tender the obligation back on a predetermined date.

Vendor Express—The U.S. Department of the Treasury program to pay vendors electronically through the ACH.

Wholesale lockboxes—Lockboxes characterized by a moderate number of large-dollar remittances, usually from company payors.

Yankee CDs—U.S. dollar-denominated CDs issued by non-domestic banks through their branches in the U.S. market.

Yield—Income divided by principal, adjusted to be expressed as an annual percentage rate of return.

Yield curve—The relationship between current market interest rates (or yields) and time to maturity.

Zero balance account (ZBA)—A disbursement bank account on which checks are written even though the balances in the accounts are maintained at zero. Debits are covered by a transfer of funds from a master account at the same bank.

Answers

Chapter 1

1. The major objectives of cash management are:

   - Maintaining liquidity
   - Conserving cash
   - Obtaining short- and long-term financing
   - Monitoring and controlling financial risk exposure
   - Coordinating decision-making with other departments in the firm

2. The major functions of cash management are:

   - Collection of cash
   - Concentration of cash
   - Disbursement of cash
   - Information management
   - Forecasting of cash
   - Investment
   - Borrowing
   - Bank relationship management

3. A firm must manage:

   - Cash inflows
   - Internal transfers

- Cash and near-cash reserves
- Cash outflows

4. The cash flow timeline represents both invoicing and check float.

5. Check float is composed of collection float and disbursement float.

6. The 1970s saw the introduction of remote disbursement and controlled disbursement.

7. The Depository Institutions Deregulation and Monetary Control Act of 1980 had a major impact on bank services and prices.

8. Securitization is the pooling and packaging of similar debt obligations into securities that can be sold to investors.

Chapter 2

1. The major decision areas are:
    - Investment decisions
    - Financing decisions
    - Dividend decisions

2. The primary objective of corporate financial management is the maximization of shareholder value.

3. GAAP (Generally Accepted Accounting Principles) are the detailed rules, developed by the Financial Accounting Standards Board, which govern financial reporting and record-keeping in the U.S.

4. The statement of cash flows shows cash from operating, investing, and financing activities.

5. A red book balance is a negative balance in a firm's cash account. A firm may avoid reporting it by combining cash and marketable securities on its balance sheet or by reporting checks written but not yet presented as a current liability.

6. The formula for present value is:

$$V = \frac{FV}{(1 + i)^n}$$

$1,500 is the future sum to be received (FV) in two years (n) and its opportunity cost is 5% (i)

The present value is:

$$PV = \frac{1500}{(1 + .05)^2} = \frac{1500}{1.1025} = \$1,360.54$$

7. A firm with a $500 invoice with terms of 2/10 net thirty will save $7.25.

Payment on day 10 = $500 x (1-.02) = $490

The present value of the payment (PV) is

$$PV = \frac{\text{Cash flow to be received in t days}}{[\,1 + r\,(t/365)\,]}$$

Where   r = interest rate - opportunity cost

t = days until payment due

χ

If it pays in 10 days =

$$= \frac{\$490}{1 + .10\frac{10}{365}}$$

$$= \frac{\$490}{1.0027} = \$488.68$$

If it pays in 30 days =

$$\frac{500}{1 + .10\frac{30}{365}} = \frac{500}{1.0082} = \$495.93$$

The firm is better off by: $495.93 - $488.68

$$= \$7.25$$

8.   The current ratio is $\underline{\text{Current Asset}}$
                           Current Liabilities

$$= \frac{970,000}{590,000} = 1.64$$

The debt to equity ratio is

$$\frac{Total\ Debt}{Shareholders\ Equity} = \frac{590,000 + 800,000}{100,000 + 400,000 + 80,00}$$

$$= \frac{1,390,000}{580,000} = 2.40$$

9.   The return on investment is $\underline{\text{Net Income}}$
                              Shareholders' Equity

$$= \frac{90,000}{100,000 + 400,000 + 80,000} =$$

$$\frac{90,000}{580,000} = 15.52\%$$

10. A firm needs liquidity in order to meet its transaction requirements, to be prepared for unanticipated cash needs, and to take advantage of investment opportunities.

11. The major areas of responsibility for the cash manager are:

     -    Funds movement

     -    Banking system administration

     -    Money market administration

     -    Forecasting

Chapter 3

1. The major roles of commercial banks are:

   1. Intermediation

   2. Payments and Collections

   3. Acting as Guarantor

   4. Acting as Agent or Fiduciary

   5. Consulting

   6. Risk Management

   7. Acting as Broker and Dealer

2. Underwriting is the principal function of an investment banking firm. It assures the issuer of stock or bonds of a definite sum of money for the issue at a definite time. The investment banker assumes the risk of price and marketability.

3. Savings and loan associations and mutual savings banks have traditionally been state chartered. The Garn-St. Germain Act of 1982 allows mutual savings banks to switch to a federal charter.

4. Unlike banks, credit unions are not-for-profit financial institutions with restricted membership.

5. A captive finance company is a subsidiary of a large industrial corporation which lends money to finance the purchase of its parent company's product.

6. U.S. banks can be regulated at both the federal and state level; consequently, the U.S. has a dual banking system.

7. The major roles of the Federal Reserve are:

   - Supervising banks

   - Conducting monetary policy

- Providing services for banks
- Acting as the fiscal agent for the U.S. Treasury

8. National bank charters are granted by the Office of the Comptroller of the Currency (OCC).

9. The FDIC operates the Bank Insurance Fund (BIF) covering commercial banks and mutual savings banks, and the Savings Association Insurance Fund (SAIF), covering savings and loan associations.

10. The Edge Act allows U.S. banks to invest in corporations engaged in international banking.

11. McFadden Act.

12. Glass-Steagall Act.

13. The Depository Institutions Deregulation and Monetary Control Act (DIDMCA).

14. The Financial Institutions Reform Recovery and Enforcement Act (FIRREA).

15. Regulation Q.

16. Regulation CC.

17. Article 3.

18. 30 days.

19. No, unless the bank agrees in writing to assume this liability.

Chapter 4

1. The payee is the party to whom a payment is made.

2. This is the Transit Routing Number.

3. A cash letter is a bundle of checks, accompanied by a list of individual items and dollar amounts, together with deposit tickets and other control documents.

4. A direct send is a cash letter that bypasses the local Federal Reserve. A bank sends it directly to a correspondent bank or a non-local Federal Reserve bank.

5. An on-us item is a check deposited in the same bank on which it is drawn.

6. A country item is a check drawn on a bank located outside the area served by a Federal Reserve city or the RCPC.

7. A ledger balance reflects accounting entries to a bank account while collected balances reflect the transfer of value after the appropriate delay specified by the availability schedule.

8. Deposit float may be calculated on an item-by-item basis, as an average of all the bank's customers or on the basis of a sample of the company's deposited checks. In some cases availability maybe negotiated.

9. Factors that determine availability include:
   - Drawee's location
   - Time of deposit
   - Degree of customer sorting

- Pre-encoding by the customer
- Checks rejected during processing

10. Federal Reserve float represents the difference between the availability granted the clearing bank and the time required to debit the drawee bank's account.

11. A PTD is drawn against the payor and not a bank.

12. A sight draft is payable when presented while a time draft is payable at a specified future date.

13. The most commonly used ACH formats are:
   - Prearranged Payment and Deposit (PPD) used for consumer transactions
   - Cash Concentration and Disbursement (CCD) used to move funds within or between companies
   - Cash Concentration and Disbursement plus Addendum (CCD+) used for the U.S. Treasury Department's Vendor Express program and corporate-to-corporate payments
   - Corporate Trade Payments (CTP) used for corporate-to-corporate payments
   - Corporate Trade Exchange (CTX) used for corporate-to-corporate payments

14. In an ACH transaction settlement occurs one or two days after transmission of the payment information, with the debit and credit occurring simultaneously.

15. Settlement through Fedwire is immediate rather than on a one- or two-day cycle like the ACH.

16. A repetitive wire transfer is used when a company makes a transfer frequently between the same debit and credit parties. A line number is

used to identify each transfer with only the date and dollar amount allowed to be changed.

17. CHIPS is both a message and a settlement system, while SWIFT is not a funds transfer network. SWIFT sends payment instructions, while settlement occurs through another means like Fedwire, CHIPS or a correspondent bank account.

18. A daylight overdraft is an intra-day exposure that occurs when an account is overdrawn during a business day. Because the Federal Reserve is guarantor of a wire transfer to the receiving bank, it could be forced to make good a wire transfer initiated by a bank that subsequently fails. The Federal Reserve has set a cap on the daylight overdraft allowed for each financial institution to lessen the risk.

Chapter 5

1. The major objectives of credit management are:
   - Setting credit policies
   - Making customer credit decisions
   - Ensuring prompt and accurate billing
   - Maintaining account receivable records
   - Establishing and implementing collection procedures

2. A credit policy consists of setting credit standards, specifying credit terms, and establishing a collection policy.

3. Revolving credit terms involve the granting of credit without requiring specific approval of each transaction as long as the credit limit is not exceeded, and payments are made on time.

4. Seasonal dating is a special credit term used in industries with highly seasonal sales. Payment is due near the end of the buyer's selling season although sliding discounts may be used to encourage early payment.

5. $i = \dfrac{d}{1-d} \times \dfrac{365}{n-t}$

    Where   i = effective interest rate

             d = discount percentage

             n = date payment is made

             t = last date discount may be taken

    With terms of 3/20 net 60, the effective cost of passing up the discount is:

    $$i = \dfrac{.03}{.97} \; x \; \dfrac{365}{60 - 20} =$$

    $= .0309 \times 9.1250 = .2822$ or 28.22%

6. The five Cs are:
    -   Character - willingness to pay
    -   Capacity - ability to pay
    -   Capital - financial strength
    -   Collateral - protection for the lender
    -   Conditions - economic environment

7. Credit scoring is a technique used to estimate the creditworthiness of credit applicants based on a statistical profile of a successful credit, which is used to weight various elements on the applications.

8. (1) Additional sales

    100,000 x .15 = $15,000

    (2) Marginal profitability of additional sales

    .20 x $15,000 = $3,000

(3) Additional investment in receivables

$$\frac{\$115,000}{365} \, x35 \; (\text{-}) \; \frac{\$100,000}{365} \, x15$$

= $11,027 (-) $4,110

= $6,917

(4) Cost of additional investment in receivables

$6,917 X .10 = $692

(5) Additional bad debt loss

= .02 X $15,000 = $300

(6) Net change in pretax profits

$3,000 - ($692 + $300)

=$2,008

Yes, the change in terms is profitable.

9.   Factoring is the sale of an accounts receivable to a factoring company. The factoring company provides credit evaluation and collection services. Title to the accounts receivable is transferred to the factoring company.

10. Average daily sales

$$\frac{\$75,000 + \$100,000 + \$90,000}{90} = \$2944.44$$

$$DSO = \frac{\$125,000}{\$2944.44} = 42.5 \; days$$

11. The Robinson-Patman Act.

12. The Truth-in-Lending Act.

Chapter 6

1. The major objectives of a collection system are to mobilize funds, provide timely and accurate information, update accounts receivable, and support audit trails for both internal and external auditors.

2. Companies may collect through an over-the-counter/field deposit system, by mail payments to the company, to a lockbox, or electronically via a wire transfer or an ACH.

3. A wire transfer is the fastest and most secure but is relatively expensive for the payor.

4. Collection float is composed of mail float, processing float and availability float.

5. Availability float is determined by the depository bank's availability schedule.

6. Average daily float = $\frac{\$2,120,000}{30} = \$70,667$

   Annual cost of float = $70,667 X .07 = $4,947

7. The selection of either a company processing center or a lockbox is a function of the volume of checks processed and the dollar size of the checks. For example, a low volume of checks with large dollar amounts usually supports the use of a lockbox system.

8. A lockbox system reduces mail, processing and availability float, provides economies of scale in processing and establishes an audit trail outside the company.

9. A wholesale lockbox is used primarily for corporate-to-corporate payments where large-dollar remittances are involved. A retail lockbox is used for large-volume, small-dollar remittance payments like consumer payments.

10. Float Cost with lockbox

= Average Float = $\frac{\$1,010,000}{30}$ = $33,667

$33,667 X .07 = $2,357

Float savings with lockbox = $4,947 - 2,357	= $2,590
Fixed lockbox cost	= (1,000)
Variable-lockbox cost (6,000 x .30)	(1,800)
Savings-internal processing cost(6,000 x . 20)	1,200
Net benefit of lockbox	$ 990

A lockbox is profitable in this situation.

11. Lockbox studies are used to determine the optimal number and location of lockbox collecting points that will minimize collection float.

12. An electronic lockbox allows companies to receive customer payments by wire transfer or through the ACH.

13. An over-the-counter field deposit system is a collection system in which funds are received and deposited by local operating units of the firm such as division offices or retail stores.

14. A pre-authorized debit involves the advance approval of a payor for the payee to transfer funds from the payor's account via the ACH. An example of this application is the automatic withdrawal of insurance premiums from a policyholder's account.

15. Net settlement systems benefit firms in the same industry that buy and sell from each other on a regular basis by requiring only periodic transfers of the net amount due to other firms.

16. The two types of computer analysis used in lockbox studies are exhaustive searches and discrete searches. Exhaustive searches involve the consideration of many more possible combinations of lockboxes than the discrete approach.

Chapter 7

1. The objectives of a cash concentration system include:
   - Simplifying cash management
   - Improving control of funds
   - Pooling funds for investment or debt reduction
   - Minimizing excess balances
   - Reducing transfer expenses

2. Over-the-counter/field banking systems and lockbox banking systems are the two major types of banking systems.

3. EDT is an electronic depository transfer which is the use of an ACH transaction for concentrating funds. These transactions are transmitted in the CCD format.

4. Wire transfers may also be used for concentration. They are generally used when the amounts are large enough to justify their cost.

5. A depository transfer check (DTC) is an unsigned, restricted payee instrument used to concentrate funds. It may be used in field banking system concentration.

6. The major cost components of a cash concentration system are excess balances in the firm's banks, costs to transfer funds and the administrative costs of arranging the concentration system.

7. Excess balances may arise through delays in deposit reporting, clearing or the initiation of transfers.

8. Anticipation is the initiation of a transfer before funds become available at the deposit bank. Availability anticipation initiates the transfers on the basis of actual deposit information, while deposit anticipation is done on the basis of unreported, expected deposits.

9. Threshold concentration allows bank balances to build to a predetermined level and then a transfer is initiated to the concentration bank.

10. Minimum Transfers = $\dfrac{\text{Wire Cost - EDT Cost}}{\text{Days Accelerated} \times \text{Opportunity Cost}}$

$$= \frac{\$22.00 - \$1.00}{1 \times \dfrac{.08}{365}} = \frac{21}{.0002191} = \$95,847$$

11. Fraud may be prevented by (1) having different reports prepared by different people, (2) conducting surprise audits requiring daily reporting, and (3) instructing banks to allow no overdrafts.

12. Pooling funds is a valuable objective of cash concentration because pooling permits a firm to buy larger blocks of short-term securities which tend to earn higher yields.

Chapter 8

1. A cash disbursement system should:

   - Reduce the net cost of making payments

   - Provide timely information

- Help maintain good payee relations
- Protect against fraud
- Manage disbursement float

2. Disbursement systems may be centralized or decentralized. In a centralized system check writing and account reconciliation are controlled from headquarters, while in a decentralized system checks are drawn on a local disbursement bank and account reconciliation is performed at the local level.

3. Disbursement float is composed of mail float, processing float and clearing float (availability float plus clearing slippage float).

4. Remote disbursement is the use of banks with longer clearing times for the purpose or delaying collection and final settlement of checks. DIDMCA mandates to reduce float have made it less effective.

5. A zero balance account is a bank disbursement product which is an account on which checks are written even though the balance in the account is zero. The checks are covered by a transfer of funds from the company's master account in that bank.

6. A multiple drawee check, also known as a payable-if-desired check, is a check that can be presented for payment at a bank other than the drawee bank. It is typically used for payroll and dividend applications.

7. Controlled disbursement is a service that provides same-day notification of the dollar amount of checks that will clear, permitting earlier determination of amounts that can be invested or need to be borrowed. Remote disbursement is using bank locations with longer clearing times to delay the collection of checks.

8. Payor bank services are an information service provided by the Federal Reserve to notify banks of a day's presentments.

9. A controlled disbursement bank should be evaluated on the following criteria:

   - Timeliness of reporting

   - Accuracy in processing

   - Volume capacity

   - Reporting detail and reconciliation services

   - Cost effectiveness

   - Customer service support

10. Positive Pay is a service used for fraud control. The firm transmits a file of checks issued. The bank matches serial numbers and dollar amounts and pays only those checks that match.

11. In sort only account reconciliation the bank sorts the checks only by check serial number.

Chapter 9

1. A treasury management information system (TMIS) is designed to:

   - Collect information

   - Organize information

   - Provide tools to analyze information

   - Provide decision support

   - Initiate transactions

2. A TMIS provides the following advantages:

   - Increased access to information

   - Improved productivity

   - Better bank relationship data

   - Increased security

3. Information from external sources about collections, check clearing and the company's cash position should be monitored. This information stream will consist of both previous day/historical and same-day data.

4. A TMIS may be used to initiate a number of different transactions such as funds transfers, automated clearing house (ACH) debits and credits, stop payments, foreign exchange transactions, and tax payments.

5. Treasury management software packages often consist of modules to handle applications such as:

   - Account analysis
   - Cash position worksheets
   - Cash ledger accounting interface
   - Forecasting
   - Reconciliation
   - International transactions
   - Debt and investment tracking
   - Bank relationship management

6. Cash management software can be licensed from banks or other vendors, developed in-house or off-the-shelf packages can be adapted to treasury needs.

7. A disaster recovery plan is a blueprint for reconstructing a TMIS in the event it is disabled or destroyed, or in the event a similar disaster occurs at one of the company's banks. Such a plan should include regular back-up of data and the plan should also be tested regularly.

8. The most common security procedures used in connection with electronic funds transfers are use of personal identification numbers, call-backs, data encryption, and message authentication.

9. Electronic data interchange (EDI) is computer-to-computer communication for routine business transactions. Electronic transmission, in stan-

dard formats, replaces paper documents throughout the business transaction cycle.

10. EDI can provide benefits which include:

   - Improved response time
   - Reduced clerical expense
   - Fewer errors because rekeying is unnecessary
   - Decreased order lead time
   - Improved cash forecasting accuracy
   - Elimination of uncertainty regarding mail and check clearing times

11. A value added network (VAN) is a third-party communications provider that acts as an intermediary between the trading partners in an EDI transaction.

12. Transaction sets are electronic analogs of paper business documents. ANSI X12 transaction set standards include 810 (Invoice), 820 (Payment Order/Remittance Advice) and 823 (Lockbox Transaction).

13. The physical process of electronic data interchange requires translation of data from the sender's format to a mutually-agreed machine-readable format, communication of that data through a medium acceptable to both companies' computers, and translation from the agreed format to the internal format of the receiver.

14. A TMIS may be used to monitor same-day information such as clearings to be funded in controlled disbursement systems, reporting of lockbox deposits and ACH transactions as well as incoming and outgoing wire transfers.

Chapter 10

1. The major objectives of cash forecasting include:

    -   Managing liquidity

    -   Obtaining financial control

    -   Meeting strategic objectives

    -   Achieving capital budgeting

    -   Minimizing net cost of funds

2. Cash forecasting can be done on a short -, medium -, or long-term basis. Short-term forecasts are done on a   daily or weekly basis for a 30-day horizon. Medium-term forecasts cover periods from one-month to one year, and long-term forecasting goes beyond one year.

3. The steps in the cash forecasting process are:

    -   Dividing cash flows into their major components

    -   Determining the degree of certainty of each component

    -   Identifying sources from which data may be gathered

    -   Organizing data into meaningful categories

    -   Selecting the appropriate forecasting method after determining the relationship between the available data and the cash flow components to be forecast

    -   The model should then be validated using in-sample and out-of-sample validation. This validation should be continuous.

4. Short-term forecasts can be prepared using either the receipts and disbursements method or the distribution method.

5. A pro-forma statement is prepared using the percentage-of-sales method. This presumes the next financial statement period will retain the same relationship between sales and other income statement and balance sheet items as it did in the prior period.

6. The major sources of cash are cash flows from operations, decreases in assets and increases in liabilities. The major uses of cash are increases in assets, decreases in liabilities, capital expenditures and dividend payments.

7. Time series forecasting predicts a variable based only on past observations of that variable.

8. The moving average forecast is

    $(100+150+250+210) \div 4 = 177.5$

9. Exponential smoothing is a variation on the simple moving average that weights each observation with more recent observations given heavier weights. This enables trends and seasonality to be captured in the forecast.

Chapter 11

1. A firm has a short-term investment portfolio in order to preserve liquidity and generate income with an acceptable degree of risk.

2. A company's investment policy is influenced by:
    -   Objectives for short-term investments
    -   Timing of cash flows
    -   Tax status of firm
    -   Qualified staff
    -   Legal or internal restrictions
    -   Financial reporting requirements

3. A company will examine the time to maturity, credit quality, and marketability of a financial instrument in order to determine its fit with the company's short-term investment portfolio.

4. Crisis management refers to the steps to be taken if a default by an issuer of a security or insolvency of a broker or dealer is encountered. The object of such action is to limit losses to the extent possible.

5. Yield is influenced by:

    -   Maturity - normally the shorter the time to maturity, the lower the yield

    -   Marketability - securities without an active secondary market tend to have higher yields

    -   Default Risk - the lower the credit rating of the instrument, the higher its yield

    -   Tax-Status - tax-exempt securities, like municipal securities, will have a lower pre-tax yield than a taxable instrument of similar risk

6. An inverted yield curve means yields on long-term securities are not as high as those of short-term securities. This is due to investor expectations of falling short-term interest rates.

7. Financial markets may be divided into long-term or capital markets with instruments that mature in more than one year, and the money market, which consists of short-term debt instruments maturing in one year or less.

8. In a book entry transaction, the physical securities do not move when traded. In the case of treasury securities they remain in a vault at the Federal Reserve Bank of New York, and book entries are made when ownership changes.

9. The U.S. Treasury issues T-Bills with maturities of 3 months to one year, T-Notes with maturities from 2 to 10 years, and T-Bonds with maturities of 10 to 30 years.

10. Federal agency securities are debt instruments issued by agencies of the U.S. Government. They act as financial intermediaries in certain credit markets. For example, the Federal National Mortgage Association (Fannie Mae) helps provide liquidity to the mortgage market.

11. Municipal securities are classified as general obligation securities or revenue securities. General obligation securities are backed by the taxing power of the issuing entity, while revenue securities pay their principal and interest from proceeds of a specific project.

12. The income from municipal obligations is exempt from federal income tax and is often exempt from taxes in the state in which they are issued.

13. Eurodollar CDs are U.S. dollar denominated certificates of deposit issued by banks, including branches of U.S. banks, outside the U.S.

14. Banker's acceptances are short-term obligations of a bank created in financing an international trade transaction.

15. A repo is an abbreviation for a repurchase agreement which is a transaction between a securities dealer and an investor in which the dealer sells securities to the investor with an agreement to repurchase them at a specific time and price to produce a pre-determined yield to the investor.

16. Commercial paper is an unsecured promissory note which matures in 270 days or less.

17. Money market preferred is preferred stock in which the dividend rate is adjusted every 49 days on the basis of current Treasury yields.

18. Discount = (discount rate X face value) X $\dfrac{\text{days to maturity}}{360}$

$$= (.0453 \text{ X } \$100{,}000) \text{ X } \dfrac{182}{360}$$

$$= \$4530 \text{ X } .5055$$

$$= \$2{,}289.92$$

Purchase Price = $97,710.08

19. Bond Equivalent = $\dfrac{\text{Discount}}{\text{Purchase Price}} \times \dfrac{365}{\text{Days to Maturity}}$
      Yield

$= \dfrac{\$2,289.92}{\$97,710.08} \times \dfrac{365}{182}$

$= .0234 \times 2.0055$

$= 4.69\%$

20. Banks provide sweep accounts, which automatically transfer excess balances into an interest-earning account.

21. The two major active investment strategies are matching which involves purchasing a security. This matures on the date funds are required. The other is riding the yield curve, which will require purchasing a security maturing beyond the cash need with a normal yield curve or maturing prior to the cash need if the yield curve is inverted.

22. A matching strategy would involve purchasing the 90-day T-Bill.

Discount = (Discount Rate x Face Value) X $\dfrac{\text{Days to Maturity}}{360}$

$= (.0475 \times \$10,000) \times \dfrac{90}{360}$

$= \$475 \times .25$

$= \$118.75$

Purchase Price = Face Value - Discount
$= \$10,000 - 118.75$
$= \$9881.25$

Bond Equivalent Yield = $\dfrac{\text{Discount}}{\text{Purchase Price}} \times \dfrac{365}{90}$

$$= \frac{\$118.75}{\$9881.25} \times \frac{365}{90}$$

$$= .0120 \times 4.0556$$

$$= 4.87\%$$

If the company is riding the yield curve then the 180-day T-Bill would be purchased and sold after 90 days.

First, find the purchase price of the 180-day T-Bill

$$\text{Discount} = (.0500 \times \$10,000) \times \frac{180}{360}$$

$$= \$500 \times .50$$

$$= \$250$$

Purchase Price = $10,000 - $250 = $9750

Find the bond equivalent yield of riding the yield curve:

$$\text{Bond Equivalent Yield} = \frac{\$9,881.25 - \$9,750}{\$9,750} \times \frac{365}{90}$$

$$= .0135 \times 4.0556$$

$$= 5.48\%$$

The bond equivalent yield of riding the yield curve is:

$$= 5.48\% - 4.87\% = .61\% \text{ or}$$

61 basis points higher than the matching strategy.

Chapter 12

1. The major objectives of a company's borrowing program include:
    - Ensuring continued availability of borrowed funds
    - Minimizing borrowing costs

- Balancing the risks of unfavorable interest rate movements and not having sufficient financing

- Maintaining flexibility in borrowing

2. The London Interbank Offered Rate (LIBOR) is the rate offered by banks in the Eurodollar market for the short- term placement of funds by other banks.

3. Credit enhancement is a process in which a bank or an insurance company guarantees the debt obligation of the borrower using an indemnity bond or letter of credit. The borrower's debt is traded with the credit rating of the guarantor.

4. A committed line of credit involves a formal loan agreement with the bank requiring balance or fee compensation and obligating the bank to provide funding up to the established credit limit.

5. $$\text{Effective Annual Interest Rate} = \frac{\$ \text{ interest paid} + \text{fees}}{\text{Average usable loan}} \times \frac{365}{\text{days loan outstanding}}$$

$$= \frac{.07(200,000) + .0025(300,000)}{200,000} \times \frac{365}{365}$$

$$= \frac{\$14,000 + 750}{\$200,000} \times \frac{365}{365}$$

$$= 7.38\%$$

6. Commercial paper issuers have lines of credit to be used if market conditions are not conducive to issuing commercial paper.

7. First, find the amount of usable funds:

    Usable funds =

    Face Value - (fare value X disc. rate) $\underline{\text{(days to maturing)}}$
    $\qquad\qquad\qquad\qquad\qquad\qquad\qquad$ 360

    $\qquad\qquad$ = \$1,000,000 - (\$1,000,000 X .06) $\underline{(\ 60)}$
    $\qquad\qquad\qquad\qquad\qquad\qquad\qquad\qquad\qquad$ 360

    $\qquad\qquad$ = \$990,000

    Next, find the dealer cost:

    $\qquad\qquad$ = (.0025 X \$1,000,000)X$\underline{(\ 60)}$
    $\qquad\qquad\qquad\qquad\qquad\qquad\qquad$ 360

    $\qquad\qquad$ = \$416.67

    Finally, find the effective annual cost:

    $\qquad\qquad$ = $\underline{\text{\$interest paid + fees}}$ X $\underline{\ \ 365\ \ }$
    $\qquad\qquad\quad$ usable funds $\qquad$ days to
    $\qquad\qquad\qquad\qquad\qquad\qquad$ maturity

    $\qquad\qquad$ = $\underline{\text{\$10,000 + \$416.67}}$ X $\underline{365}$
    $\qquad\qquad\qquad$ \$990,000 $\qquad\qquad$ 60

    $\qquad\qquad$ = 6.40%

8. A loan participation is an arrangement whereby a bank signs an agreement to share part of an existing loan with another lender. This is generally done with the borrower's approval.

9. Floor planning is a type of asset-based lending in which inventory of high value, such as automobiles, trucks and farm equipment, is used as collateral.

10. An asset suitable for securitization should have a predictable, steady cash flow and a low level of historical loss experience.

11. A bond indenture is the formal agreement among all parties to a bond issue defining the details of the issue, such as the collateral, if any, and the duties of the trustee.

12. Covenants are provisions in loan agreements, which restrict the borrower's activities in ways that protect the lender. Some examples include maximums or minimums on financial ratios, limitations on capital expenditures or asset sales.

13. A company issues convertible bonds in order to borrow at a lower rate than possible with non-convertible bonds and to be able to convert debt to equity on the balance sheet.

14. If a default occurs the lender may demand repayment of the debt prior to maturity, terminate the agreement, or do both.

Chapter 13

1. The purpose of the Bretton Woods Conference was to create a stable world economic environment after World War II. It established the International Monetary Fund, the World Bank and the gold-exchange standard.

2. A quote of SF 1.59 - .64 = $1 means the bank will pay (bid) 1.59 Swiss francs for one U.S. dollar. The offer rate of 1.64 Swiss francs is the rate at which it will sell one U.S. dollar.

3. Delivery on a spot transaction is usually two business days from the date of the transaction. In this case, delivery will be on Monday.

4. Forward exchange rates are based on the spot exchange rate and the level of borrowing and lending interest rates in the two currencies.

5. Translation exposure is created by the need to consolidate non-U.S. subsidiaries' financial statements into the parent company's financial statement.

6. Foreign exchange exposure can be hedged using forward contracts, futures, options, or currency swaps.

7. No. Foreign exchange futures are highly standardized contracts that are offered for only a few major currencies.

8. The underlying currency has a market price above the strike price if the call option (right-to-buy) is in-the-money.

9. An investor worrying about falling interest rates should buy an interest rate call option. If rates do fall, the value of the underlying future will rise, and the profit on exercising the option will offset the loss of investment income.

10. An interest rate swap allows one party to convert a fixed rate payment into a floating rate payment, while the other party reverses that position.

11. Interest rate collars are combinations of caps and floors, setting maximum and minimum interest rates.

Chapter 14

1. Bank relationship management seeks to:
   - Ensure the firm has adequate credit facilities
   - Provide a firm with necessary banking services
   - Manage total banking costs
   - Ensure fair and reasonable bank compensation
   - Control risk exposure to banks

2. Among the criteria for bank selection are:

   - Provision of credit at competitive prices, with flexibility in structuring terms and conditions

   - Knowledge of the firm and its industry

   - Responsiveness to the firm's needs and questions

   - Quality of bank management and the bank's financial strength

3. The major documents associated with a banking relationship are the account resolution, signature cards and service agreements.

4. A bank report card should include evaluations of:

   - Number of errors by service

   - Bank reporting times for information reporting services

   - Responsiveness to questions posed by the company

   - Timeliness of error resolution by the bank

   - Effectiveness of bank personnel

5. Bank relationship audit and control issues include:

   - Procedures for opening accounts

   - Policies for account reconciliation

   - Maintenance of account documentation

6. Banks may be compensated with fees, balances or a combination of fees and balances.

7. $$-CB = \frac{\text{Service Charges}}{(\text{Earnings Credit Rate} \times \frac{\text{Days in Month}}{365}) \times (1-\text{Reserve Req})}$$

$$CB = \frac{\$4,000}{(.06 \times \frac{30}{365}) \times (1-.10)}$$

$$= \frac{\$4,000}{(.0049)\,(.90)}$$

$$= \frac{\$4,000}{.0044}$$

$$= \$909,091$$

8. From the information in Question 8:

     Average ledger balance $100,000

     Less: Deposit float   (19,000)

     Equals: Average collected balance $ 81,000

     Earnings Credit=

     Collect Bal.X(1-Reserve Req.)X(earnings credit X Days in $\frac{Month}{365}$)

$$= \$81,000 \times (1-.10) \times (.06 \times \frac{30}{365})$$

$$= \$81,000 \times (.90) \times (.0049)$$

$$= \$357.21$$

     Earnings credit $ 357.21

     Less service charges (650.00)

     Deficiency   (292.79)

Therefore, earnings credits are not sufficient to cover the service charges.

9. From the corporate perspective fee compensation is preferred for the following reasons:

     - Companies can generally earn higher rates on balances than the bank can pay in earnings credits

- Fee compensation permits tighter cost control
- Excess balances represent a form of overpayment which can't occur with fee compensation

10. Target balances are the desired average balances a company may maintain to compensate the bank for services provided. Target balances may be as low as zero if the firm wishes to compensate only with fees.

11. An account analysis is a statement, prepared by a bank, summarizing a company's transaction activity, average balances and service charges.

12. Bundling is charging for a group of related services whether or not the customer uses all of them.

13. Bank credit analysis is divided into the following components:
    - Liquidity
    - Asset quality
    - Earnings
    - Capital
    - Holding company

14. A company will want to optimize the number of banks with whom it has a relationship because there are internal and external costs for each banking relationship and so there is an incentive not to have any more relationships than are necessary.

Chapter 15

1. International cash management may be centralized or decentralized depending on the degree of control sought by the company and the firm's structural relationship with its subsidiaries.

2. A company may seek off shore financing in order to:

    -   Diversify its funding sources

    -   Hedge long-term investments in that currency

    -   Borrow at lower rates

    -   Gain tax advantages

3. There are differences in payment practices outside the U.S. These include greater use of electronic payments, the existence of giro systems, and variations in the way banks collect payments.

4. Pooling is the practice of allowing excess balances in the accounts of some subsidiaries to be used to offset deficits in the accounts of other subsidiaries.

5. Value dating is the practice of banks setting dates on which credit is granted or an account is debited on a basis other than the actual clearing date. For example, checks may be debited, based on the date they were written.

6. A check drawn in a different country cannot be cleared through normal channels, but must be submitted to a bank for collection.

7. A multi-currency account allows for the transfer of payments in any readily convertible currency to and from one designated account.

8. A netting system reduces the number of foreign exchange transactions and therefore lowers the transactions cost. There is favorable pricing for larger foreign exchange transactions, and cash forecasting is improved. Netting can eliminate float and result in greater certainty regarding value dating.

9. A reinvoicing center is a company-owned subsidiary that buys goods from the exporter and sells goods to the importer. Each party conducts the transaction in its own currency.

10. A letter of credit substitutes a bank's credit for that of the buyer. Consequently, it eliminates the risk of non-payment to the seller.

11. An irrevocable letter of credit requires the issuing bank to honor all drafts presented by the seller as long as all necessary documentation is provided.

12. A stand-by letter of credit states a bank will pay the beneficiary upon presentation of a signed statement by the beneficiary that the bank's customer has not fulfilled the terms of the contract.

13. Banks under a documentary collection do not assume credit risk but act only as agents in the collection process.

14. Counter trade is a method of payment in which countries with an insufficient amount of hard currency agree to exchange merchandise for sale in the buyer's country rather than making a money payment.

15. To be eligible for discount at the Federal Reserve, a banker's acceptance may not have a maturity of more than 180 days.

16. The Export-Import Bank of the United States (Eximbank) is an independent agency of the United States government established to finance and guarantee U.S. export loans.

Index

A

B

S

T

U